D1111919

HOUGHTON MIFFLIN BOOKS
IN AMERICAN HISTORY

Under the editorship of
GEORGE E. MOWRY

Between the Wars: America,

HISTORY

1919-1941

David A. Shannon

UNIVERSITY OF WISCONSIN

HOUGHTON MIFFLIN COMPANY • *Boston*

To the memory of

FRED ALBERT SHANNON

Editorial Foreword

This is the first of a series of brief volumes which together will cover the history of the United States from the first settlements of the continent to the present. Each will be written by an authority on the period, and each will seek to give both the student and the general reader an understanding of the dominant personalities and the major forces which together have given direction to the American journey down through some of the most exciting years in human history.

Since there have been not a few such projects in the past, it may be questioned — why still another? In explaining why societies change Ralph Waldo Emerson commented that new times virtually demand "new measures and new men." He might also have added to his imperatives, new history. For just as men search the past better to understand the present, the ever-changing present continues to throw new light on the past. Far from being a "restless idiot," time has a remorseless and interconnected logic. From the changing perspectives of each new cluster of years come new interpretations of the past and from such interpretations new insights into the present and the future. To that extent no history has ever been definitive; all are to a degree mythic. And like myth, history needs to be changed to encompass the present and make it understandable.

This present volume might well be subtitled "a study in recent historical myth and counter-myth." For at the start of each chapter Professor Shannon has listed the misconceptions about the period between the two great World Wars which prevailed among contemporaries. The most important of these, according to the author, were the assumptions that the Republicans were responsible for inaugurating post-World War I conservatism, that these same Republicans sought to turn social progress back to the nineteenth century, that Franklin Roosevelt was victorious over the great depression, and that he was either a far-sighted statesman who early understood the necessity of our entry into the war against Germany or that he was an unprincipled demagogue who led us into an unnecessary and unwanted war. With cool and critical detachment, the author proceeds to examine each of these beliefs and many more in the light of the most recent scholarship to which he himself has substantially contributed. His book, therefore, is an important addition both to the knowledge of the past and to an understanding of the present.

GEORGE E. MOWRY

Los Angeles, California

Contents

Part Two · BUST YEARS

Introduction:

History and Myth

Interpretation of history is no mere academic exercise. Nor is it an irrelevant and pedantic dialogue to be conducted in an ivory tower. Granted that some of the fine distinctions and disagreements over details that divide professional historical opinion do not excite the layman, nevertheless interpretation of the past lies at the heart of an individual's or a society's decisions. Every conscious decision and consciously adopted point of view necessarily involves an interpretation of at least a part of history.

Examples will illustrate the point. First, an individual example: A man deciding whether or not to accept a new job has to estimate the future, try to predict what his life would be like with the new employer. But he has to compare the predicted future with the actual past, with how happy or unhappy he was in the old job. This looking at the past record actually means interpreting the past, interpreting a small slice of history, for objective conditions mean different things to different people. Social examples are usually more complex but no less real. For example, since 1945 American society has consciously adopted policies and attitudes toward the Soviet Union. Those responsible for shaping foreign policy have necessarily interpreted the history of Soviet-American relations in making decisions about the contemporary situation. To a considerable extent, they have also reasoned by analogy from the democratic nations' relations with Hitler's Germany and thereby involved an interpretation of another aspect of history. In considering the domestic implications of a possible foreign policy decision, foreign policy makers interpret American domestic history as well. Another social example: During World War II President Roosevelt and his close advisers, in pondering the shape of the postwar world and their desire for a world organization, quite obviously bore constantly in mind the defeat of Woodrow Wilson's desires for United States membership in the League of Nations. To avoid Wilson's mistakes was Roosevelt's purpose, and to identify those mistakes involved an interpretation of Wilson's actions. In other words, FDR interpreted history when he made historical decisions. The overwhelmingly favorable popular response to the proposal to help create and participate in the United Nations involved the American people generally in historical interpretation. Whether we are always aware of it or not, all of us constantly heed Lincoln's dictum that to understand the present we must understand the past. And understanding the past really means interpreting the past in a meaningful way.

Now, unless one begins with the philosophic assumption that "wishing will make it so," a kind of mind-over-matter way of thinking, it is important that historical interpretation conform with the real world, the real past. Operating from false assumptions is a sure path to disaster unless one is extremely lucky. It is here that historical myths can and often do lead society astray. A large section of the German people in the 1920's and 1930's cherished the myth, or wrong-headed interpretation of the past, that they had lost the war in 1918 because of Bolshevik and Jewish machinations at home; the ultimate fruit of their myth was destruction. The assumption throughout the Western world that colonial imperialism was beneficent, and was so regarded by colonial people, ill prepared the white man for the colonial revolt of the mid-twentieth century. In a more remote era, the myth of the invincibility of American arms against the British during the American Revolution was a significant misreading of recent history when the young United States engaged the British in war again in 1812. (Incidentally, the War of 1812 is a part of history that is studiously ignored by those who hold to the myth that "the United States never lost a war nor won a peace.")

Parts of the American population—regions, ethnic groups, organizations of various kinds—have time and again held to a misinterpretation of the past that has been a handicap in dealing with problems confronting them. The South's fondly cherished myth that life on a plantation before the Civil War was idyllic and that *ante-bellum* southern culture was the high point of western civilization seriously handicapped that region's adjustment to the real world of the late nineteenth and early twentieth centuries. The

Negro's belief that the Republican party had selflessly engaged in a crusade for his emancipation caused him to give his almost total allegiance to that party and thereby limited the range of his political decisions. For decades American farm organizations misinterpreted American economic history and attributed industrial and commercial growth solely to protective tariffs and the monetary system. Therefore, they believed that the way to agricultural prosperity was through tariff protection for the farm, even though few foreign farm products were competitive in the American market in any circumstances, and through reversal of the monetary policies of the "gold bugs."

But there is a paradox about myths. By definition unreal, widely and deeply believed myths can be an actual force, and a factor with which the historian must reckon. One cannot understand the history of the South after the Civil War unless one understands the way that most southerners interpreted their region's past. One cannot understand Negro politics between the Civil War and the Great Depression if one ignores the myths about the war and the Republican party that Negroes believed. One cannot understand late nineteenth and early twentieth-century politics without understanding the farmers' economic theories, mistaken though they were. This is not to take the mind-over-matter position. It is to say that one cannot understand a society without understanding its beliefs, its assumptions, even if these beliefs be fallacious.

Most widely held myths have at least some evidence to support them and are cases of distortion or improper emphasis rather than utter fabrications. An outright forgery, such as the Protocols of the Elders of Zion, can have a serious effect, to be sure, but myths that have no foundation whatsoever rarely have the impact of those that a reasonable man might believe.

The myths about the 1920's and 1930's discussed in this volume were not products of pure imagination and therefore were and are all the more widely held. The following chapters are not devoted exclusively to fables about the past. Relevant myths will be discussed, but the main emphasis will be upon historical evidence which, it is to be hoped, will lead to a realistic interpretation of the recent past.

Much, but by no means all, of this book is about politics. When people discuss politics they frequently become involved in a semantic bog, especially when they use such communications shortcuts as *conservative, reactionary, liberal,* and *radical,* all useful terms only if there is agreement about what they mean. In order to avoid confusion let us agree now to certain arbitrary definitions. Unless otherwise indicated, the noun *conservative* in this book will mean a person whose primary goal in economic affairs is to advance the short-term interest of a majority of the business community, especially big corporations, by opposing such countervailing forces to corporate power as government regulation and trade unions or by advancing government measures to strengthen or protect corporate power. An economic conservative, as used here, is not necessarily a conservative in matters of civil liberty and individual conscience. A conservative in these fields is one who would limit or restrict the Bill of Rights. A *reactionary* will mean an extreme conservative, one who in economic matters would abolish those countervailing forces to corporate power that have become customary and generally accepted. Both conservatives and reactionaries, the former mildly and the latter strongly, usually distrust the ability of the mass of people to govern themselves wisely. *Liberals* or *progressives,* here used interchangeably, are those who in economic matters would use the power of government to regulate corporate power and private property to advance and protect the interests of a majority of people. They would modify capitalism from its classic model to achieve this end, but they would not abolish it. They are defenders of civil liberty and of the right of the citizen to advocate whatever doctrines he wishes. The term *radical* in this book will mean a person who rejects capitalism as a desirable economic arrangement.

Boom Years

Part One

Boom
Years

1

Woodrow Wilson and Postwar Conservatism

FOR ROUGHLY THE SECOND DECADE of the twentieth century Woodrow Wilson was the central figure of national politics and the symbol about which political warriors clashed. His influence lived on after his public career. The popular memory of him remained sharp for years after he left the White House in 1921.

He was a remarkable man by any standards. By the standards normally used to judge national political figures he was almost unique. With the possible exception of Theodore Roosevelt, Wilson's contemporary and the dominant figure in the Republican party until his death in 1919, no president had possessed such intellectual qualifications and background since the early nineteenth century. Wilson was a southern gentleman (nothing very unusual in politics), a seemingly aloof and cold intellectual of outstanding academic background (unique in national politics), and a stern, conscious, and deep moralist (rare but not unique among prominent politicians).

Wilson was born in Virginia in the last days of 1856. His boyhood in that state coincided with the Civil War and Reconstruction. His father and his maternal grandfather were Calvinist Presbyterian ministers, and his Calvinist upbringing left its mark on his personality and his social assumptions. He graduated from Princeton University, which had been founded in the Presby-

3

terian fervor of the Great Awakening and was not to lose its early tone and become "Ivy League" until the twentieth century. Wilson then went to law school at the University of Virginia, graduating in 1882. After practicing law in Atlanta for a year he earned a Ph.D. in political science at The Johns Hopkins University in Baltimore. His dissertation was published as *Congressional Government* in 1885, quickly became a standard work in its field, and went through many editions. After five years of professorial apprenticeship at Bryn Mawr and Wesleyan, he went back to Princeton as a professor of government. In 1902, when just forty-two years old, he became president of Princeton. Wilson was a vigorous and able university president. He improved the faculty and the intellectual tone of the campus, but he resigned after eight years when he lost a sharply contested issue of campus politics. Besides, he was ready to try his hand at the politics of government.

As Princeton's president, an outstanding political scientist, and an articulate writer and lecturer, Wilson commanded a national audience. When he left Princeton he was an intellectually acute, conservative Democrat. But after he was elected governor of New Jersey in 1910, a year of general Democratic good fortune, he quickly established a reputation as a high-minded reformer. As governor he was an advocate of democratic political process, an opponent of corrupt machine politicians, and a mild critic of flagrant governmental privilege for vested economic interests. He was not a militant opponent of big commercial and industrial corporations; he was not of the wing of the Democratic party that looked to William Jennings Bryan as its champion. He barely received the Democratic presidential nomination in 1912 and won because the Republicans split into the Taft and Roosevelt tickets.

In his first White House years Wilson established a reputation as a progressive through his domestic legislative program, although he did not advance proposals as far-reaching as many liberals desired and he was often willing to compromise his original demands. In the 1916 elections the voters, impressed with his legislative achievements and his record of keeping the nation neutral through twenty-six months of raging war in Europe, re-elected him by a small margin despite the healing of the breach between regular and Roosevelt Republicans. After America entered World War I in 1917 Wilson emerged as a national leader such as no president had been since Lincoln and as an international statesman. No previous American president had had such international influence.

The essence of Wilson's appeal was his middle-class idealism. Whether Wilson was urging a tariff reform, dealing with a revolutionary situation in Mexico, leading a nation at war against imperial Germany, or announcing American war aims, he always made his appeal in terms of morality, justice, and fairness as these concepts were understood by his contemporary middle-class Americans. He also appealed directly to the people, both at home and abroad, which enhanced his personal popularity and prestige. His high-mindedness well fitted the popular American mood until the postwar disillusionment. It was a period in which serious people of good will believed that politics could and should be above economic interest, that right would conquer all, that clean living and high thinking were the greatest of virtues, that a millennium such as John Calvin would have approved was not beyond quick realization. It was a time when the YMCA was a most popular institution among soldiers. It was a time when President Wilson could in all seriousness tell a British diplomat during the difficulties with Mexico that he would "teach the South American republics to elect good men." It was a time when a large part of the population believed that the effective prohibition of alcoholic drinks was possible and desirable, when Americans could believe that the war they were suffering would "make the world safe for democracy," when high-school boys could flock to a youth organization called the ACL, which stood for Anti-Cigarette League and A Clean Life. It was a perfect time for Woodrow Wilson to be President of the United States.

Such was the contrast of Wilson with his predecessors in the Democratic leadership—and of Theodore Roosevelt with his predecessors in the Republican leadership—and such was the contrast with the national mood and the characteristics of national politics in the immediately subsequent era that myths about Wilson came easily.

The Wilson Myth

The popular myth about Wilson's last presidential years runs along these lines. Wilson, a progressive in domestic matters and an internationalist in foreign policy, faced a powerful group of domestically conservative or reactionary Republicans who were isolationist in their views about America's relations with the rest of the world. These conservatives were concentrated in the Senate, where they were able to defeat approval of the liberal and internationalist Treaty of Versailles. Their defeat of the treaty, which prevented United States membership in the League of Nations, signaled the beginning of an ostrich-like head-in-the-sand policy toward Europe which was not to disappear until Hitler threatened the world's peace in the late 1930's. Had America not been isolationist during these years, had it been a member of the League of Nations, Hitler probably never would have become a threat and there would have been no World War II. Wilson foresaw these consequences of the treaty's defeat. In a valiant effort to prevent his enemies in the Senate from blocking the treaty, he took his case to the people in an exhausting speaking tour. His stroke, incurred from overwork, incapacitated him and enabled his Senate opponents to defeat the League. The election of 1920 constituted a national referendum on the League issue, and the voters upheld the Senate's refusal to ratify the treaty by choosing the archconservative Republican candidate, Warren Gamaliel Harding. Harding, elected on a foreign policy issue, inaugurated an era of domestic conservatism and economic nearsightedness that brought about the crash of 1929 and the Great Depression. Progressivism was dead. The American people concurred in these old-fashioned, nineteenth-century government economic policies because in the short run, until the fall of 1929, they brought about a shining prosperity. Rich, soft, pleasure-seeking, and complacent America did not awaken until the stock-market crash and then it paid its retribution for its ten-year binge.

This view of the immediate postwar era persists strongly, despite the writings of several historians, for several reasons. In the first place, it is not entirely false. Republicans in the Senate did oppose the treaty and defeat it, Wilson did take his case to the people, he did suffer an incapacitating stroke, the League of Nations was one of the issues in the 1920 election, and the Republican administrations of the following decade pursued policies most people would characterize as conservative. Another reason for the myth's vitality is that it is comforting to ardent Democrats. It puts the Democratic party in the role of the defender of what was wise and right and the Republican opposition as the advocate of folly and wrong-headedness. And the myth simplifies history and makes it a clear-cut struggle between good and evil, capable of being understood by the person of little political or historical sophistication.

But the myth is such an oversimplification that no serious student of history can accept it. Life is not simple, and therefore history, which is past life, is not simple. No political party has a monopoly on wisdom and right and none is wholly foolish or wrong. And life and history seldom if ever resolve into a clear-cut struggle between the forces of good and evil.

The balance of this chapter will treat the Treaty of Versailles issue from its beginning through the election of 1920 as well as the domestic policies of the Wilson administration from the end of the war to its end in 1921. (Subsequent chapters on the eras of Harding and his successors will indirectly treat other aspects of the Wilson legend.) This chapter will indicate that the era's politics was complex, that both major parties were sometimes wise and sometimes foolish both in aims and strategy, that neither side was consistently liberal or conservative, and that neither Wilson nor his opponents were shining knights of wisdom and virtue.

America and the World

A part of the myth about isolationism and the defeat of the Treaty of Versailles by the Senate lies in the assumption that the treaty—and the League of Nations it established—was wholly liberal, enlightened, and noble. Actually, it was rather less than that. Some background about war aims and the writing of the treaty is necessary.

Before the United States entered the war in April 1917, the Allies had signed a number of secret treaties among themselves. The British informed Wilson about these treaties immediately after the American declaration of war. These treaties provided that the Allies would take slices of the territories of the Central Powers (Germany, Austria-Hungary, and Turkey) and divide up the German colonial empire among themselves. Quite obviously, Wilson did not approve of these treaties, although he did not make their abrogation a condition of American military effort in France. In January 1918, after the Bolsheviks of Russia had recently come to power and published the secret treaties they had found in the Czarist archives, Wilson announced the American war aims in the Fourteen Points. Wilson called for a League of Nations "for the purpose of affording mutual guaranties of political independence and territorial integrity to great and small states alike"; the removal of trade barriers and equality of trade conditions among the members of the League; an end to secret diplomacy; freedom of the seas during both wartime and peacetime; reduction of armaments; opportunity for Russia to develop as she saw fit; impartial adjustment of colonial claims, with the voice of the colonial people to have "equal weight" with the power asserting the claim; evacuation of Belgium; the return of Alsace-Lorraine to France; the creation of a Polish national state; and a redrawing of the map of Europe to create a national state for each national cultural group, "national self-determination." In October 1918 Germany approached Wilson with an appeal for an armistice based upon the Fourteen Points. Britain flatly refused an armistice with an express promise of freedom of the seas, and France insisted that Germany agree to reparations for its damages to French property. Germany accepted an armistice with these conditions.

While negotiations for the armistice were still underway and while the fighting was still fierce in the trenches of France, Wilson put his prestige on the line with the American voters. Urged by Democratic candidates in the 1918 elections to give them a campaign boost, Wilson declined to help them as individuals and made a blanket appeal for a Democratic Congress. "The return of a Republican majority to either house of the Congress," Wilson said in an official statement, "would . . . be interpreted on the other side of the water as a repudiation of my leadership." Just six days before the armistice the voters elected Republican majorities to each house of Congress. Thus, by his own assessment, Wilson went to Paris repudiated by the American people. Wilson failed to alleviate the situation presented him by a hostile Senate, which would have to ratify any treaty, when he named the members of the peace commission. No senator and no prominent Republican went with the President to the peace table.

Four men, Prime Minister David Lloyd George of Great Britain, Premier Georges Clemenceau of France, Premier Vittorio Orlando of Italy, and Wilson, made the basic decisions in writing the Treaty of Versailles. The Allied peacemakers were in varying degrees old-fashioned nationalists and imperialists who wished to shape the postwar world as much like the prewar world as possible, only eliminating Germany as a power. Wilson was not in agreement with them. His Fourteen Points well summarized his position. But he did agree with his adversaries in opposing the new government of Russia and communists elsewhere. Indeed, Wilson had already agreed long before the peace conference to cooperate with the Allies in a military expedition into the Soviet Union, thus making his point about Russia in the Fourteen Points inoperative. This military expedition left a legacy of distrust and fear of the West among the Russian Communists that is not yet dissipated. The Treaty of Versailles was the work of representatives of western Europe and the

United States. Germany, the main nation of central Europe, had no real alternative to accepting what her former enemies dictated. Nations of eastern Europe and other parts of the world, such as Latin America and Asia, either were not represented at the conference at all or had little influence there. The treaty most emphatically was not a world document.

In several respects the Treaty of Versailles did not fulfill the Fourteen Points. Freedom of the seas and a hands-off-Russia policy had disappeared even before the peace conference met. The Treaty of Versailles was by no means a secret treaty, but the conference fell short of Wilson's goal of "open convenants openly arrived at" when it all but excluded the press from the negotiations. Colonial people had no voice at Versailles whatsoever, much less an equal voice, in dealing with the problem of colonies. Indeed, the solution of how to dispose of Germany's former colonies smacked strongly of old-fashioned colonialism and power politics. Germany's colonies in every case went to the Allied power that had wrested them by force or had been promised them by secret treaty. The only concession to anti-colonialism was that the Allies received the colonies as mandates from the League of Nations rather than as outright colonial possessions. But whether their colonial administrators governed them by mandate from the League or by the traditional authority made little difference to the colonial people who were governed by outsiders. Non-Caucasians suffered another defeat when Japan was defeated in its bid to get an explicit statement of racial equality into the final document. Wilson firmly opposed the Japanese request. Nor did Wilson gain anything firm in his demand for equality of trade opportunity. The treaty did not explicitly extend the idea of the "Open Door" to the entire world as Wilson wished it to. Wilson had not included opposition to heavy war reparations from Germany in his Fourteen Points, but he did oppose them at the peace conference and again he was defeated. The treaty created a special reparations commission to set the amount Germany was to pay after the document was signed. In 1921 the commission set the figure at an astronomical $33 billion.

Those parts of the Fourteen Points that were written into the treaty were the ones that France and England wanted. Alsace-Lorraine went back to France. Germany withdrew from Belgium. New countries came into being on the basis of national cultures—Poland, Yugoslavia, Czechoslovakia, Lithuania, Estonia, and Latvia. These new national entities were consistent with "national self-determination," but they also created a buffer zone around the Soviet Union, whose containment was a primary goal of the peacemakers. And, of course, the treaty created the League of Nations, which was uppermost in Wilson's mind.

All too often, the opponents of the treaty and the League in the United States have simply been lumped together as "isolationists." The precise meaning of that word is vague. If it means a person who wishes the United States to have nothing to do with the rest of the world, who has no interest in foreign affairs whether they be economic, political, social, or cultural, then there were precious few "isolationists" among the leaders of the fight against the treaty. Opponents of the treaty and the League in 1919 and 1920 were moved by considerably diverse motives. All that they had in common was opposition to the idea of collective security as represented by the League of Nations.

Some of the League's opponents were intense American nationalists wary of yielding any national decision-making whatsoever to an international body. Former Senator Albert Beveridge of Indiana, an ardent imperialist in 1898 and a Theodore Roosevelt Progressive, and the publisher William Randolph Hearst were good examples of this kind of chauvinistic League opponent. Some were merely highly partisan Republican leaders who sensed that the League was really not very popular with the voters and who saw a way to turn the Democrats out of the White House by making the League the main issue of politics. Henry Cabot Lodge of Massachusetts, who was chairman of the key Senate Committee on Foreign Relations, was never candid about his motives, but probably a large part of his opposition to the League derived from Republican partisanship. On domestic policy those against the League ranged from the far left to the far right. Socialists and Communists opposed the League, largely because of the treaty's restrictions upon the Soviet Union. Non-Marxist progressive Republicans such as Senators William E. Borah of Idaho, Hiram Johnson of California, Robert M. La Follette of Wisconsin, and George W. Norris of Nebraska were among the "irreconcilable" opponents of the League. Both *The Nation* and *The New Republic* opposed ratification of the treaty. From the right end of the political spectrum in opposition to the treaty were the *Chicago Tribune*, Henry Clay Frick, Andrew Mellon, and Philander C. Knox, then a senator from Pennsylvania and once President Taft's Secretary of State. Several American ethnic groups objected to ratification. Many Jews were disappointed by the treaty's failure to create a Jewish national state in Palestine. Irish-Americans were angry about the refusal of Great Britain to countenance independence for Ireland, and when they "twisted the lion's tail" with a vengeance during the national debate over the treaty they evoked a wide response. Parts of the German-American community thought the treaty too Carthaginian toward Germany. Even a few friends of independence for India fought ratification.

But even though opponents of the League represented a cross-section of the population, they had an uphill fight to defeat the treaty, and they probably would not have won if President Wilson had not refused any kind of compromise. Soon after Germany signed the treaty in June 1919, American public opinion seemed to support ratification. A poll of newspaper editors conducted by the *Literary Digest* indicated widespread support. About thirty state legislatures and governors had come out in favor of the League. Consequently, the League's opponents in the Senate stalled for time while they endeavored to change public opinion. Senator Lodge even read the treaty aloud to his colleagues in the Committee on Foreign Relations. Going through the 246-page document word by word consumed two weeks. Then the committee began extensive hearings, which took up another six weeks. When Wilson conferred with several Republican senators in mid-August he saw that opposition to the League was growing. The President decided that an appeal to the electorate was the best approach he could take. He would build a fire of public opinion under the Senate that would force it to ratify the treaty.

In early September Wilson left Washington for a speaking tour to build pro-League sentiment. He was not in good health, and his physician had advised against the trip. He had had a bad bout with influenza when he was in Paris and had been troubled by headaches throughout the summer. In three weeks Wilson gave thirty-seven major addresses and traveled over 8,000 miles. His health was destroyed, and he had to abandon the tour and return to Washington, where one week later he suffered a serious stroke. He was completely incapacitated for several days, and when he began to recover he was partly paralyzed. If anyone was able to build public opinion for the League it was the President, and now even he was unable to work effectively. Furthermore, illness and adversity seemed only to strengthen his Calvinist will to win a complete victory or none at all.

Senate maneuvering on the treaty vote was complicated. One should remember that more than two thirds of the senators, enough to ratify the treaty, and perhaps as many as three fourths of them, were ready to vote for the treaty and the League either as it had been written or with some revisions. Yet the treaty was never ratified. While Wilson was still on his speaking tour the Committee on Foreign Relations presented its reports to the full Senate. Ten of the committee's seventeen members signed the majority report, which called for ratification of the treaty with forty-five amendments and reservations. The minority report, signed only by Democrats, called for ratification with revisions. Only a simple majority was necessary to reject any revision, and a combination of Democrats and "mild reservationist" Republicans voted down the forty-five amendments.

On November 6 Senator Lodge introduced fourteen other reservations. This time the Senate accepted the revisions. Again only a simple majority was necessary. The division in the Senate was almost altogether on party lines, the Democrats voting to reject the amendments and the Republicans voting to accept them. Gilbert M. Hitchcock of Nebraska, the Democratic leader in the Senate, twice visited the President in his sickroom to see what Wilson advised, for in accepting the Lodge reservations without putting the whole treaty to a ratification vote the Republicans had left the initiative up to the Democrats and the White House. On November 18 Wilson made public a letter he had written to Senator Hitchcock. The Lodge reservations, he wrote, do "not provide for ratification, but, rather for the nullification of the treaty. I sincerely hope that the friends and supporters of the treaty will vote against the Lodge resolution of ratification." The President had drawn the line: all or nothing.

The next day the Senate voted three times on ratification. The first vote was on the treaty with the Lodge reservations. The Democrats accepted Wilson's urgings. Their votes against the Lodge resolution, plus those of the Republicans who opposed the treaty even with the Lodge reservations, defeated ratification by a vote of 39 for and 55 against. Then Senator Hitchcock, ignoring the advice of the President, introduced a resolution calling for ratification with five minor reservations. The Senate defeated this resolution, 41 for and 51 against. Finally, there was a vote on ratification without any reservations. It was foredoomed to failure. Thirty-eight Senators voted for it, 53 against.

There matters stood for the tense winter of 1919-1920. No one yet considered the treaty a dead issue. Public opinion demanded another test in the upper house. Neither the Senate Republicans nor Wilson would back down from their November positions. The Republicans strongly supported the Lodge reservations—some of them would not vote for the treaty even with the reservations—and public opinion was steadily building behind the Republicans. Wilson would not back down an inch. His close friend and adviser Colonel Edward M. House urged him to leave the treaty up to the Senate. House wrote Wilson that he need not "be a party to those reservations." He could just leave responsibility up to the Senate, which House predicted would ratify the treaty without serious amendments "in a form acceptable to both you and the Allies." Wilson and House ceased to be friends after this note. One of the arguments against ratifying the treaty with reservations was that such an action would make necessary new negotiations among the Allies, perhaps even another peace conference. The Allies sought to assure the United States on this point. Viscount Edward Grey, former British foreign affairs secretary, was ambassador in Washington that winter, and it was common knowledge that his mission was to urge Wilson to compromise. Wilson refused to see him, saying that his health did not permit it. Grey wrote a letter to the editor of the London *Times* in which he stated that American failure to ratify the treaty would wreck the League of Nations and that the Allies were ready to accept the Lodge reservations without new negotiations. Wilson still refused to see Grey and refused to depart from his opposition to any reservations whatsoever.

Finally, in mid-February the Senate began to debate the treaty. Wilson's health had improved to a degree, and he continued to oppose anything except ratification of the treaty in its original version. On March 19, 1920, the treaty came to a vote in the Senate for the fourth and last time. This time the vote was on ratification with the fourteen Lodge reservations plus an expression of sympathy with Irish independence. Twenty of the forty-seven Senate Democrats, figuring that this vote was the showdown and that the treaty would either be ratified with the Lodge reservations or not at all, bolted Wilson's orders and voted for ratification. The other Democrats voted with the "irreconcilables," those who would vote against the treaty in any form. The ratification fell short of the necessary two-thirds majority. Forty-nine Senators voted for the resolution with the fifteen reservations; thirty-five voted against it. If seven more Democrats had deserted Wilson's orders and voted for the resolution, the treaty would have been ratified on March 19, 1920. If seven "irreconcilables" had changed their votes the treaty would have been ratified. If Senator Lodge had rescinded his reservations the treaty would have been ratified. If President Wilson had consented to the reservations the treaty would have been ratified. Who can say upon whom the responsibility for the treaty's defeat must rest? In any event, the normal constitutional process had developed into a Senate deadlock from which neither the Republicans nor Wilson nor most Democrats would retreat, and the treaty went down to defeat.

But even after March 1920, those who hoped for ratification and American membership in the League of Nations continued to think there was a chance of ratification. President Wilson had sent a message to the Jackson Day dinner in Washington, an annual Democratic jubilee, in which he said that if the Senate defeated the treaty the elections of 1920 would be "a great and solemn referendum" on the treaty and the League. Actually, the President, a former professor of political science and a candidate in two presidential elections, should have known that an election in the United States is not and never has been a great referendum on any single issue, much less a solemn one. Personalities, other national issues, and regional and local issues come into play in a presidential election, and one can never say with precision just what, if anything, election results indicate about the public's thinking on any given issue. Yet Wilson looked toward the elections as a possible vindication of his position. In May 1920, when upon the motion of Senator Knox of Pennsylvania, Congress by a simple majority declared the war was over without a treaty by simply rescinding the war resolutions of April 1917, President Wilson replied with a veto. Technically, the war was still on when the voters went to the polls in November 1920.

The campaign had only served to show how foolish was the idea of "a great and solemn referendum." The Republican national convention, as was to be expected, adopted a platform that both supporters and opponents of the League interpreted as favoring their position, but the platform did not even mention the League of Nations by name. The Democratic platform, again as was to be expected, also straddled. It stated support of the League and the treaty but also indicated that the party would not oppose reservations. During the campaign both major party candidates, Republican Warren G. Harding and Democrat James M. Cox, hedged over the League in an effort to attract votes both from those who wanted and those who did not want the United States to join it. Some pro-League Republicans argued during the fall of 1920 that a vote for Harding was a vote for the League with reservations. Cox, late in the campaign, began publicly to back away from his earlier Wilsonian principles. It is probably true that most Republicans who supported the League voted for Harding and most Democrats who supported it voted for Cox. Harding won in a landslide. Cox and the Democrats were smothered, receiving less than 40 per cent of the popular vote.

Yet no one could say with any assurance what the verdict of the people had been in so far as the treaty and the League were concerned. More than anything else, they were probably tired of the whole dragged-out issue. Two days after the election Harding declared that the League issue was as "dead as slavery." Surely a realistic analysis of the election did not warrant such a statement. But it had been none other than President Wilson who had declared the election a referendum on the League, and thus he had no choice but to accept the election as a defeat for the League.

The rest of the story was anticlimax. On July 21, 1921, Congress passed a joint resolution simply declaring that the war was over. The treaty never again came to a vote. Neither political party thereafter adopted a platform that advocated membership in the League of Nations.

Given the complexity of the League issue in American politics, the fact that the treaty fell short of the principles enunciated in the Fourteen Points, the fact that a vast majority of the Senate had favored ratification with reservations but had failed to ratify because of Wilson's unbending refusal to compromise even in the slightest, and the complex and diverse motives of those who opposed the treaty, it is clear that the view of the treaty fight which sees Wilsonian international idealism defeated by Republican isolationism is too oversimplified and partisan to be respected. But it is not clear that American failure to join the League of Nations led ineluctably to World War II. It is impossible to say what would have happened if the United States had been a member of the League. Whether or not the way the treaty fight ended made any great difference for the next generation we shall never know.

Wilson's Postwar Domestic Policies

That part of the Wilson myth and of the Roaring Twenties myth that sees Republican reaction killing Wilsonian liberalism is more than oversimplification. It is clear distortion. The myth presents Wilson as a thoroughly frustrated figure in his last two years in office. Isolationist, vindictive, and fiercely partisan Republicans in Congress, strong because of a general postwar disillusionment with noble sentiments, prevented the ratification of the Versailles Treaty and took the issue to the voters in 1920. Having won endorsement on their foreign policy position, the Republican administrations undertook a program of domestic conservatism. The Republican party killed the New Freedom after it had killed the League, and progressivism thereafter lay dormant until the Great Depression evoked the New Deal. Thus, in general outline, runs the myth.

The main difficulty with this interpretation of the early postwar years is that it ignores Wilson's domestic policies during his last two years in office. Wilson was the first postwar president, and the last quarter of his presidency cannot by any reasonable standard be judged progressive or liberal in domestic affairs in either results or intent. Wilson, not Harding, inaugurated postwar conservatism. Harding did not kill the New Freedom. The New Freedom was a victim of infanticide at the hands of its father and its Democratic godfathers, aided by Republican uncles who had never thought highly of the child. From the winter of 1918-1919 to Harding's inauguration in March 1921, the federal government's policies, both executive and legislative, that affected business, labor, agriculture, and the consumer were thoroughly conservative. In matters of civil liberty, the Republican administrations of the 1920's were more liberal than Wilson's after the declaration of war. Indeed, no other American president ever left office with as poor a civil-liberties record as Woodrow Wilson's.

Many of the economic problems the government had to face were connected in one way or another with postwar demobilization. The economy and the government's role in it had never changed so rapidly in a similar period as it had in 1917-1918. With the coming of peace, the economy had to change again to a peacetime basis.

The war had not been long declared before it became apparent that the nation's productive and distributive facilities were inadequate to the wartime task if they operated traditionally. To produce the arms necessary to defeat Germany and to transport them across the Atlantic to the French and English as well as the American forces was a task that required great planning and coordination. It became necessary to rationalize (i.e., to reorganize for greatest efficiency) the country's economy. Some industries, notably those engaged in heavy manufacturing, had already rationalized their production in the interest of greater efficiency and profits. But never before had it been necessary to rationalize the entire economy of the United States. Only the federal government could undertake so large a task, making the tremendous productive facilities of the nation operate under forced draft toward a specific purpose. The government's efforts were never fully adequate, its direction of the economy was often makeshift and without intelligent comprehensive planning, and the war ended before the nation's productive capacities were completely harnessed. Nevertheless, on Armistice Day the United States government was the prime mover and coordinator of the American economy.

Neither the Wilson administration nor Congress seriously considered maintaining the government's economic role while shifting its function from war to the economic welfare of the whole population. But the government could relinquish its economic powers and functions in several ways. The demobilization policies actually pursued were in every case except taxation ones that conservatives might applaud, measures that benefited the economic interests of invested capital in the short run. In most aspects of economic demobilization the government merely turned over its wartime functions to private business.

Government wartime spending had been a tremendous stimulation to the economy. This spending ceased as quickly as the administration could stop it. The War Department had $4 billion in outstanding and unfilled orders on Armistice Day. The administration canceled more than half these orders within a month after the last shot. Construction of all government buildings less than 70 per cent completed halted before the end of the year. Instead of engaging upon a federal public works program to ease the economy into peacetime and employ returning servicemen, as many liberals urged, President Wilson called a conference of governors and mayors and urged them to undertake more public works. Needless to say, the efforts of state and local government in this respect had no economic impact.

The War Department had considered a plan of releasing servicemen in such a way as to minimize unemployment, first mustering out men who had jobs waiting for them and then others as jobs were available. But in the end the army simply discharged the soldiers by military units and ignored both their length of service and their employment possibilities. Of the four million men in the service half were gone in less than six months. Within a year after the armistice the armed forces were down to normal peacetime size. The United States Employment Service, be-

gun during the war to help rationalize manpower, set about finding jobs for released soldiers and did the job remarkably well.
But in January 1919, Congress reduced the Employment Service's
appropriation by four fifths when Wilson made no vigorous fight
for the service's function, and the government's activity in this
field faded to insignificance. Before all the soldiers were released,
an unofficial Emergency Committee on Employment for Soldiers
and Sailors had taken over the task. This organization restricted
itself to a promotion campaign that urged employers to hire returning servicemen.

The federal government showed greater consideration to capital that had been enlisted or conscripted into the economic army
than it did to the citizen-soldier. During the war the government
had assumed control of three critical industries; telephones and
telegraphs, railroading, and oceanic shipping and shipbuilding.
Government control of the communications industry had been
more or less accidental. A strike of telephone and telegraph
workers had seemed imminent, and to prevent a disruption of
this vital wartime service the government had assumed control of
the industry (the practice in most other industrial nations) and
put it under the Post Office Department. The government returned the industry to private control on August 1, 1919. The
only condition of the government's relinquishment was that rates
could not be increased for four months.

What to do about the railroads was a considerably more complex problem because the plain fact was that the government
had operated the railroads more efficiently and with better and
safer service than had private enterprise before the war. Indeed,
private management's inefficiency had been the cause of the federal government's assuming control of railroading. In December
1917, American railroads were in a frightful crisis that jeopardized the success of the whole war effort. While manufacturers
were unable to get empty freight cars and both passenger and
freight service was wildly unreliable, eastern freight yards were
jammed to capacity. Some essential industries such as steel ran
short of fuel. Basically, the trains were not where they were supposed to be at the right time. The chief difficulty was that there
was no over-all direction of the nation's roads. Some systems
were integrated, such as the New York Central and the Pennsylvania, but there was no coordination among the systems. The
situation demanded national integration and rationalization. Unfavorable weather in December 1917 brought matters to a head.
The government took control of the industry through the United
States Railroad Administration. William G. McAdoo resigned as

Secretary of the Treasury and became its head. McAdoo integrated the systems, but it soon became apparent that railroad equipment was inadequate and sometimes in dangerously poor condition. The federal government spent over a half billion dollars on capital improvements. Railroad capital continued to receive a return on its investment. The government paid railroad companies a rental based on prewar earnings.

Several people and interests came forward with plans to continue the railroad efficiency born of wartime urgency. McAdoo and Walker D. Hines, who succeeded to the railroad post in January 1919, proposed that the wartime arrangement be continued for another five years while the whole transportation problem was studied. Others recommended government ownership and operation of the railroads, which was common practice in Europe. Glenn Plumb, legal counsel of the economically conservative railroad labor brotherhoods, suggested a scheme of nationalization. Under the Plumb plan, the government would create a wholly federally owned corporation, which would run and operate all the railroads in a single system. A third of the members of the corporation's board of directors would represent the government, a third the railroad managers, and a third railroad labor. Owners of private enterprise railroad securities would exchange them for bonds of the new corporation, which would continue to be regulated by the Interstate Commerce Commission. The Plumb plan had the strong support of the railroad brotherhoods—not because of any ideological committment to industrial nationalization but because they believed that an efficient rail system would be able to pay better wages. But the plan had little support in Congress, none from the administration, and highly vocal opposition from private railroad investors.

The investors were divided about how control should be returned to private business although they were nearly unanimous in wanting it returned. Railroad securities were highly popular investments; insurance companies and banks had much of their capital in the railroads. Some railroads had a large bonded indebtedness and were in financial difficulty, particularly if they served areas that were in economic decline. Holders of weak railroad securities, such as the New York, New Haven and Hartford, the Erie, the Missouri Pacific, and the Chicago, Milwaukee and St. Paul, wanted some kind of consolidation with stronger railroad companies so as to protect their investment. Those who had interests in the strong railroad lines had no desire to become burdened with unprofitable ones.

The national discussion of railroad problems indicated remarkably little concern for railroad efficiency. Economic interest, whether that of railroad labor or of investors in strong or weak rail companies, determined the main positions. On the day before Christmas 1919, President Wilson further complicated the already involved problem by giving Congress a deadline: on March 1, 1920, he would simply return control of the railroads to management unless Congress meanwhile took action. This would mean a return to the situation that had been the root of the problem in 1917. Liberals could see no valid reasons for Wilson's demand for quick action.

Congress enacted the Esch-Cummins or Transportation Act of 1920 the day before the President's deadline. The measure was a compromise mishmash. It clearly rejected the idea of the Plumb plan or of continued government direction of any kind. As it worked out in practice, it neither provided for greater transportation rationalization nor protected investors in the weak lines. In other words, the main beneficiaries of the act were the stock and bond holders of the already strong railroad companies. The government's answer to the railroad problem was nearly as conservative as any other solution that had been advanced. The Transportation Act did not meet the challenge. Although the Interstate Commerce Commission in 1920 approved freight rate increases of 35 per cent and passenger fare hikes of 20 per cent, railroad companies still failed to make the 6 per cent return on investment the ICC established as fair. The basic railroad law poorly prepared the roads to meet the increasingly competitive challenge of trucks and cars. By midcentury American railroad passenger service was the worst of any major industrial country in the Western world.

The problem of the shipping industry differed from the railroad problem because the government had not merely rented and directed shipping facilities as it had the railroads. It had to a considerable extent created a merchant marine. The federal government had built and operated about 2,000 ships totaling about 15 million tons. Prewar experience had demonstrated that American shipping companies were not competitive with those of European maritime powers. Unless they were subsidized in some manner, American private shipping companies could not maintain a strong merchant marine, which wartime experience had demonstrated was necessary for national defense. The issue boiled down, then, to the question of whether the federal government should subsidize private merchant shipping in the interest of long-run national defense or whether it should continue to engage itself directly in the shipping business with the same object in mind. Shipping remained a minor issue of politics throughout the 1920's, but Wilson and the Republican Congress elected in 1918 made the bipartisan basic decision to withdraw the federal government from operation of the merchant marine and to subsidize privately owned companies.

In June 1920, Congress passed and Wilson signed the Jones Merchant Marine Act. It was more favorable to shipping capital than the Transportation Act had been to railroad investors. It directed the government to sell its ships at bargain prices and, on easy terms, set up a twenty-five-million-dollar loan fund for American shippers, offered shippers very generous mail contracts, exempted them from corporation income taxes if they used the funds saved for construction of new ships, and granted them a monopoly on shipping between colonial territories and the United States mainland—this last provision no different in principle from the English navigation acts of the colonial period of American history. Even the governmental largesse of this measure was not sufficient to maintain a healthy merchant marine, and the shipping companies came back to Congress to ask for and receive even more generous subsidies. American shipping thrived briefly in the late 1920's, but it was hard hit by the depression and it was in poor condition again when war broke out in Europe in 1939. As with railroading, the conservative decisions made immediately after World War I failed ultimately to protect the national interest.

Two measures of the Wilson administration significantly altered antitrust law to the advantage of big corporations. The Webb-Pomerene Act of 1918 exempted foreign operations of American business from the antitrust laws. Thereafter it was entirely legal for American firms to combine to restrain trade in their foreign operations or to effect combinations with foreign corporations. There is ample evidence that corporations which cooperated legally to limit competition abroad found it easier to establish a community of interest for their domestic operations as well. The Edge Act of 1919 applied a similar exemption to banking.

Of all the policies developed late in the Wilson administration affecting the relationship of the federal government with business, only the taxation policies could be considered not in the typical conservative mold. The Revenue Act of February 24, 1919, increased corporation income taxes slightly as well as taxes on large personal incomes. The administration had asked for the legislation while the war still raged. The rationale behind the increase in taxes had nothing to do with "soaking the rich," redistributing wealth, or regulating the economy. The administration and Congress simply wanted to balance the budget and make a start at reducing the war-swollen national debt. The administration cannot fairly be criticized for pursuing a taxation policy which was wrong according to the thought of economists of the next generation, but since the late 1930's most economists have argued that it was ill-advised to try to balance the budget so quickly after World War I. During the war, of course, the federal government operated at a deficit. In the last half of 1918 the deficit amounted to almost $9 billion. In the last part of 1919 the government began to have a surplus. This abrupt about-face in fiscal policy had a sharply deflationary impact on the economy and was a major factor in bringing about the depression of 1920-1921.

The government under President Wilson withdrew from its wartime functions on terms that were quite generous to the business community, but it displayed no similar generosity in its peacetime policies toward agriculture and labor. Toward agriculture it was merely neutral; toward labor unions it became outright hostile.

Agriculture prospered during the war as it never had before. Three forces operated to increase farm prices: the government's support of prices to stimulate farm production; the disruption of agriculture in Europe brought about by the conflict; and the reduction to a trickle of farm products from Australia and Argentina brought about by a wartime shortage of shipping. American farmers foolishly thought they had entered a new era. Many farmers mortgaged themselves heavily to buy more land and equipment. Then after the war European agriculture began to revive and the Australian and Argentinian surpluses hit the world market. At the same time the federal government reverted to its traditional hands-off policy toward agricultural prices and stopped price supports. Farm prices began to sag in 1919, dropped precipitously in 1920, and hit bottom in 1921. Corn fell to 23 per cent of its 1919 price, wheat to less than 40 per cent. Forced farm sales and country bank failures in agricultural regions became commonplace. In 1922 prices began to pick up, but American agriculture did not really recover fully until World War II. The Democratic administration and the Republican Congress were sympathetic with the hard-pressed farmer, but they were also inactive.

Organized labor after the war found only a few people in

government who were even sympathetic. During the war the relations between organized labor and the federal government had been harmonious. The administration, eager to keep production uninterrupted, made such concessions to trade unions as recognition and the eight-hour day in the areas of the economy where government could do so. The American Federation of Labor vigorously supported the war effort. Samuel Gompers, president of the AFL, served on wartime governmental boards and worked to prevent production disruptions.

But labor's wartime advances were by no means universal. Unorganized labor received little in the way of an assist except full employment, and most workers in basic and mass-production industry were unorganized. When in 1919 steady employment and a full work week ceased to be the rule and when prices continued to rise, unorganized labor especially became restless. Established trade unions were eager to entrench themselves and consolidate their wartime gains. The first postwar year was one of unprecedented industrial strife. Over four million workers were on strike sometime during 1919. Even the actors of Broadway went out on strike. Labor lost its 1919 struggles with only a few exceptions, and the new hostility of the Wilson administration was an important factor in the major labor defeats. Another important factor was the general hysteria of the period about the possibility of revolution. Although trade unionism had nothing to do with revolutionary upheaval, many people equated unionism with revolutionary radicalism and anti-union employers made the most of the misapprehension.

The most important strikes of 1919 were in the steel and coal industries. Steel management had defeated unionism in 1892, and the industry was virtually without labor organization. Working conditions and wages were poor. The average work week was 68.7 hours. Most steel mills operated with two twelve-hour shifts, and thousands of steel workers put in a twenty-four-hour work day every month when they changed from the day to the night shift. Their thirty-six hour break when they went into the day shift, likewise a change that occurred once a month, was their longest period off. The AFL established a National Committee for the Organizing of the Iron and Steel Industry, and put a prewar former left-winger named William Z. Foster in charge of the group. In September 1918, the National Committee began to sign up steel workers. In July 1919, the National Committee asked United States Steel Officials to meet with it about its demands, which were the abolition of the twenty-four-hour shift, the substitution of an eight-hour day and a forty-eight-hour week, and a wage-rate increase. The committee did not ask for a union shop. United States Steel simply ignored the request. The strike began September 22. Not all employees joined the strike, but production decreased significantly and management fought back fiercely.

Management argued that the steel workers were well paid — that they went on strike only because they wanted a holiday — and that the strike leaders were nothing but Reds. Skillfully aligning his side with "Americanism," a very popular if nebulous concept the first year after the war, Elbert H. Gary, chairman of the board of United States Steel, charged that the strikers wanted "the closed shop, Soviets, and the forcible distribution of property." Although he was wide of the mark on each point, his charge helped swing public opinion to management's side. It had been a tactical error of the AFL to put Foster, a former Socialist and syndicalist, in charge of the National Committee. (Two years after the strike Foster joined the Communists and later became their national leader.)

The strikers probably would have lost the strike in any case because their resources were greatly inferior to management's and because the press almost universally maligned them. But government, including the Wilson administration, aided their defeat. A greater proportion of the workers in the Chicago area went on strike than they did in and near Pittsburgh. The big United States Steel plant in Gary, Indiana, near Chicago on Lake Michigan, was all but closed down. Management imported southern Negroes, who did not understand the issues and who wanted to move to the North, to break the strike. The governor of Indiana sent units of the national guard to the plant gates to ease the strikebreakers' entrance into the plant. When the guardsmen proved inadequate, the governor appealed to Washington for help. The administration dispatched General Leonard Wood and a detachment of federal troops. General Wood declared martial law in Gary and got the strikebreakers into the plant. Political opposition to the strikers was bipartisan. The Republican administration of Allegheny County (Pittsburgh), Pennsylvania, and the Pennsylvania state troopers cooperated closely with steel management. The strikers gave up entirely in January 1920, and the steel industry did not become unionized until 1937. A 1922 investigation and report by the Interchurch World Movement, however, revealed many management abuses and condemned the long working hours of the industry. Public opinion began to swing in favor of steel labor, although the union was by then soundly defeated.

The Wilson administration's actions in the 1919 coal strike were a vital factor in the union's essential defeat. Soft-coal miners had not had a pay increase since 1917, and the soaring cost of living was lowering their living standards. A convention of the United Mine Workers in September 1919 called for a strike on November 1 unless the miners got a new contract giving them a 60 per cent wage increase and a thirty-hour week. The wartime Fuel Administration had stopped controlling coal prices early in 1919 and had not been active at all since June. Coal prices rose sharply; labor was determined to get some benefits from the higher prices.

President Wilson said a coal strike would be "morally and legally wrong" and asserted that the Fuel Administration was still active. On October 30 he renewed wartime controls on coal prices and directed Attorney General A. Mitchell Palmer to seek a federal court injunction against a strike. Nevertheless, the miners struck and effectively stopped production. Two days after the judge changed the sweeping injunction from a temporary restraining order to a permanent one, John L. Lewis, the new president of the UMW, surrendered and called off the strike, saying, "We cannot fight the government." But the miners themselves thought they could. They refused to return to the pits until early December, when the now revived Fuel Administration granted a 14 per cent wage increase. This small gain for the miners was the result of the developing coal shortage, not any change of heart in the White House.

When one considers this record of economic conservatism in the last years of Wilson's presidency one wonders why he is generally remembered as a great liberal. The answer of course is that from 1913 to 1916 Wilson was in the progressive tradition and that thereafter foreign rather than domestic affairs provided most of the drama of national politics and relegated into the background the kind of domestic considerations that divide conservatives and liberals. But Wilson's later domestic record is clear, and students of twentieth-century history should have no illusions that Wilson maintained the New Freedom's spirit and policies throughout his tenure.

The Wilson Administration and Civil Liberties

The Bill of Rights is one of the glories of the Consititution of the United States, and the American tradition of toleration of dissenting opinion, freedom of thought, absence of a political police, and legal rights and safeguards for accused persons is one which on the whole compares favorably with the traditions of other nations. Yet the American people and their government have upon occasion departed from this tradition of tolerance and even from constitutional restraint. The passage of the Alien and Sedition Acts in 1798 was a sharp deviation from the heritage of freedom, as were some of the measures undertaken under the Lincoln administration while the nation was undergoing its most serious crisis. In the late 1940's and early 1950's the domestic reaction to the Cold War brought another wave of hysterical fear and hate that sometimes defied sound judgment and denied fair play to dissenters. But by far the most serious wave of tolerance, of high-handed governmental disregard of individual rights, and of popular hysteria occurred during the Wilson administration. Ironically, Woodrow Wilson, one of the heroes of liberal mythology, was President of the United States during its most illiberal period.

The roots of the postwar hysteria about the "Reds" went deep. Both the natural anxieties of a nation at war and the government's forced and calculated fanning of the war fever led an otherwise sensible people into a state of passion that made dissent dangerous. The federal government jailed those who openly expressed opposition to the war even if they did nothing overt to hinder its prosecution, rifled the mail of citizens it suspected and denied the use of the mails to leftwing publications, and even banned a Hollywood film about the American Revolution on the grounds that it would tend to reduce popular faith in the British ally. The people themselves, without government action, smeared the houses of American citizens of German descent with yellow paint, exerted the threat of economic and physical force to get poor men to buy war bonds, and condoned, even demanded, the abolition of the study of the German language in the public high schools. Such wartime passions could not be turned off as one would extinguish an electric light.

Added to the residue of war fever was a deep fear of revolution. In November 1917 the Bolshevik faction of the Russian revolutionary movement overturned the revolutionists who had overthrown the autocratic czar the previous March. The Bolsheviks fanatically believed that their initial success would spark similar revolutions elsewhere in the capitalist world, as indeed they did momentarily in central and eastern Europe. Even the United States had a very small but vociferous Communist movement, which split off from the older Socialist party late in the war and became a separate entity in 1919. American anxiety about the "Red menace" was greatly out of proportion to the number of

"Reds." Although total membership of all the Marxist parties in 1919 constituted only one fifth of one per cent of the population — and it fell precipitously in the following years — many people thought the United States stood at the edge of violent revolution.

The Seattle general strike of February and the bomb scare of April 1919 magnified in the public mind the strength of the left although the Seattle strike involved ordinary nonpolitical trade unionists and there was no evidence that radicals had been behind the bomb outrages. Seattle Mayor Ole Hanson denounced all the strikers as revolutionary Bolsheviks while he ruthlessly suppressed the strike, and the public believed him. The bomb scare developed when the maid of a Georgia senator opened a package addressed to her employer and had her hands blown off. A quick investigation of the mails turned up thirty- six other bomb packages, all of them addressed to political and business leaders. The culprits were never discovered, but the general public assumed that Bolsheviks or "Wobblies," as members of the Industrial Workers of the World were called, had been the perpetrators and that overthrow of the government had been their purpose. The public easily came to believe that radicals were the instigators of the many strikes of 1919. Perhaps the peak of such suspicion came in September 1919, when the Boston police went on strike. The police strike had serious consequences, to be sure, but to attribute revolutionary intent to Boston Irish Catholic cops required a departure from normal rational processes. (Incidentally, when the Republican governor of Massachusetts, Calvin Coolidge, fired off a telegram to American Federation of Labor president Samuel Gompers declaring, "There is no right to strike against the public safety by anybody, anywhere, any time," a rather irrelevant remark inasmuch as the strike was already over, he became a national hero. President Wilson publicly congratulated Governor Coolidge for his stand.)

The combination of war passion and hysterical fear of revolution was a potent one indeed. Popular, nongovernmental violence against suspected radicals became commonplace; mobs frequently broke up meetings all over the nation. On May 1, 1919, a crowd of men in service uniforms surged into the offices of *The Call*, a Socialist party daily newspaper in New York City, terrorized the people working there, emptied the filing cabinets, and threw the typewriters out the windows. A vigilante group in San Diego horribly beat and tortured a Wobbly who had been giving a soapbox speech. The most serious violence took place at Centralia, Washington. On Armistice Day 1919, an American Legion parade (one of the purposes of the Legion at its foundation earlier in the year was to war against Bolshevism) moved toward the local IWW hall. The Wobblies in the hall thought they were under attack, as they had been before, and fired guns into the parade, killing three marchers. Twelve IWW's in the building were arrested. A lynch mob killed one of them; the others received sentences of from 25 to 40 years.

State and local governments responded quickly to the wave of antiradical sentiment and to a considerable degree stimulated intolerant excesses. Thirty-two states adopted so-called criminal syndicalism laws forbidding membership in organizations dedicated to revolution. The laws were used most extensively against the IWW, which had been under prosecution throughout the war; the organization all but disappeared in the Red scare. Twenty-eight states passed laws forbidding the display of red flags, hardly the most efficient way of preventing revolution. The spirit of the vigilante was by no means restricted to the provincial back country. The New York State legislature passed a series of sweeping bills of doubtful constitutionality that punished Marxists of various descriptions. Governor Alfred E. Smith vetoed the measures, and the proponents of them were unable to override him. The state Assembly, however, indicated its faith in representative government by refusing to seat five duly elected Socialists from New York City districts. The governor was powerless to act in this case.

The Wilson administration not only failed to speak out against such infringements of civil liberty and constitutional process, to a considerable extent it led the wave of Know-Nothing reaction. The President himself, a former professional student of the Constitution, must bear the burden of responsibility for his administration's excesses. Thomas W. Gregory, Attorney General during most of the war, had to restrain his chief upon occasion in his requests that radical critics of the war be prosecuted for minor irritations.

When Gregory left office Wilson replaced him with his floor manager at the 1912 Democratic convention, A. Mitchell Palmer of Pennsylvania. This war-like Quaker instituted an unprecedented reign of federal repression. Secretary of Labor William B. Wilson, given the administration of the immigration laws, rounded up a large number of alien radicals during 1919, charged them with being illegally in the United States, and had them deported. The aliens, among them the famous anarchist Emma Goldman, left on a ship popularly known as the "Soviet Ark." Palmer, who had ambitions for the 1920 Democratic presidential nomination and thought a reputation as a vigorous antiradical would help him politically, soon made Secretary Wilson seem a model of restraint. On the night of January 2, 1920, and again three nights later, Department of Justice agents in thirty-three American cities conducted raids on known local radicals. More than five thousand people were arrested. Whether there was an arrest warrant or not, whether the person arrested was an alien or not, made no difference. In some communities even those who came to jail to visit relatives and friends were thrown behind bars. The deportation of the aliens caught up in the Palmer raids was the task of the Department of Labor. Louis F. Post, top assistant of the Labor Secretary, brought a measure of restraint to the proceedings, and only 556 of the arrested persons were deported. State governments prosecuted about one third of the others.

A reasonable man in early 1920 would have predicted that the excesses of the Red scare would continue for a long time, but the hysteria died down rather quickly. Such betrayals of constitutional tradition as the Palmer raids and the refusal of the New York Assembly to seat the elected Socialists shocked responsible men to take counter action. Charles Evans Hughes, Republican presidential candidate in 1916 and later to be Secretary of State and Chief Justice of the Supreme Court, issued a report sponsored by the New York State Bar Association that denounced the Assembly for its high-handed refusal to heed representative principles and the state consitution. A committee of twelve distinguished attorneys and law professors criticized Attorney General Palmer and said that under his administration the Department of Justice, instead of administering justice, had actually "committed continual illegal acts." When such respected people spoke out the excesses subsided even if the mood of intolerance was to linger for years.

Indeed, the Red scare abated so quickly that the worst and most outrageous violent incident of the era failed to evoke more than a flurry of indignation. On September 16, 1920, a wagon of explosives blew up in Wall Street outside the offices of the House of Morgan. The blast killed thirty-eight people, injured two hundred and caused two million dollars' worth of property damage. The deed was generally and promptly attributed to the Bolsheviks, but the guilty person or persons were never apprehended. Even with such an awful event as the Wall Street explosion at the beginning of the election campaign, the 1920 canvass had relatively little Red hysteria.

Eugene V. Debs, who had been the presidential candidate of

the Socialist party in four previous elections, ran again, this time from his cell in Atlanta penitentiary, and polled 919,000 votes, 3.5 per cent of the total ballots cast. In the early summer of 1918 Debs had been mildly critical of the war in a speech to Ohio socialists. Attorney General Gregory doubted that Debs's speech constituted a violation of the wartime laws, but he did not forbid the Ohio district attorney to seek an indictment. Debs was easily convicted and after an unsuccessful appeal to the Supreme Court went to prison in April 1919.

An incident involving Debs reveals a great deal about Wilson's state of mind in his last months in the White House. After the 1920 elections there developed a considerable movement to release the Socialist leader from prison. He was an old and feeble man and the best known of the jailed war critics; his imprisonment symbolized the whole wartime and postwar reaction. None other than Attorney General Palmer himself prepared for Wilson's signature a document to commute Debs's sentence and release him. Wilson's cabinet had discussed clemency for Debs, and a majority of those speaking to the subject had favored the idea. The President shut off the cabinet discussion. Wilson denied the request to release Debs.

Debs, when informed by a reporter that Wilson had refused to release him, replied that it was Wilson, not he, who needed a pardon, a pardon from the American people. Thinking of the recent elections, Debs stated that no president had ever left office so thoroughly repudiated. It was an impolitic statement for a federal prisoner to make about the nation's chief executive, but it was a fairly accurate if emotional evaluation of Wilson's twilight. For this public indiscretion, the Federal Bureau of Prisons limited Debs's visiting and mailing privileges and did not restore them until Warren G. Harding became president in March. Harding, usually seen as a reactionary contrast to Wilson, released Debs on his first Christmas in office.

2

Government and Business in
the Republican Era

IN THE LAST PRESIDENTIAL ELECTION of the predepression era the
Republicans pointed proudly to their record since 1921 and declared that they had inaugurated a "new era." There was much
to this 1928 Republican claim. The years of Republican ascendancy had brought innovations and a new kind of relationship between the federal government and the American economy.

The men ultimately responsible for the "new era" were the two
Republican presidents, Warren G. Harding and Calvin Coolidge,
and the 1928 presidential candidate of the party, Herbert Hoover,
who had served prominently as Secretary of Commerce since
1921. The Republicans in 1928, however, refrained from talking
about President Harding. He had become embarrassing. Indeed,
after he died in office in 1923 it was years before his friends and
followers in his home town in Ohio were successful in getting a
prominent Republican figure to give an address for the dedication
of the Harding Memorial.

In retrospect at least, Harding was a tragic figure. His was
simply a case of having more responsibilities and powers than his
ability and character justified. He should never have been Presi-

31

dent of the United States; he should never have been nominated for the office. He was, in fact, a last-minute dark-horse choice.

Warren Gamaliel Harding was the son of a hard-headed Ohio farmer who recognized early his boy's special charm and essentially weak character. He is supposed to have told his son it was fortunate that he was not a girl. He was constitutionally unable to say no, judged the father, and consequently would always have been in what the farmer called "a family way." But the young man had charm. He was warm-hearted and generous, vigorous and handsome, extroverted and affable, the essence of the "nice guy," but not much more. He married a widow of small-town wealth and became publisher of the Marion, Ohio, *Star*. (One of his newspaper carriers was the son of the local Presbyterian minister, a boy named Norman Thomas, later to run for the presidency six times on the Socialist ticket.) Harding went into local politics as a Republican—it was a strongly Republican area—served in the state legislature and became lieutenant governor. He ran for governor in 1910 but was defeated in the Democratic and liberal Republican wave of that year. (Wilson became governor of New Jersey in that election, and in Dutchess County, New York, a young Democrat named Franklin D. Roosevelt won his first office when he was elected to the state Senate.) In 1914 Harding won election to the United States Senate, where he fitted in well with the Senate "club" spirit, was a GOP regular, and was generally inconspicuous but for his attractive appearance.

After the Republicans won the 1918 congressional elections they were convinced they would win in 1920. Consequently, the battle for the nomination was fierce. The major candidates deadlocked at the Chicago convention, and the party leaders, fearful of possible bad blood from a long floor fight such as Democrats frequently indulge in, called for a recess. At a secret caucus the party leaders gave the nomination to Harding, who had done nothing to antagonize anyone. Governor Calvin Coolidge of Massachusetts became Harding's running mate. Perhaps sitting mate is a more accurate term in this case, because the Republican leadership easily persuaded Harding not to campaign and thereby reveal himself as the shallow man he was. Wilson was a millstone around the neck of the Democratic candidates, Governor James M. Cox of Ohio and Assistant Secretary of the Navy Franklin D. Roosevelt, and the Republican strategists calculated that all they had to do to win was to keep from losing votes. The strategy worked beautifully. Harding and Coolidge lost only eleven states, all of them southern.

The corruption of the Harding administration was so spectacular that many accounts of it tend to minimize its other important features. But since Harding's policies did not differ significantly from those of his successors, they will be considered here as a unit. The Harding and Coolidge administrations and the first several months of Hoover's presidency had a strong continuity. Harding's administration was unique only in its corruption.

Much of the corruption was the work of the "Ohio gang." Harry M. Daugherty had long been a close friend of Harding's and his chief political adviser; Harding made him his Attorney General. A friend of Daugherty's, Jesse Smith, held no office of any kind but was in fact the assistant Attorney General in charge of graft. He had office space in the Department of Justice, where he arranged bribes for the Alien Property Custodian. One of the most thoroughly crooked Harding appointees was Charles R. Forbes, head of the Veterans Bureau, who required bribes before letting hospital contracts and who sold Bureau equipment to friends and then had the Bureau buy it back at a much higher price. When Harding discovered irregularities in Forbes's office in early 1923 he allowed him to resign and go to Europe. After Harding's death, when the Bureau's corruption became generally known, Forbes went to prison. The most spectacular fraud of the Harding administration involved naval oil reserves. Harding's Secretary of the Interior, former senator from New Mexico Albert B. Fall, persuaded Navy Secretary Edward Denby, a former Michigan congressman, to transfer control of the Elk Hills naval oil reserve in California and the Teapot Dome reserve in Wyoming to Fall's department. For a $100,000 "loan" delivered in a little black bag, Fall leased the Elk Hills reserve to Edward L. Doheny of the Pan American Petroleum Company; for $200,000 in Liberty bonds and $85,000 in cash, he leased the Teapot Dome oil rights to Harry F. Sinclair, who represented the Continental Trading Company. Ultimately, a jury convicted Fall for bribery.

Knowledge of at least some of the corrupt practices of his henchmen and worry about it probably contributed to Harding's death in August 1923, of pneumonia and a stroke, at the age of 58. The nation, however, did not learn of his administration's moral softness until after his death. None of the evidence about corruption in high places implicated Harding himself. Harding was the victim of his friends. But, on the other hand, he did not crack down hard on the grafters he knew about.

Vice-President Calvin Coolidge was vacationing at his father's farm in Vermont when Harding died, and his father, a rural justice of the peace, administered the presidential oath of office. It was fitting that Coolidge took the oath in a Vermont farmhouse by the light of a kerosene lamp. A dour, unbelievably thrifty, rustic, stringy, vinegary little man, Coolidge remained always a rural New England Puritan. He was spare with his words, his emotions, and his money. So thrifty was he that he saved much of his presidential salary (he was the only modern president able to do so) and borrowed nickels from secret service men and failed to repay them. So sour was he that when Alice Roosevelt Longworth, Theodore Roosevelt's daughter and the wife of Speaker of the House Nicholas Longworth, said that Coolidge appeared to have been "weaned on a dill pickle" the whole nation could appreciate the remark. He utterly lacked color or flair. He was thoroughly honest and responsible, but he was limited in imagination.

Herbert Clark Hoover was the third president of the "new era" and quite a contrast to Harding and Coolidge. Hoover had superb qualities for business leadership and had been a highly successful engineer and executive. Vigorous, industrious, and logical, Hoover had first served in government under Democratic auspices. He was in Europe when the war began in 1914. His sense of public service prompted him first to help the American embassies at London and Paris to evacuate American citizens who wished to return to the states and then to organize relief for the overrun Belgians. He performed these tasks so ably that Wilson made him Food Administrator in 1917, an office which he directed efficiently and as effectively as the somewhat defective legislation allowed. There was some Democratic talk of nominating him for the presidency in 1920 until he announced his Republican affiliation. As Secretary of Commerce under both Harding and Coolidge with a strong voice in foreign affairs pertaining to the domestic economy, the Iowa-born Stanford University graduate was the "new era's" chief architect. But though a man of generally recognized great ability, Hoover did not have the qualities to be a popular figure. He was a little cold personally, rather formal and distant. He had been a successful engineer and business administrator, not a successful salesman.

Two lesser figures of the "new era" deserve special attention: Charles Evans Hughes, Secretary of State under both Harding and Coolidge, and Andrew Mellon, who served as Secretary of the Treasury under all three Republican presidents of the 1920's. Hughes was one of the nation's ablest lawyers. A man of striking dignity and force, he had almost been elected president in 1916. Mellon, a lean and handsome man, came into government when he was past sixty years old. He was a prominent Pittsburgh banker, one of the richest half-dozen men in America, and the leading investor in the Aluminum Corporation of America and

the Gulf Oil Company. Mellon was very much the top businessman in government: able, conservative, and dedicated to running government by the same principles and toward the same
ends that one would direct a corporation, unmindful that a corporation's primary purpose is to make a profit and that the republic's purpose is to "establish justice, insure domestic tranquil-
ity, provide for the common defense, promote the general welfare, and secure the blessings of liberty . . ."

Republican Tradition

A widely held view of the Republican administrations of the
1920's is that they represented a return to an old order that had
existed before Theodore Roosevelt and Woodrow Wilson became
the nation's chief executives. Harding and Coolidge especially
are seen as latter-day McKinleys, political mediocrities who peopled their cabinets with routine, conservative party hacks of the
kind almost universal in Washington from the end of the Civil
War until the early twentieth century. In this view, the 1920's
politically were an effort to set back the clock, or turn back the
calendar, to the 1890's, an effort momentarily successful because
of the decade's general prosperity but ultimately disastrous when
the economy underwent a crisis in 1929. The crash of 1929 and
the subsequent dreary months of despair are seen as the result of
a failure to adjust government policies to fit contemporary life
and of failure to lead the economy wisely.

Certainly there is much to commend this interpretation of the
decade's politics. The policies of these administrations were the
most conservative the nation had seen since the days of McKinley. The government returned to a high-tariff policy. It ceased
to reflect concern about the power of great concentrations of
wealth and of giant corporations. Economic privilege bothered
these presidents little if at all. Their administrations could not
by any means be considered sympathetic to the labor movement
or even to laboring men except in election campaigns. The federal government displayed during the 1920's much the same
kind of distrust of the farmer's political ambitions that the Republicans and Cleveland Democrats had shown in the 1890's.
There was even a certain similarity of style between McKinley's
administration and those of the 1920's: they were not exciting,
they tended to be complacent, and they made little effort either
to lead Congress vigorously or to stir the electorate broadly to
new departures.

Yet, for all the similarities, there was a great deal that was new—new but not dramatic—about the "new era." The innovations were in the area of government's relations with the business community, and the key figure was the engineer, Herbert Hoover. Hoover was no ordinary Secretary of Commerce. So relatively inconspicuous is the usual head of the Commerce Department that is seems incongruous to think of a man in that position as one of Washington's movers and shakers, but Hoover clearly was one of the most important members of the Harding and Coolidge administrations. His importance is indicated by, if nothing else, his moving from that cabinet post to the White House.

Let us examine briefly what was conventional or traditional about the Republican administrations in the area of economic policy before we look into what was new. Perhaps Republican tariff and taxation policies in the 1920's came closest to a return to McKinleyism. Even here, however, there were some significant breaks with tradition.

Everyone expected an increase in tariff rates with the return of the Republican party to power. Historically, the Republicans had been protectionists. The Democrats, although not free traders, were in favor of far more modest tariff protection. In 1913 the Wilson administration had seen through Congress the first downward tariff revision since the 1890's and the first important one since the Civil War, but this Democratic tariff had operated only briefly under normal circumstances. The outbreak of war in Europe the year after its passage prevented more than a trickle of European manufactures from being exported to the United States, and Europe was the main source of manufactured imports. With the end of the war and the resumption of normal production in the Old World, American manufacturers feared foreign competition.

Farmers had long been at best lukewarm about tariffs on manufactures, on items they had to purchase, and a group of senators and representatives from agricultural states had organized themselves informally into what was known as the farm bloc. To get farm bloc votes for a manufacturer's tariff, protectionists had to offer a farmer's tariff. The Emergency Tariff Act of May 1921 imposed higher duties on several agricultural items and thereby bound the farm bloc to the idea of protection in general. Real protection of the domestic agricultural market was ephemeral. Sugar and wool were the only important American farm products that could be significantly subsidized by eliminating or handicapping foreign competitors.

Then the protectionists went to work on the matter really

dear to their hearts and purses. In September 1922 the Fordney-McCumber Tariff Act became law. It was the highest American tariff up to that time. Duties on imported chemicals and dyes were almost prohibitive, designed to save the domestic market for the new American chemical industry, which had hardly existed until the war. It even imposed a stiff duty on foreign books. This much of the new tariff was traditional protectionism.

One feature of the 1922 tariff was new: a crude instrument to create the kind of piecemeal, informal, neomercantilism that was typical of Hoover's activities in the 1920's. A special tariff commission had come into being in 1916. The 1922 act directed the tariff commission to keep constant check on the differences in production costs of American and foreign manufacturers and empowered the President, upon the recommendation of the commission, to increase or decrease any given duty by as much as one-half. This feature was an effort to make protectionism "scientific" or precise and more readily adjustable than the cumbersome congressional process could make it. The President, upon the commission's suggestion, could even shift the base for figuring duties from the foreign manufacturer's price to the "American valuation." This was the price that an American manufacturer would have to charge for the product if he had made it, and the duty would then be over and above that figure. This power of the executive to adjust the tariff was, as it worked out in practice, a clumsy tool indeed. Presidents Harding and Coolidge made only thirty-seven changes in duty rates, all but five of them upward.

Also entirely traditional were the taxation and spending policies of the 1920's. The Sixteenth Amendment to the Constitution, which empowered Congress to levy taxes on incomes, went into effect in early 1913. Soon thereafter a low income tax passed Congress. During the war income taxes went up sharply, as of course did federal expenditures. After the war almost everyone favored reducing federal spending and lowering the national debt, but there was disagreement about what kind of taxpayer should receive the lion's share of tax reductions. Some advocated sharply decreasing corporation taxes and the tax rate on big incomes; others wanted tax relief for families of modest means.

Secretary Mellon urged a tax program that would leave the rates on low incomes where they stood but would decrease the tax bills of corporations and receivers of large personal incomes. Congress balked enough to raise the exemption for heads of families with incomes up to $5,000 from $2,000 to $2,500, but Mellon got through most of his desires in his first tax request of 1921 and continued to do so throughout the decade. By 1926 a person who made a million a year paid less than one third the income tax he did in 1921. The tax laws were also riddled with loopholes. An investigation early in the depression revealed that J. P. Morgan, one of the nation's richest men, had in some years paid no income tax whatsoever.

This tax program of Mellon's was thoroughly conservative in the old-fashioned sense of the Cleveland-McKinley era, but it is interesting to note that Mellon felt obligated to defend the program in terms of the "new era" rather than the old era. He argued that low taxes on great wealth were necessary to bring about new investment, which was necessary to create more jobs and further the economy's prosperity. In other words, taxation policy was related to the health of the economy and economic growth was one of the government's primary goals. (As things worked out, a large part of the funds that wealthy people saved from paying lower taxes did not actually go into new investment; it went into speculation that created neither more jobs nor more real wealth.)

A brief word about government spending: federal expenditures declined sharply from their wartime level but were not as low as they had been before the war. The only categories of spending that decreased were those of health, welfare, and public works. Spending for the aid of business enterprise, such as for the activities of the Department of Commerce (to be described in the next section) and for subsidies to shipping companies, expanded enormously. Law enforcement cost more than it had before the war, mostly because of the costs of enforcing prohibition—or rather attempting to enforce it.

Republican Innovation

What was new about the "new era?" What did Hoover, who was in practice the "assistant president" for business affairs both domestic and foreign, seek to accomplish and how? How did the relations of the government with the business community during the 1920's differ from what they had been before the Progressive Era and under Presidents Roosevelt and Wilson?

In sum, Hoover envisioned a new mercantilism, both internally and externally. But this modern Richelieu stopped short of wanting to use governmental power to force business to do or not to do certain things. Quite the reverse. Hoover's plan was for government benignly to show, induce, and help business to adopt methods that would increase its efficiency and profits. Business would not only make better profits if it operated with maximum efficiency but it would also, Hoover firmly believed, help the prosperity of all and strengthen the nation generally. President Coolidge said, with his customary economy of language, "The business of America is business." Secretary Hoover certainly agreed, and had he been given to such efforts to capsule his philosophy he might have said, "The business of American government is to help business by showing it how to rationalize itself."

Throughout the nineteenth century, many firms had slowly rationalized their manufacturing processes. In the late nineteenth century some men became professional specialists at rationalizing manufacturing processes. The most famous of these "efficiency experts" was Frederick W. Taylor, and sometimes rationalization is called *Taylorization*. Taylor and others like him began to extend their system beyond the manufacturing process into business management generally and into distribution particularly. Some large firms "integrated vertically." United States Steel, for example, besides actually producing steel, moved back in the industrial process to mining and transporting ore and coal and forward to fabricating steel articles. Thus United State Steel controlled the entire process of making a steel bridge, from the extraction of the raw materials to the erection of the span.

Some well-rationalized firms discovered it was advantageous to move beyond their own corporate boundaries and to rationalize their whole industry. By arranging some kind of community of interest of firms in the same industry they could eliminate the inefficiences that arose from competition, or "cut-throat competition" as they labeled it when disadvantageous to themselves. United States Steel was such a giant in its field that it could easily force its wishes upon other firms in the industry. When it raised its prices all steel firms by common consent raised theirs; to have attempted to compete with the giant would have meant ruin. Other devices to bring about rationalization of a whole industry were interlocking directorates and holding companies.

Yet as late as World War I and the 1920's several industries, most of them engaged in manufacturing light consumer goods, were far from rationally organized although many individual firms within an industry were efficient. During the war the War Industries Board rationalized industries by governmental edict in order to facilitate war production. Automobile wheels and tires came in 287 different sizes until the WIB reduced the number to nine. It similarly standardized the size and shape of bricks.

Herbert Hoover, as an engineer and business executive, was greatly impressed by wartime rationalization. It was no quirk of his personality that one of his greatest heroes was Woodrow Wilson and that a generation after he left the White House he should write a book highly laudatory of his wartime chief. Hoover drew back from the kind of economic rule by edict that government had found necessary during the fighting, but he wanted to continue the governmental program of industrial and commercial rationalization. As Secretary of Commerce he did so.

How did Hoover's policies toward business differ from government policies of the late nineteenth century? Certainly the McKinley administration was never accused of hostility toward business. The main difference between Hoover's and, for instance, McKinley's policies was that Hoover's were more positive. Late-nineteenth-century statesmen thought it generally sufficient to provide the conditions favorable to business enterprise: granting them the domestic market through a protective tariff, following fiscal and banking policies favorable to creditors, stimulating the expansion of transportation necessary for an industrial economy, and discouraging trade unionism. Hoover thought it necessary to go beyond creating a favorable climate for business and actively and positively aid the business community.

If one rereads the history of the Progressive Era critically, avoiding the stereotyped interpretations of Theodore Roosevelt and Woodrow Wilson, one can see many continuities between Progressive Era and Hooverian governmental policies. But this is not the place for a review of early twentieth-century history. Certainly Hoover's desire to foster industrial efficiency by reducing competition was contrary to the philosophies of many prominent figures of the Progressive Era, notably Robert Marion La Follette and William Jennings Bryan. Hoover did have a new idea in the 1920's—unless one counts the special wartime economic policies—and Hoover did play the major role in government's business policies.

In his memoirs, published in the early 1950's, Hoover nicely summarized his activities as Secretary of Commerce. It was "not the function of government to manage business," he wrote, but it was proper for government "to recruit and distribute economic information; to investigate economic and scientific problems; to point out the remedy for economic failure or the road to progress; to inspire and assist in cooperative action." Recruiting and distributing economic information were among the Department of Commerce's main occupations. It gathered statistics on prices, costs, markets, and volume of production and published the information in some cases or distributed it only among interested parties in other cases. When firms in the same industry shared such essential information about their business they were better able to rationalize the whole industry rather than just their own. The idea of supposedly competing firms in an industry cooperating to rationalize their field, which might involve such practices as dividing markets among themselves or reaching harmony on prices, certainly was in conflict with the model of laissez-faire capitalism as Adam Smith had envisioned it, but that is just the point. Herbert Hoover was not a devotee of Adam Smith. Competition in the nineteenth-century sense had no appeal for him. It was too disorganized and too likely to be irrational.

Investigating economic and scientific problems and pointing the way to their solution was the main activity of the Department's economists, the specialists in its Bureau of Standards, and the personnel in the Bureau of Foreign and Domestic Commerce. Professionally trained economists worked for Commerce by the dozens, turning out studies of various aspects of the economy that had utility to businessmen. (It is interesting to note that the "special interest" departments of the federal government, Commerce, Labor, and Agriculture, first used large numbers of professional economists, rather than the Treasury, and it was not until after World War II that federal law specifically recognized the role of economists in supervising the general health of the entire economy.) The Bureau of Standards under Hoover became one of the nation's important scientific research institutions. In the 1920's it was particularly concerned with engineering standardization and with standardizing, simplifying, and reducing the number of styles, sizes, and designs. It seems surprising in retrospect how slowly engineering standardization became widespread in industrial America. As late as 1920 the machine tools used in the automobile industry were so lacking in precision that an engine made from mass-produced parts could develop only one half the horsepower of one assembled from hand-tooled components. The tolerances were too great to permit a high degree of engine efficiency. During the 1920's the auto industry as well as others, under the guidance of the Bureau of Standards, adopted Johansson measuring blocks, made of a high-grade steel that reduced expansion and contraction under heat and cold to a minimum. With this better measuring standard, as well as with better cutting tools, mass-produced engines by the end of the 1920's were nearly as efficient as hand-tooled ones. The Bureau of Foreign and Domestic Commerce actively sought foreign markets for American products and advised investors thinking of putting some of their capital to work abroad about the probable safety of the investment.

Of all the functions of the Department of Commerce it was Hoover's efforts "to inspire and assist in cooperative action" among businessmen that drew the heaviest criticism from those parts of the public that thought the antitrust laws meant what they said. Hoover was particularly active at stimulating the organization of trade associations and invigorating and expanding already existing ones. A trade association is an organization of firms in a single industry, and it is an outgrowth of the natural tendency for men who have common interests, economic or otherwise, to associate with one another. Trade associations have periodic meetings and usually publish a trade magazine. The first such national trade association in the United States was one created by the brewers during the Civil War. By 1920 over two thousand such associations were in existence. Under Hoover the Department of Commerce actively encouraged the formation of hundreds of new associations by calling industrial conferences at which Department personnel explained the advantages of the trade association and showed how one should be organized. The Department published a handbook explaining how a trade association should function.

In industries that were characterized by a multitude of relatively small firms, none of them strong enough to lead their entire industry the way United States Steel led in its field, the trade association was the most effective way to minimize competition. The Department of Commerce advised trade associations to urge their members to adopt a uniform cost accounting system. In industries that got most of their contracts by bids, trade associations often set a uniform formula for figuring costs. With either method, prices tended to be common throughout the industry and to be set by the conditions of the industry rather than by the laws of supply and demand described by the classical economists.

All these trade-association techniques to minimize price competition would seem, on their face, to violate the antitrust laws at least in spirit. But the Supreme Court held otherwise. In the American Column and Lumber Company case in 1921 and the

American Linseed Oil Company case in 1923 the Court disapproved of the trade-association practices of furnishing an official interpretation of the price information that came from the constituent firms and of penalizing firms that did not price according to the association's policies. But later, the Supreme Court in the Cement Manufacturers' Protective Association and Maple Flooring Manufacturers' Association cases in 1925 made it clearly legal for associations to publish all critical cost and price information so long as the explicit purpose was not to standardize the industry's prices. Thereafter trade associations could merely refrain from saying outright, for example, what a bag of cement should cost, meanwhile furnishing all the price information necessary for anyone with a minimum of ability at arithmetic to arrive at the common price. Cement manufacturers had no difficulty staying within the law and establishing a common price. Consistently, cement bids for public works were identical, down to a fraction of a cent.

While Hoover actively pursued his program "to inspire and assist in cooperative action" other branches of government consistently refrained from rigid enforcement of the antitrust laws and from regulation. The Antitrust Division of the Department of Justice took a relaxed view of its responsibilities. Although it filed slightly more actions during the 1920's than had the Wilson administration, few of the cases were against major companies, some of them were against labor unions, and many were settled by consent decree. Indeed, half the cases in the Coolidge administration were settled in this manner. A consent decree stops further action in an antitrust suit. In an informal conference that has no public record, officers of the allegedly offending company meet with Department of Justice lawyers and agree upon what is legal and illegal. The company agrees to stop whatever practice the Antitrust Division has objected to, and there is no further punitive action. The most important concern involved in an antitrust suit during the 1920's was the National Cash Register Company. A federal court imposed a $2,000 fine against an officer of the company, but a higher court reduced the fine to $50, and the White House forgave even that penalty.

Presidential appointments to regulatory commissions, most of which were first cleared with Secretary Hoover, consistently went to men who were not expected to be tough with business. Many of the new members of the commissions had been officers or lawyers for firms which the regulatory commissions had been designed to supervise. Senator George Norris of Nebraska, a progressive Republican, charged that the Harding and Coolidge administrations were actually indirectly repealing the regulatory legislation by their appointments and that they took this method rather than outright legislative repeal because being open about their intention would be politically unwise. The record contains much to support Norris' argument.

One of Harding's first commission appointments was T. O. Marvin, who joined the Tariff Commission. Marvin was the editor of a magazine called *The Protectionist*. Harding's first appointment to the Federal Trade Commission was V. W. Van Fleet of Indiana. Van Fleet, a special assistant to Attorney General Daugherty, was a close friend and political ally of Senator James E. Watson of Indiana, a man who yielded to no one in his defense of business. Watson's opposition to the Federal Trade Commission became clear when he claimed, on the Senate floor where he was immune from slander charges, that many of the FTC personnel appointed by the Wilson administration were anarchists and seditionists. Undoubtedly the ablest and staunchest business representative on a federal regulatory commission was William E. Humphrey, whom Coolidge put on the FTC in 1925. The FTC under Humphrey's influence, far from protecting the consumer or regulating business in the public interest, actually became a device to protect business from what it considered "unfair competition." Humphrey later became something of a celebrity among businessmen when President Franklin D. Roosevelt tried unsuccessfully to remove him from office before his term had expired.

With Secretary Hoover encouraging business cooperation on the one hand and the Department of Justice and regulatory commissions doing very little to enforce competition on the other, government provided an ideal climate for the growth of corporate concentration. Concentration of corporate wealth and power in the hands of a relatively few corporate entities—the "trusts," to use the late-nineteenth-century term—was nothing new in the 1920's. The trend had been under way ever since the Civil War; it only became accentuated during the postwar decade. Nor is it clear that the long-term trend toward monopoly or oligopoly would have been halted or reversed if Washington's attitude had been more hostile. Fundamental economic forces operated to give tremendous advantage to the integrated, rationally organized, large-scale corporation. But it is clear that the long "trustification" process hastened its pace during the 1920's and that government policies were a significant stimulus to the quicker step.

By 1929 the two hundred biggest corporations of America owned almost half the total corporate wealth and about one fifth the total national wealth. Furthermore, these powerful companies were growing far more rapidly than smaller firms; one study estimated their growth at three times the rate of all corporations. Concentration was most outstanding in industries devoted to manufacturing and mining, but other business areas had the same tendency in not quite as marked a degree. The public utilities field had a spectacular surge toward concentration in the 1920's. The number of banks in the nation declined by over five thousand during the decade, and the assets of the biggest banks became even larger than they had been early in the Wilson administration when the Pujo investigation's revelations shocked the nation. Even retailing, long thought to be a secure refuge for the small entrepreneur, gave way to big corporations establishing chains of retail outlets. By the end of the 1920's Americans bought more than one fourth of their food and clothes, about one fifth of their drugs, and almost one third of their tobacco from "chain stores."

The holding-company device for effecting concentration was the one most commonly used. (A holding company is a corporation that owns stock in another corporation; it may or may not actually operate as an ordinary firm, producing goods or services.) Of the nation's ninety-seven most powerful corporations in 1929, all but four were holding companies. Five were companies that produced nothing themselves; they merely owned a controlling part of the stock of companies that did produce.

The holding-company scheme was prevalent in manufacturing (United States Steel, Allied Chemical and Dye, for example), but the most spectacular holding-company empires of the 1920's were built in public utilities and in railroads. Samuel Insull built a fantastic electric-power structure with the holding-company device. There were more than one hundred companies in Insull's corporate pyramid, so intricately interwoven that it took months after the crazily built structure collapsed during the Great Depression to figure out how it had fit together. But Insull was not alone in building holding-company empires in public utilities. At the end of the 1920's, just ten holding-company empires controlled almost three fourths of the nation's electric generating and transmitting facilities.

Ownership of a maximum of 51 per cent of the stock of a corporation afforded control. Actually, ownership of a much smaller percentage would mean control. Holding companies could be built upon holding companies, and the leverage exerted at the top could control corporations all the way to the bottom even if the percentage of equity at the bottom was extremely small. O. P. and M. J. Van Sweringen, brothers from Cleveland who made a fortune in real estate and then went into railroad investing, illustrated what could be done with holding companies. They began with $1 million, half of which they borrowed from a syndicate of financial supporters. With this sum they bought control of the Nickel Plate Railroad. Then they branched out and eventually acquired control of the Erie, the Chicago and Eastern Illinois, the Chesapeake and Ohio, the Wheeling and Lake Erie, the Hocking Valley, the Kansas City Southern, and the Pere Marquette. Through an intricate series of holding companies, the Van Sweringen brothers were able to control the Chesapeake and Ohio even though they personally owned only .98 per cent of the stock of the C & O. Their control of the Hocking Valley came with only .04 per cent of its total equity.

A holding-company structure such as that of United States Steel could be defended on grounds of efficiency. The steel giant integrated the operations of its constituent companies and produced steel more efficiently than a less powerful firm could have. (Empires such as Insull's and the Van Sweringens' could not be defended on these grounds because they made no effort actually to integrate or otherwise make more efficient the operating companies in their network.) Efficiently produced goods and services were certainly in the public interest if the public received the benefits of rationalization in the form of higher wages, better products, or lower prices. Industry in general during the 1920's raised money wages slightly and improved the quality of their products. On the other hand, prices of industrial products tended to be set by management and maintained at a fairly stable level, relatively unresponsive to supply and demand. When demand lagged, manufacturers decreased the supply of their product—that is to say, they cut production by partially shutting down and laying off workers. This practice was to be disastrous during the following decade of depression.

Not only had the most important parts of the American nonagricultural economy come under the control of large corporations by 1929, but also the nature of the corporations themselves had changed. There had been a time in the late nineteenth century when a huge corporation was something that an ordinary man could visualize, could personalize. The men of "big business" were national figures with strong personalities: Rockefeller, Gould, Carnegie, Morgan. Henry Ford survived into the postwar era of corporate anonymity, but what man in the street could name the president of General Motors or chairman of the board of Westinghouse Electric? Big corporations to a remarkable degree became anonymous and impersonal in fact as well as in the public mind. Corporation management became highly specialized. There was a strong tendency for the management of a large firm to be directed by standardized, replaceable "management units" rather than by personalities, just as the individual worker on the assembly line had become a specialized, highly skilled, wondrous machine but a machine nevertheless. Men still made basic decisions, of course, and to an extent corporations bore the stamp of a particular mind or character. But, on the whole, systems came to replace men. The advantage was that the system could go on forever while no man could; all that was necessary was to replace "management units" in the system when they wore out. A really good management system even had adjustment to change built into it. But there were also disadvantages from the point of view of society as a whole. As corporations lost their human scale and became systems, they could be amended, modified, or counterbalanced only by systems bigger than the human scale. Big, systematized business developed before big, systematized government and labor. One might even say that the business system called the governmental and labor systems into being.

Republican Foreign Policies

The most popular interpretation of America's foreign policy during the 1920's is that it was "isolationist." The main evidence to support this contention is that the United States was not a member of the League of Nations. But other aspects of American policy in the decade support no such generalization. Indeed, it is difficult to see how the United States, the most powerful nation in the world economically, could have operated exclusively within its continental boundaries even theoretically, and in fact it did not. It traded and invested the world over. It was very much involved in the tangle of European debts and reparations. It took the initiative in bringing about an agreement of the major powers about naval strength and stabilized, for the time being, the imperial situation in Asia. It continued to exert great influence in the affairs of its sister republics of Latin America, although it gradually became less bumptious than it had been before the war. If these policies and actions were "isolationist" then it was only because that much abused term means nothing but refusal to participate in an international association of nations with the purpose of collective security.

The outstanding fact about world affairs after World War I was America's great strength relative to other powers for the first time in history. America was not the world's greatest military power during the decade; it had no need to be to gain its economic ends. It was about on a par with the world's great naval powers. But economically—and it is basically economic muscle that underlies a nation's strength in world affairs—the United States stood at the top. This was a new situation.

America's top position in the international economic hierarchy came about both because the old powers, Great Britain, France, Germany, and Russia, had been reduced in economic strength by the war and because America's economic might grew tremendously. Throughout the nineteenth century the United States had been, to a degree, "economically underdeveloped." Much of the capital that had gone into building America had come from abroad. In the 1840's the American economy had reached what some economic historians have recently begun to call "the take-off point," and thereafter America's industrial power began to grow very rapidly. But still as late as 1914 foreign investments in the United States (mostly from Europe, indeed mostly from Great Britain) were about $3 billion more than the amount of capital Americans had invested abroad. In other words, the United States was a debtor nation. But the war changed that situation abruptly. By the end of 1919 the situation was reversed: Americans had almost $3 billion more invested abroad than foreigners had invested in the United States. Further, European governments owed a debt of about $10 billion to the United States government. The gap between America's international credits and debts continued to grow throughout the 1920's. Leaving aside intergovernmental debts for the moment, by mid-1929 American investors had over $8 billion more invested abroad than foreign investors had in the United States.

Foreign investments are not the only measure of a nation's relative economic power although they are a good measure of a nation's surplus capital. By the end of World War I the United

States produced more goods and services than any other nation of the world, not only in total but also per capita. Americans had more steel, food, fiber, coal per capita—indeed, more of practically everything—than even the richest foreign nations. America's might in these terms also continued to grow in the 1920's. By 1920 United States national income was greater than the combined national incomes of Great Britain, France, Germany, Japan, Canada, and seventeen small countries. The plain fact was that the United States was far and away the richest nation in the world. Perhaps the gap between the wealth of America and the wealth of the next richest nation was greater in the 1920's than the difference in economic power between the world's two richest nations since the Middle Ages. There was no question but that the United States evoked the respect of other world powers, respect because the other powers were fully aware of how poorly they measured up to America in economic strength.

Toward what purposes did the Republican administrations of the decade endeavor to use this strength? What were the goals of their foreign policy? There were three interrelated, mutually dependent purposes. First, the United States was more than eager to expand abroad economically, to sell its products in other parts of the world, and to invest its capital beyond the continental boundaries. Such expansion was a necessity if the domestic economy was to work smoothly. It is the nature of capitalist economies that they must be dynamic. They must grow; their markets must expand. If they stand still, they stagnate. Expansion of the market can come in the form of a higher living standard domestically, a growth of the domestic population, greater sales and investment abroad, or a combination of the three. Awareness of the need of expanding markets was not restricted to high-domed economic theorists. Even President Harding, no intellectual giant, said that American business must "go on to the peaceful commercial conquest of the world." Second, international peace and stability were a major goal. A third goal was the prevention of revolution. These objectives were dependent upon one another. Economic expansion abroad was more likely to come about in a stable world than in one likely to explode into war and revolution. Foreign investments were certainly safer in a world free of revolution. Revolutions were likely to bring wars and wars were likely to bring revolutions. Besides the advantages of stability for foreign markets and investments, peace and stability were inherently desirable.

There was general agreement in the United States about these goals of foreign policy. Only very few people countenanced revolutions abroad, and then only because they thought revolution the last resort against intolerable conditions. Very few people wanted war, either for the United States or for other nations. Probably most people were not aware how important to them foreign economic expansion was, but if they stopped to think how much American wheat, cotton, tobacco, and industrial products were sold overseas they could not but see how such commerce affected their welfare. There were, of course, disagreements among Americans over how best to achieve these goals. Some citizens thought peace could best be preserved by joining the League of Nations; others thought otherwise, that membership in the League would involve America in conflict she could avoid by not joining. Some thought the best way to prevent revolution was to attack its primary causes in the social and economic conditions of potentially revolutionary societies; others thought the United States should suppress revolutions by force and contain the nations likely to export revolution, notably the new Soviet Union. Some thought the best way to achieve an expanding economy was through a high tariff; others thought that the higher the tariff the less the chance of foreign sales. Some thought they could raise both tariffs and foreign sales and investments. But even disagreements over means rather than ends were relatively mild. After the treaty fight of 1919-1920, foreign policy issues were not a major factor of national politics until the rise of Nazi Germany and the militaristic expansionism of Japan in the 1930's.

Most Americans were concerned about the possibility of a naval arms race. They believed that nations bristling with naval firepower would be tempted to use it. Besides, building battleships was an expensive business, and most people believed that federal expenditures should be kept low. Naval power was very much involved in America's position in the Far East and its relations with Japan, another rapidly industrializing and economically expanding nation and a country that clearly had colonial ambitions. The result of this concern was the Washington Naval Conference of late 1921 and 1922, which created a new complex of treaty arrangements about naval power and the Far East.

The initiative for a naval disarmament conference came almost simultaneously from the administration, Congress, and the British foreign office. In May 1921, Senator Borah introduced a resolution urging the administration to negotiate with Great Britain and Japan about naval disarmament, and the Senate passed his resolution by a large majority. The House concurred the following month. In early July, working independently of one another,

Secretary of State Hughes suggested a conference to the British and the Foreign Office suggested such a conference to Washington. Representatives of the United States, Great Britain, Japan, France, Italy, and China convened in Washington in November.

Secretary Hughes surprised the conference at its first session, which was expected to be devoted to felicitous formalities, by coming right to the point. He suggested that Great Britain, Japan, and the United States keep their naval strength in the same ratio —rough parity of British and American naval power and Japan's about three fifths as much—and that all three nations reduce the size of their fleets and agree to build no more capital ships for ten years. He declared that the United States was prepared to scrap 800,000 tons of its naval vessels, and he then went on to spell out just what Britain and Japan should scrap.

Within about a month the American, British, and Japanese delegates reached essential agreement, but it took longer to get the French and Italians to agree to accept significantly smaller navies than the other powers. In February 1922, however, delegates from those five nations signed the Five-Power Naval Treaty. The treaty provided for a ratio of roughly 5 to 5 for Great Britain and the United States, 5 to 3 for Japan, and 5 to 1.75 for France and Italy in battleships. There was less disparity in the distribution of authorized aircraft carrier strength. All five powers agreed to a ten-year holiday on construction of big naval vessels. In 1927, at the rather hasty instigation of President Coolidge, the signatory nations to the Five-Power Naval Treaty met at Geneva to consider limiting the amounts of ships smaller than battleships and aircraft carriers, the only kinds of craft affected by the 1922 treaty. The conference broke up without an agreement. In 1930 the five nations met again in London. This time Great Britain and the United States allowed Japan a slight increase in authorized cruisers and granted equality with them in submarine strength. In actuality, however, these treaty arrangements inhibited only Japan. The United States did not keep its fleet up to treaty size.

Two other treaties to which the United States was a party grew from the 1921-1922 Washington Conference. Upon the initiative of Senator Lodge, who thereby indicated he was not an opponent of all international agreements, Great Britain, Japan, France, and the United States agreed to respect one another's possessions in the Pacific and to confer with one another if any disputes among them or with an outside power should threaten the peace of that ocean area. Perhaps more important was the Nine-Power Treaty, signed like the others in February 1922. This treaty was an official international recognition of the Open Door in China, first enunciated unilaterally by the United States in 1899 and 1900. The United States, Japan, Britain, France, China, Italy, Belgium, Holland, and Portugal agreed to respect the sovereignty and territorial integrity of China and to refrain from taking advantage of China's weakened condition to seek special commercial rights or privileges at the expense of other signatory powers. The treaty did not commit its signers to any kind of action if one of them violated the agreement.

Frank B. Kellogg, who took over direction of the Department of State from Secretary Hughes in March 1925, was much involved in a noble but, as it turned out, naive attempt to eliminate war by getting all the world powers to renounce war "as an instrument of national policy in their relations with one another." A general arbitration treaty between France and the United States was about to expire when in 1927 Aristide Briand suggested to Secretary Kellogg that the two nations agree never to go to war against one another. Secretary Kellogg agreed, provided that thirteen other nations be invited to join in the no-war pact. The invitations to a conference at Paris were duly issued, and in June 1928 Great Britain and her self-governing dominions, Germany, Japan, Belgium, Czechoslovakia, Italy, and Poland, besides the United States and France, signed the Pact of Paris, often called the Kellogg-Briand Pact. Subsequently the United States invited all the other nations of the world to sign the agreement (France invited the Soviet Union, which signed, because America did not then recognize the Russian government), and all the important countries soon did so. Hailed as opening a new era of permanent peace in 1928, the Pact of Paris was not long to be so highly regarded. Eleven years after representatives of the various European nations solemnly signed the Pact, World War II erupted in full and awful force.

For a nation that was supposedly "isolationist," the United States came very close in the 1920's to being an unofficial member of the League of Nations and a member of the League-established Permanent Court of International Justice, usually called the World Court. In 1922 the Department of State dispatched two "unofficial observers" to League agencies and commissions. The observers participated in official discussions but could not vote. In 1924 the United States sent official delegates to the League's conference on opium traffic. Midway through President Hoover's administration America had five permanently assigned "unofficial observers" in Geneva and had participated in forty League conferences. As to relations with the World Court: after the Pact of Paris, Kellogg negotiated eighteen arbitration treaties that provided that certain kinds of disagreements between signatory nations and the United States would be submitted either to the Hague Court, established early in the century with funds given by Andrew Carnegie and having no connection with the League of Nations, or to another "competent tribunal." This reference was to the World Court, for it appeared that the United States was about to join that organization. In 1924 both major parties came out for adherence to the World Court in their platforms, and early in 1925 the House passed a resolution favoring American membership. In 1926 the Senate passed the resolution after modifying it. The League appointed a committee of distinguished attorneys from several countries to modify the World Court's protocol to meet the Senate's objections, and Elihu Root, who had been Secretary of State under Theodore Roosevelt, was a member of the committee. American membership in the Court appeared sure. However, in 1930 and again in 1935, after the White House and the State Department had accepted the new protocol, the Senate vote on ratification fell short of the necessary two-thirds majority, largely because of pressure created by the chauvinistic Hearst press. If willingness to join the Court is taken as an index of "isolationism," the United States was more "isolationist" in the 1930's than in the 1920's. The United States finally joined the World Court in 1946.

The postwar snarl over debts and reparations very much involved America in Europe's affairs. During the war and immediately after it the United States government had lent about $10 billion to the Allies. The biggest borrowers were Great Britain, France, and Italy, in that order. Since nearly all the loans had been used to purchase equipment and food from the United States and since American losses in the war, both in terms of men lost and money spent, were less than those of the Allies, they suggested canceling the loans. The United States would not entertain the idea. But, obviously, the loans had to be scaled down. Most of the loans called for 5 per cent compound interest. Money at 5 per cent compound interest doubles itself in fifteen years, and the Allies never would be able to get out of debt at that interest rate. During the 1920's, in a piecemeal fashion, an American debt commission worked out funding arrangements with the Allies that reduced the total debt by roughly 50 per cent.

The ability of Britain, France, and Italy to pay their debt depended in fact upon their ability to collect reparations from Germany. The total reparations due from Germany amounted to $33 billion, far beyond her power to pay. The United States never officially admitted a relation between reparations payments and Allied debt payments, but it in fact helped to work out an arrangement implicitly recognizing such a relation. In fact, the two schemes agreed to by the Allies and Germany, the Dawes Plan and the Young Plan, were named for American citizens, both financiers, Charles G. Dawes and Owen D. Young.

In 1922 Germany was unable to meet her next reparations payment and French troops occupied the Ruhr, Germany's most heavily industrialized region. Germany's economy was in a deplorable state, reduced by the worst kind of runaway inflation to futility. Because German workers, offered passive resistance to the French military occupation, France did not profit from the situation. Secretary Hughes persuaded the French to work out a new reparations scheme.

Dawes devised the plan that came to bear his name. American bankers would lend funds to Germany, which would enable that country to stabilize its currency and resume payment of reparations that the Allies had agreed to scale downward. In 1928, Germany asked for another reduction, and the Young Plan further reduced the reparations bill. The resulting situation was at best an odd one. American bankers sold German bond issues to American citizens. This enabled Germany to pay her reparations to the Allies, which enabled the Allies to pay on their war debts. Thus the money went from the United States to Germany to Britain and France and back to the United States government, investors and bankers meanwhile receiving interest and commissions. The whole scheme depended upon prosperity. If American loans dried up, then German reparations and Allied debt payments would likewise. The Great Depression ended the rickety arrangement.

It would require an odd semantics indeed to characterize United States policies and actions in Latin America during the 1920's as "isolationist." Yanquis did show signs during the decade of developing better manners in dealings with their Latin neighbors, but most Latins only wished the Yanquis really were isolationist and would restrict themselves to their continental boundaries.

American private investments south of the Rio Grande and the Theodore Roosevelt corollary to the Monroe Doctrine had been sources of considerable friction between Latin American nations and the United States earlier in the twentieth century, and they continued to cause trouble in the 1920's. Roosevelt had devised his corollary to the 1823 Monroe Doctrine in 1905 during a crisis in the finances of the Dominican Republic. The little nation was in debt to $32 million, a fantastic sum for a nation that even today has a population smaller than Chicago and far less wealth. About two thirds of the debt was held by Europeans. When the republic defaulted on the debt there was a real danger that European powers would use force to collect, as they had previously in Venezuela. Under Roosevelt's plan, with which the Senate concurred, an American was appointed collector of customs in the Dominican Republic. This collector applied 5 per cent of the revenues gained each year to the operation of his office, paid on the foreign bonds, and turned the balance over to the Dominican government. The Dominicans were not allowed to borrow further nor to change their tariff rates. Thus, while gaining protection from possible European force, the Dominicans yielded a considerable degree of control of their finances to the United States. Similar arrangements were made with other small Latin American countries. Sending American marines to protect financial arrangements of this kind became common. Needless to say, Latin American nationalists strongly resented the Roosevelt corollary.

The most serious situation in the 1920's arising from the corollary was in Nicaragua. President Taft had sent marines to that republic and appointed an American collector of customs in 1911 and 1912 when the Nicaraguans were in trouble with foreign creditors. In 1923 Secretary Hughes promised that if the Nicaraguans would conduct an honest election the United States would withdraw the marines. An American citizen wrote the law under which the elections were held, and President Coolidge withdrew the marines in 1925. The State Department was satisfied with the results of the election, but when a palace revolution overthrew the government of which it approved the United States refused to recognize the new government. The Nicaraguan Congress obligingly toppled the new government and installed a new president, Adolfo Diaz, who had been a friend of American interests and had worked closely with the State Department since the days of the first intervention under President Taft. But Diaz soon faced a revolt of considerable proportions. Coolidge sent back the marines in far greater numbers, but this time some of the Nicaraguan political factions kept up their armed opposition. Marines supervised elections in Nicaragua in 1928, 1930, and 1932. Coolidge, who always pursued a hard and nationalistic policy toward Nicaragua, sent Henry L. Stimson there in 1927. Stimson had been Secretary of War under Taft and was to become Secretary of State under Hoover and Secretary of War again in World War II. Stimson

did his utmost to bring about the administration's desires by nego-
tiation rather than by force, and when he became Secretary of
State under Hoover he began to withdraw the marines. The last
of them left the Central American republic in early 1933. Except
for a brief period in 1925, American marines had been in Nicaragua continuously since 1912.

American resolution of the difficulties with Mexico, which was
more important in terms of dollars since Mexico was the world's
second largest producer of oil in the 1920's, was somewhat less
crude than in the Nicaraguan affair. A little background is necessary. Until 1911 a dictatorial regime headed by Porfirio Diaz had
been very generous in granting concessions in Mexico to foreign
capital, and American oil and mining companies, as well as several British ones, invested heavily. The Mexican revolution, which
began in 1911 and went on intermittently for decades, now qui-
escent and now erupting, had two main objectives: greater democracy within Mexico, economic, political, and social; and overthrow, or at least control of, the foreign investors who dominated
the Mexican industrial economy. President Wilson had become
deeply embroiled in Mexican affairs and the two nations were
close to war when the Wilson administration retreated rather than
be involved in Mexico and Europe at the same time.

Article 27 of the Mexican constitution of 1917 provided that all
subsoil rights in Mexico belonged to the national state. This was a
return to the pre-Diaz custom. The Mexican government did not
invoke the article immediately, but it held the power to require all
holders of concessions, foreign or domestic, to renegotiate their
terms, and a revolutionary government was not likely to be generous with foreign oil companies. The American ambassador in
Mexico City, James Sheffield, worked closely with the United
States oil companies, but when the new duly elected president of
Mexico, Plutarco Calles, proved difficult about foreign oil concessions, Secretary Kellogg adopted a truculent attitude. He even
implied publicly that the United States would support a Mexican
anti-Calles insurrection and declared that the Mexican revolution
was Bolshevik inspired.

Public opinion in the United States was not ready to support the
kind of Mexican ventures that Wilson had engaged in. In January
1927 the Senate unanimously passed a resolution calling for arbitration of the whole oil dispute. When Sheffield resigned in June,
Coolidge replaced him with Dwight Morrow, who soon displayed
unusual diplomatic talents. Morrow arranged a compromise that
allowed concession holders who had received and worked their

concessions before the 1917 constitution to continue as before but retained for Mexico ultimate control of subsoil rights. The arrangement made while Morrow was ambassador postponed the issue for several years; it came forward again strongly in the late 1930's.

The peaceful and on the whole amicable resolution of the Mexican oil dispute and Stimson's policies in Nicaragua indicated that by the late 1920's the United States was beginning to be less truculent and quick to resort to force when dealing with Latin Americans. Indeed, the United States even officially repudiated the Roosevelt corollary. In 1928 President Coolidge requested J. Reuben Clark of the State Department to put forth precisely just what the Monroe Doctrine was. The Clark Memorandum, published in 1930, clearly omitted the corollary that Roosevelt had devised and used as a justification for Latin American intervention. Other justifications for intervention remained, of course—primarily defense of the Panama Canal—but in the last few years of the Republican administrations of the 1920's the government clearly moved toward a softer Latin American policy that was a harbinger of Franklin D. Roosevelt's "Good Neighbor policy."

3

Politics and Social Tensions
of the 1920's

THAT CONSERVATIVES DOMINATED NATIONAL POLITICS in the postwar decade is beyond question. But the debates, both contemporary and historical, over who killed progressivism were out of order because progressivism did not die. It was certainly not as alive as it had been in the prewar era or as it was to be in the following decade, but progressivism was too virile and tough to be extinguished by ten years or so of conservative dominance. Indeed, progressives were able to do a little more than just keep some coals burning in the ashes ready to flame again at a more propitious time; they were able to enact a small amount of legislation that was in the progressive tradition and to block some of the desires of the conservatives.

Progressives in Congress got help on matters that related to agriculture from the newly formed farm bloc. The farm bloc's members were not necessarily progressive. Many of them in fact held to social theories that were quite conservative. But they were ready to depart from conservatism when they believed they could advance the cause of their agricultural constituents. The farm bloc was born in May 1921 in the Washington office of the American

Farm Bureau Federation, then as now the most conservative farm pressure group. Agricultural prices had skidded badly and caused widespread hardship on the farm, and the Farm Bureau was ready to resort to congressional action to get help. The farm bloc was bipartisan, and nearly all its members came from southern or western states. Its first leader was Senator William S. Kenyon of Iowa; Senator Arthur Capper of Kansas succeeded him.

In the summer of 1921 a progressive–farm bloc alliance got two significant laws through Congress: the Packers and Stockyards Act and the Grain Futures Act. The first measure granted the Secretary of Agriculture the power to issue cease and desist orders to prevent meat packers from engaging in unfair practices toward meat producers such as rigging prices and combining to set high stockyard fees. The second measure granted him similar powers over the grain exchanges. Harding's head of the Department of Agriculture, Henry C. Wallace of Iowa, father of another Secretary of Agriculture of the 1930's, administered his powers fairly and vigorously.

The most prominent organization of progressives in the early 1920's was the Conference for Progressive Political Action (CPPA). Although the railroad brotherhoods both before the 1920's and since have been the most politically conservative of the nation's trade unions, they were the instigators of the CPPA. Still disturbed by the failure of the Plumb plan, the brotherhoods called a conference of progressives at Chicago in February 1922, at which the CPPA was founded. The CPPA decided to throw its support to progressives in either party in the 1922 elections and to meet again after the elections to consider the possibility of forming a third party. It would be difficult to prove that CPPA support provided the difference between victory and defeat, but candidates backed by the organization did very well in the fall. Among the Democrats elected to the Senate with CPPA endorsement was Burton K. Wheeler of Montana, who was soon to become one of the main investigators of the Harding administration's oil scandals. Robert La Follette, the most prominent of the Republican candidates to receive the help of the CPPA, won re-election by the greatest majority of his long career. The CPPA endorsed sixteen gubernatorial candidates and helped to elect twelve of them, among them Democrat Alfred E. Smith of New York and former Bull Mooser Gifford Pinchot of Pennsylvania, who won as a Republican. In the Senate elected that year there were thirteen who considered themselves progressives and about twice as many in the House. The CPPA met after the election and decided to postpone a decision about a third party until after the presidential election of 1924.

It would have taken a foolish man indeed to bet that the Republican national convention would nominate anyone but Coolidge. Senators La Follette and Hiram Johnson made an effort to get the nomination, but the President won easily on the first ballot. Coolidge wanted Senator Borah to accept the second place on the ticket so as to give it a little progressive coloration, but Borah flatly refused to consider the nomination. So Charles G. Dawes, a colorful Chicago banker, became Coolidge's running mate.

The Democratic national convention at New York City was a knockdown, drag-out fight that well illustrated the social conflicts of the decade. The eastern wing of the party, which at that time was controlled mostly by the big city political machines, wanted Governor Smith of New York to be the Democratic standard bearer. But Smith was a son of Irish immigrants, a Roman Catholic, and a vigorous opponent of prohibition, and this combination of characteristics was sufficient to arouse the opposition of southern and western rural delegates. These delegates supported William G. McAdoo, who was at a serious disadvantage because he had been tainted with the oil scandals. One of the oil men who bribed Secretary of the Interior Fall had retained McAdoo as his attorney. At the time McAdoo had not known of Fall's bribery, and when he learned of it he promptly canceled their contract. But to nominate him would hamper Democratic efforts to pin the corruption label on the Republicans during the campaign.

The Ku Klux Klan, which will be described in greater detail later in this chapter, alarmed the eastern Democratic delegates, many of whom were of immigrant background and Roman Catholic. Many of the delegates from the South and West were Klansmen (as were many Republicans), and others came from states where the Klan was powerful enough to make them tread easily even when they despised the organization. The convention's platform committee in its majority report included a plank that affirmed the party's allegiance to religious toleration and civil liberty but did not condemn the Klan by name. A minority report, written by eastern delegates, singled out the Klan for strong criticism. The battle over which report to adopt was only a preview of the brawl that was to develop over the nomination. The minority report was barely defeated. A shift of two votes would have put the Democratic party on record against the KKK.

The balloting for the nomination went on and on and on. The East wanted Smith and would not compromise; the other delegates wanted McAdoo and would not give in. Tammany Hall flooded the galleries with its noisy Smith partisans, who hooted and howled down speakers who opposed their hero. Fistfights were frequent. After several days of bitter urban-rural conflict, the convention on its 103rd ballot turned to a dark horse, John W. Davis "of West Virginia," who was actually an arch-conservative Wall Street lawyer. The rural delegates received a sop in the nomination of Charles W. Bryan, governor of Nebraska and younger brother of the Great Commoner.

The CPPA in February 1924 had called a nominating convention to meet at Cleveland in July. All kinds of organizations sent delegates: left-of-center farm organizations, some labor unions (including the railroad brotherhoods), the Socialist party, and Wisconsin progressive Republicans. Many, perhaps most, of the delegates wanted to form a permanent third party, but Senator La Follette, whose nomination by the convention for the presidency was assured, strongly opposed forming a party at that time. He argued that to form a special party of progressives would weaken progressives within the major parties. To nominate an independent presidential ticket was fine with La Follette in 1924, because neither the Republicans nor the Democrats had put up a slate or platform acceptable to progressives. But the convention should not work against progressive candidates for congressional and state offices on major party tickets. The convention had little choice but to accept La Follette's advice since he was their only potential candidate with a national reputation. It nominated him for the presidency, named Senator Wheeler as his running mate, and endorsed major-party progressives in other races. Some La Follette progressives ran for Congress or state offices as independents when neither major party had a candidate acceptable to the CPPA.

The La Follette platform illustrated one of the dilemmas confronting groups that attempt to unite progressives and radicals. The delegates at the Cleveland convention knew very well what they opposed: domination of government by short-sighted conservatives, war, and imperialism. But they disagreed strongly among themselves about just what they wanted in a positive way. Whereas La Follette and most agrarian progressives wanted to smash monopolies and attempt to establish an Adam Smith type of industrial competition, the Socialists wanted to nationalize monopolistic industries and preserve the economic advantages of size and rationalization. The resulting platform was the minimum acceptable to all groups. The platform condemned monopoly and abuse of monopolistic power but called for the nationalization of electric power and railroads. Labor delegates got opposition to labor injunctions into the platform, as well as a government guarantee of the right of collective bargaining. In the area of foreign policy the platform condemned war, urged the further reduction of armaments, and called for a revision of the Treaty of Versailles to bring it more into conformity with the Fourteen Points.

No independent presidential ticket—apart from a split in a major party such as with the Democrats in 1860 or the Republicans in 1912—ever had such widespread support as La Follette and Wheeler had. The American Federation of Labor endorsed La Follette's candidacy, although it advanced the cause only a token amount of financial support and was lukewarm generally. Prominent Republican progressives stumped for La Follette: Fiorello La Guardia of New York City, Senator Hiram Johnson of California, and Senator Smith W. Brookhart of Iowa. Senator Norris expressed his sympathy with La Follette but did not campaign for him. The erratic Senator Borah campaigned for Coolidge.

No one really expected La Follette to win, least of all the Senator himself. The Republicans had too many advantages. First, they had about $4 million in their campaign chest, compared to the Democrats' $1 million and the Progressives' $250,000. Second, the Republicans had prosperity as an issue. By 1924 the postwar depression was long past, and they could point with pride to the economy and warn against any political upheaval that might "rock the boat." Third, the Republicans rode hard the possibility that a large vote for La Follette might throw the presidential election into the House of Representatives, as had happened in 1824 when John Quincy Adams nosed out Andrew Jackson. Why this would have been such an awful eventuality they never explained. Fourth, the Republicans hurt La Follette's candidacy by emphasizing his vote against the war in 1917 and trying to identify him with irresponsible radicalism. Candidate Dawes likened La Follette to the Russian Communists, although La Follette had vigorously rejected the American Communists and prevented their participation at the Cleveland convention. Smearing one's opponent with a red brush, so common in the early 1950's, has a long record in the annals of American politics. Fifth, the CPPA had no local political organizations except in Wisconsin and a few other places to provide such necessary services as taking voters to the polls and supervising the counting.

Nevertheless, La Follette polled a respectable vote, the best vote of an independent presidential candidate in the modern era. He received 4,826,471 popular votes—almost one sixth of the total—and the thirteen electoral votes of his home state of Wisconsin. Except for those in Wisconsin, most of La Follette's supporters were voters who usually voted Democratic. Davis received only 8,385,586 popular votes and carried just twelve states with 136 votes in the electoral college. La Follette ran ahead of Davis and came in second behind Coolidge in eleven states: Minnesota, Iowa, North and South Dakota, Montana, Wyoming, Idaho, Nevada, Washington, Oregon, and California. Indeed, in California La Follette outpolled Davis better than four to one.

The election results had an obvious lesson for the Democratic party: nomination of a presidential candidate with a reputation for conservatism was to be avoided. It was unlikely that the Democrats could have won in 1924 with any other candidate—Franklin D. Roosevelt wrote a friend after the election that he did not think the Democrats would elect a president until the business cycle took a significant downswing—but Davis ran worse than any Democrat in the party's history, even worse than Horatio Seymour in 1868, Winfield Scott Hancock in 1880, or Alton B. Parker in 1904. He received only 28.8 per cent of the popular vote. Thereafter, the Democratic party consistently nominated men who seemed more in tune with the views of the nation's liberals than were the Republican candidates.

Senator La Follette opposed the formation of a permanent party after the election, and the CPPA fell apart completely. As the economy became even more prosperous in Coolidge's second term progressivism sank further, to its lowest ebb in the twentieth century. Even so, liberals were able to frustrate some conservative programs and to unite with the farm bloc to get some farm legislation through Congress.

Congressional progressives, especially George W. Norris, chairman of the Senate Committee on Agriculture, were able to prevent the transfer of Wilson Dam at Muscle Shoals on the Tennessee River to private hands and thereby preserve the installation and eventually, in 1930's, make it the nucleus of the Tennessee Valley Authority (TVA). During World War I the government had been hard pressed to find enough nitrogen for the manufacture of explosives. It had built nitrogen plants at Muscle Shoals and begun construction on Wilson Dam to provide power for the plants. President Harding, in his first weeks in office, ordered construction of the dam to cease, and his administration began proceedings to sell it. Henry Ford, the automobile manufacturer who had been defeated as the Democratic candidate for the Senate from Michigan in 1918, proposed to buy the installation at a fraction of its cost, and the administration was prepared to sell it to him. Ford evoked some enthusiasm in the South because he proposed to manufacture fertilizer at the plants and sell it cheaply. Southern farmers needed fertilizer badly. Senator Norris blocked the sale when the proposal was referred to his committee and urged the completion of the dam which was, in fact, finished in 1925.

Then Norris opened his campaign to have the government operate the dam's hydroelectric facilities and sell power to the depressed region. Despite the strength of conservatism in Congress, Norris was able to get his legislation through both houses twice. In 1928 Congress passed a Muscle Shoals bill; Coolidge killed it with a pocket veto after Congress adjourned. The next year Norris steered another bill through Congress, and this time President Hoover killed it with a veto. Hoover's veto message roundly condemned government activity in such a field. But still Norris and Congress had saved the installation for the government, and a more sympathetic administration four years later would accept Norris' idea and even expand upon it.

Farm politics plagued the complacent Coolidge throughout his second term. The nation's farmers suffered from low prices for their output and high prices for their purchases throughout the decade. Two officers of the Moline Plow Company, George N. Peek and Hugh S. Johnson, understood that their business was dependent upon farm prosperity and devised a plan they thought would ease the farmer's plight. The plan was complex, and its details need not concern us here. Its goal was to create a special domestic price for certain agricultural commodities higher than the world price. In other words, it sought through a complicated arrangement to create the same kind of price situation for agriculture that industry had through the protective tariff. The attempt to provide protection for agriculture with the tariff acts of the Harding administration had been an utter failure, as farmers should have been able to predict before the laws were passed.

Senator Charles L. McNary of Oregon and Representative Gilbert N. Haugen of Iowa, both Republicans, introduced a series of measures that embodied the Peek-Johnson scheme to a greater or lesser degree. They introduced their first bill in 1924, but they did not include in it enough advantages for southern farmers, and southern Democratic representatives teamed up with conservative eastern Republicans to defeat the proposal. In 1927 McNary and Haugen introduced their measure again, amending it this time so as to offer more to farmers outside the Middle and Far West. This time enough southern Democrats voted for the bill to pass it. President Coolidge vetoed it with a strong message in which he enumerated many kinds of objections. The farm bloc decided to push through legislation that would meet the President's specific objections. In 1928 they got through the third of the McNary-Haugen bills, only to run into an even more severe veto message. McNary-Haugenism was dead.

The McNary-Haugen vetoes indicated clearly that the administration Republicans in the 1920's could think of all kinds of objections to using the power of the federal government to aid the farmer but were quite willing to aid industrial managers and investors with tariff protection, the guidance of the Department of Commerce, and lax administration of regulatory commissions. If farmers in 1928 had voted as their economic interests indicated and completely disregarded all the other considerations that lead voters to mark their ballots the way they do, surely the farm vote would have gone against the Republicans in 1928. However, as we shall see in the last section of this chapter, complex social conditions and traditions prevented most of the nation's farmers from voting according to their pocketbooks, and in 1928 they rewarded the party that had rejected their economic demands.

Prohibition

The fate of the McNary-Haugen bills indicated that agricultural America still had political strength sufficient to carry a majority in Congress but insufficient to control or override the executive branch. In rural states farmers still utterly controlled politics. Conflicts between agricultural and urban interests played a major part in the decade's politics. Indeed, the conflict between rural and urban folkways underlay most of the social tensions of the period.

Rural areas generally are slower to accept new ways and social values than urban areas, and, in a manner of speaking, the American city entered the twentieth century at least a decade or two before the rural part of the nation. To be sure, rural America in the 1920's was rapidly changing. The automobile, better roads, and the radio tended gradually to make the life of the farmer less different from that of his city cousin than it had been traditionally. Yet one should remember that, especially early in the decade and especially in the poorer and more isolated agricultural areas, life for most farmers was not significantly different from what it had been in the late nineteenth century. The American horse and mule population was at its peak in 1918, surprisingly late in view of the large numbers of automobiles on the road by the end of the war. Most rural children in the West and South still attended one-room schools for their first six or eight grades, and these schools were less different from the rural schools their parents had attended than from the consolidated institutions their children today go to in a modern bus. Most of all, one should remember that most farmers in the 1920's had formed their social values in a day when rural values had been the generally accepted ones throughout the nation, in a less hurried, less complex, and more stable era. Rural-urban differences were very much involved in the controversies between Yankees and immigrants, between Protestants and Catholics, between religious fundamentalists and those who had accommodated their religious faith to recent scientific theories. Certainly rural-urban differences were a major aspect of the struggle between drys and wets.

The social forces behind the movement for prohibition were so complex and, on the surface, so uniquely American—evangelical Protestantism, the widespread notion that the world could eliminate evil, Negro-white tension, rural distrust of the city, and a degree of class conflict or fear of class conflict—that it is easy to forget that prohibitionist sentiment was strong in other Western nations at about the same time as it was in the United States. The Scandinavian nations, for instance, adopted prohibition. Great Britain's dry forces were never able to do more than regulate the hours of pubs, but they were strong nevertheless. And it was during this same period in France, where wine-making is one of the nation's major industries, that the government banned the production of absinthe on grounds of health. To most people today the idea of legislating drinking habits seems absurd, but from about 1825 until the 1930's a large part of the Western world vigorously supported prohibiting strong drink by law.

In the generation before the Civil War most temperance workers did not press for prohibition legislation, but Maine adopted a statewide bone-dry law. Prohibitionist groups suffered a bad setback during the Civil War, but they came back strong in the late nineteenth century. By 1900 five states had full prohibition and many others had local option laws.

The ladies of the Women's Christian Temperance Union and the men and women in the Temperance Society of the Methodist Episcopal Church and the Anti-Saloon League found the climate of opinion quite favorable during the Progressive Era. Prohibition had a strong attraction for middle-class reformers. Whiskey dealers and saloon owners frequently were behind corrupt municipal machines. Those who wanted to help the poor were often impressed by how much of a poor family's income went for alcohol. Those who feared working-class revolt thought that the abolition of strong drink would make ugly incidents of class conflict less likely. Southern whites were eager to cut off the Negro's access to liquor in the belief that docility went hand in hand with sobriety. Those who wanted to stop the flow of immigrants from Europe were frequently prohibitionists. Italians drank wine as a table beverage; eastern European millworkers crowded working-class saloons on Saturday night; the Germans drank beer even on Sunday.

The Anti-Saloon League claimed the credit for most of the prohibitionist laws. Its goal was an absolutely alcohol-free United States. If it could not get national prohibition, it would work for state prohibition. If that was impossible to achieve, it would work for local option. If that proved out of the question, it would endeavor to get legislation regulating the saloons. The League was active in politics and did an effective job in some areas of organizing prohibitionists into a voting bloc. To the League's officers a political candidate's desirability depended entirely upon his position on the liquor question. Nothing else mattered. The combination of the general climate of opinion and the League's pressure tactics was potent. By 1915 not a state of the forty-eight was left that did not have at least local option. Eleven states had total prohibition. Saloons were illegal in about three fourths of the nation's area, affecting about one half of the population. In 1913 temperance forces were strong enough in Congress to get the Webb-Kenyon Act, which prohibited the transport of liquor into dry areas, enacted over President Taft's veto. The prohibitionists then concentrated their efforts behind a great drive for national prohibition. The difficulty was that the Constitution did not grant Congress the express power to ban liquor; there had to be an amendment to the Constitution.

Without the war and the frenzy of a kind of idealism that accompanied it in the United States it is dubious that the Eighteenth Amendment ever would have been appended to the Constitution. The production of liquor required the use of grains that were needed for food, and Congress in 1917 prohibited in the Lever Act the further manufacture of liquor for the duration of the war. On December 1, 1917, it adopted the Eighteenth Amendment and submitted it to the states. The amendment provided that within a year after its ratification by three fourths of the states the importation, sale, transport, and manufacture of "intoxicating liquors" would be prohibited. The thirty-sixth state ratified the amendment in January 1919. Then Congress passed enabling legislation to enforce prohibition and to define it. The Volstead Act, passed over Wilson's veto in October 1919, declared that after New Year's Day of 1920 all traffic in beverages that contained more than one-half of one per cent of alcohol by volume was illegal.

Legislating prohibition, difficult and slow as it had been, turned out to be easier than enforcing it. The basic difficulty with prohibition enforcement was that large numbers of people, at least occasionally, wanted a drink more than they wanted to observe the law. Given this large market, the low capital requirements necessary to become a minor bootlegger, the capitalist tradition of commercial enterprise, and American attitudes toward law and authority, the development of a major illegal liquor traffic was almost inevitable. The existence of bootlegging after the adoption of the Volstead Act should not have surprised the prohibitionists. It had existed in dry states before the adoption of national prohibition.

For many reasons, violating the law without penalty was relatively easy. First, let us look at the law enforcers. The federal Prohibition Bureau was a farce until the Hoover administration. Outside the civil service system, the Bureau had a higher proportion of incompetents than other federal agencies. Because there was so much profit to be made in bootlegging, bribery of officers was common. One twelfth of the members of the Prohibition Bureau were dismissed for cause, and how many went undetected and remained in service will never be known. Despite the observation of a dry senator that not even the Disciples had had a better personnel record, this was a high ratio of corruption. Another difficulty with enforcement lay in the federal system. State enforcement officers frequently did not cooperate with the "feds," and some states even repealed the "baby Volstead" acts that required state enforcement.

But even if law-enforcement officers had been honest, efficient, and dedicated, their task would have been well-nigh impossible. Bringing liquor across the long, almost unguarded Canadian border was no difficult trick. The Caribbean was another major smuggling area. Diverting industrial alcohol to beverages was difficult to prevent. (It was also dangerous for the drinker since bootleggers often failed to remove all the denaturants from industrial alcohol before they put their product on the market, and these compounds, rather than the alcohol, sometimes caused blindness, paralysis, and death.) It was easy to avoid detection of illicit distilling if one kept the still small. We are prone to think of "alky cooking" as a rural practice, but there was a great deal of it in cities as well. Preventing home production of beer and wine and even of stronger stuff could not be done short of Hitlerian police state methods. Making alcoholic beverages of quality required skill and experience, but little skill was necessary to make a barely potable product. Senator Jim Reed of Kansas City circulated instructions for making applejack and "pumpkin gin." (Applejack was simple: you merely let hard cider freeze and poured off the liquid. To make the dubious pumpkin concoction you cut a plug in the pumpkin, removed the seeds, filled the cavity with sugar, plugged the hole, sealed it with paraffin, and waited a month.)

That there was a great deal of illicit alcohol consumed is abundantly clear, but precisely how widely the Volstead Act was violated is impossible to say. One could buy a drink without much difficulty in most cities of the nation, and even in most small towns an enterprising and thirsty man did not have to go dry for long. But it is another thing to know how many people frequented speakeasies and did business with bootleggers and how often. Statistics just do not exist. It is probable that there was less alcohol per capita consumed in the United States during prohibition than there had been before the ratification of the Eighteenth Amendment or after repeal, but being outside the law made the whole matter of drinking more deleterious to public and private health and heightened public hypocrisy. Some commentators have argued that prohibition and widespread flouting of it increased American contempt for law. Certainly, the prohibition experiment did nothing to increase popular respect for law. But lynch mobs, bribery of legislators and city officials, and adulteration of foods and drugs, for example, all existed before prohibition and all indicated disrespect for law. It was Cornelius Vanderbilt, founder of the New York Central Railroad, not Al Capone, who is famous for saying when questioned about the legality of one of his business operations, "Law! What do I care about law? Hain't I got the power?"

By the middle 1920's it was apparent to almost everyone but the Women's Christian Temperance Union that dissatisfaction with prohibition was widespread. Prosecuting attorneys found it increasingly difficult to get juries to find accused bootleggers guilty. Politicians, particularly urban Democrats, began to speak out against prohibition, which they would not have done if they had not thought such statements politically advantageous. Indeed, at least in retrospect, the most relevant question to ask about prohibition after about 1927 was why did it last as long as it did rather than why was it not more rigidly enforced.

Fundamentally, the reason why repeal was delayed until 1933 was that many voters disapproved of prohibition for themselves but approved of it for other people. In Mississippi, which at that time was more than half Negro, the whites insisted upon enforcing prohibition among Negroes and winking at violations by whites. As Will Rogers said, "Mississippi will vote dry and drink wet as long as it can stagger to the polls." Everywhere, middle-class families that enjoyed a good wine with dinner saw nothing wrong in personally violating the law, but many of them thought the continuation of prohibition would be a good thing for the working class. The English man of letters G. K. Chesterton reported widespread thinking of this sort when he visited the United States in 1922. And the middle classes and southern whites effectively dominated politics. The Republican party, in which the middle classes were stronger than they were in the other major party, refused to come out for repeal until the very end. President Hoover appointed a special commission headed by former Attorney General George W. Wickersham to investigate the whole problem of prohibition and its enforcement. The commission's evidence indicated that effective prohibition was almost impossible so long as a large part of the nation wanted to violate the law, but it refused to recommend repeal. It only indicated some ways to make the administration of the enforcement more effective.

The political forces for the repeal of prohibition grew rapidly after the advent of the Great Depression in the fall of 1929. Some opponents—the "wringing wets"—continued to be for outright repeal; others made "light wines and beer" their battle cry. The argument that repeal would enlarge the market for grain and thereby raise farm prices and that the manufacture of liquor and beer would put some men back to work had an effect. But still prohibitionists held firm and Congress did not start the repeal process.

After the election of the Democrats in 1932, mostly because of conditions that had nothing to do with the prohibition question, repeal of some kind was only a matter of time. In late February 1933 the old Congress elected in 1930 passed the Twenty-first Amendment, which had the effect of repealing the Eighteenth, and submitted it to the states. In March the new Congress amended the Volstead Act to allow the manufacture and sale of beverages with as much as 3.2 per cent alcoholic content, and the nation's breweries either went back to work or came out in the open. The thirty-sixth state ratified the new repealing amendment in December 1933 and national prohibition was dead. State laws, however, were something else. Most of the states that had been strongly prohibitionist passed legislation closely regulating the liquor traffic, and a few adopted full prohibition. The tendency since the late 1930's has been for the states to become increasingly wet.

One popular myth about prohibition deserves special attention. Many writers for the screen and press have asserted that prohibition brought gangsters and organized crime into being. This is nonsense. Organized crime and gangsters existed before prohibition was ever a glint in some Calvinist's eye, and they continued to flourish after the adoption of the Twenty-first Amendment. Gangsters did move into the bootlegging business in great numbers, leaving less profitable enterprises for the better money to be made in the new market; they may even have become more numerous and powerful, but the evidence is scanty. More interesting than a possible increase in organized crime brought by prohibition was the development—in miniature, illegally and crudely —of a kind of business system that within-the-law businessmen had found necessary to adopt in a more respectable and less bloody way.

Businessmen in legal fields had long known that resort to law, which means ultimately resort to legalized force, is necessary to the orderly and stable conduct of business. But the extra-legal bootleggers had no resort to courts to enforce contracts, seek restraining orders, or protect their property. If they could use the police for their purposes they could do so only by illegal payoffs. For bootleggers the only way to enforce contracts and agreements was through private and illegal force. Hence the gunmen, the "gangland slayings" in the newspaper headlines, the Valentine's Day massacre. In Chicago, where organized armed violence relating to bootlegging was most frequent—in other words, where competition among bootlegger-gangsters was the keenest— the administration of Republican Mayor William H. Thompson was thoroughly corrupt and made little effort to prevent gang wars or punish gang murderers. Chicago police did not arrest and bring to trial a single murderer involved in the 130 gang killings in that city in 1926 and 1927. The most famous and powerful of the Chicago bootlegger barons, actually the head of a large but illegal business, Al Capone, was finally sent to prison by the federal government for income-tax evasion.

With the end of prohibition, organized crime moved into other fields, notably narcotics and gambling. Gangsters, to be sure, lent an element of spectacular drama to the prohibition epoch, but the charge that prohibition created gangsterism will not stand up under scrutiny.

Immigration Restriction

Perhaps no element in the conflict between the city and the country was sharper than that of immigrant versus Yankee. Many city people, of course, were strongly anti-immigrant and favored cutting off further immigration, but opposition to recent arrivals, especially those from southern and eastern Europe, was even more pronounced in rural areas. Most rural people were Protestant, and most recent immigrants were Catholic or Jewish.

The United States had always been a land of immigrants. A Bureau of the Census official in the early 1920's estimated that about one half of the American population was descended from people who had been in the United States at the time of the first census in 1790 and the other half came from those who had immigrated later. But there had been so much intermarriage between the original Yankees and immigrants from Great Britain and northwestern Europe in the nineteenth century and their descendants had been assimilated so thoroughly into the general culture that by 1920 most people who were not of rather recent immigrant background —since, say, 1890—considered themselves Yankees. The Irish, who had first come to the United States in great numbers in the 1840's, were an exception to this generalization. Indeed, because they were not Protestant, were usually poor, and were prone to stick to the ways of the Auld Sod, the Irish were in many respects like the "new immigrants" who had begun to arrive in significant volume in the 1880's.

Except for the Irish, immigrants had not usually strongly antagonized older-stock Americans until they began to come from eastern and southern Europe in large numbers during the early years of the twentieth century. These "new immigrants" were rarely Protestant, less well educated than most Americans, and far more poverty-stricken. Their folkways were less like the usual American folkways than were those of the people from northwestern Europe. Over two million Italians immigrated to the United States in this century's first decade, most of them from the poorest and most backward parts of the peninsula. Over two million came from Austria-Hungary, most of them Slavs. Nearly as many came from Russia. A brief examination of the foreign-born population in the census of 1920 is revealing. The total population was roughly 105,700,000. The total foreign-born population was nearly 14,000,000, of which about 8,046,000 had come from central, eastern, or southern Europe.

The movement for restriction of immigration began to grow rapidly almost from the time that the "new immigrants" started to become numerically significant. All kinds of people with all kinds of motives, even conflicting ones, came to support restriction. Some were outright racists, such as Madison Grant, author of *The Passing of the Great Race* (1916), who had elaborate "scientific" theories to support his arguments. Racism was a strong current in the Immigration Restriction League, which Henry Cabot Lodge helped organize in 1894. Others, especially anti-Semites, only reflected the traditional and ignorant kind of prejudice. Some argued for immigration restriction on the grounds that immigrants were radicals who endangered American social stability; contradictorily, others argued they were hopelessly conservative or reactionary and prevented social progress. Although most big employers favored immigration because it provided a source of cheap labor, some of them feared that immigrants would strengthen the trade-union movement. Many trade unionists, on the other hand, supported restriction and argued that a more homogeneous labor force would be easier to organize and more likely to demand a higher level of wages. There were even a few advocates of long-range social and economic planning who advanced the thesis that population control was a prerequisite to a good society and that immigration regulation was necessarily part of population control. From such diverse elements the immigration restriction movement grew to such force that it could not be denied.

Three times restrictionists pushed bills through Congress that required literacy tests of immigrants—over one fourth of the immigrants arriving between 1899 and 1909 were unable to read or write any language—but Presidents Cleveland, Taft, and Wilson vetoed each one. Finally, in January 1917, Congress passed its fourth literacy test bill and overrode Wilson's second veto. By that time, however, the war in Europe had greatly reduced the tide of immigration.

It is unlikely that the restrictive legislation of the 1920's would have been as severe as it was had it not been for the war and its immediate aftermath. War-stimulated nationalists demanded that the heat be turned up under the "melting pot" and that no new ingredients be added to it. (Relatively few people until the 1930's supported the idea of "cultural pluralism," that it was desirable for the nation to have a variety of cultures within it.) Immediately after the war the new-born American Legion inaugurated a major campaign to halt immigration from Germany and from those nations, mostly in Scandinavia, that had been neutral during the war. Many aliens from neutral powers had taken advantage of the legislation that allowed them to escape the draft by forfeiting their right to become American citizens. Legion pressure on what it called "alien slackers" was intense. The Red scare of 1919-1920 also heightened demands for restriction from those who equated immigrants with radicalism. Many people were alarmed when immigration resumed after the war in almost the volume of before 1914. Altogether over four million people immigrated to the United States in the 1920's, not many fewer than had come in the 1880's, and most of them came in the first part of the postwar decade.

Restrictionists in Congress worked hard in the last years of the Wilson administration. For the first time Congress seriously considered the idea of a quota system: all immigration would be kept at a specific minimum with allotment quotas for each foreign country. Congress passed such a bill, but Wilson refused to sign it. President Harding was for immigration restriction, and Congress quickly passed a measure quite similar to the one Wilson had just vetoed. Harding signed the Emergency Quota Act, sometimes called the Johnson Act, in May 1921. The new law, intended to be only temporary, provided that the number of aliens of any nationality to be admitted to the United States in any year could not exceed 3 per cent of the number of foreign-born of that nationality counted by the census of 1910.

Although the scheme was designed to discriminate against immigration from southern and eastern Europe, quotas for that part of the world were consistently filled while those for northwestern Europe went begging. In other words, although the volume of immigration slowed considerably, the new law in practice did not, in the opinion of most restrictionists, sufficiently reduce the percentage of immigrants from the nations they held to be least desirable. Congress responded with the National Origins Act of 1924, which President Coolidge eagerly signed. (The dour Coolidge had told Congress that "America must be kept American," which, when translated from the sloganese to which the President was addicted, meant that Catholic and Jewish immigrants from Italy and eastern Europe must be excluded.) The 1924 legislation was a complex administrative horror. Until 1927, each nation would have an immigration quota equal to 2 per cent of the foreign-born of that nation residing in the United States in 1890. Pushing the base date back twenty years had the effect of further discriminating against immigration from southern and eastern Europe since most of it had been after 1890. The total of the quota until 1927 was 164,-000. In 1927, under the law, a new system was to go into effect. It set a top limit of 150,000 immigrants a year. The national quotas within this total were to be calculated by finding the ratio of "the number of inhabitants in the continental United States having that national origin" to the total population. Note that the term was "national origin" rather than foreign-born residing in the United States at any particular time. This meant that the "nationality" of all the people in the United States in 1920 had somehow to be determined. With intermarriage between "nationalities" having been common for over two centuries and genealogical records being what they were, it was quite impossible precisely to measure how many people in the United States were of English or German or Scottish ancestry. Millions of them were of all three. The immigration authorities threw up the job as impossible and begged Congress to rewrite the law so as to make it administratively practical. Congress refused to amend its handiwork, although it did agree to grant the executive branch another two years, until 1929, to wrestle in the genealogical and statistical mire.

The quotas that went into effect in 1929 were necessarily rather arbitrary, but they clearly did have the effect of reducing total immigration and of proportioning it so that most immigration came from the sources providing it in the era before the "new immigration." The quota for Great Britain was 65,721, for Germany 25,957, and for the Scandinavian nations 7,501; Poland received only 6,524, Italy 5,802, and Russia 2,712. European immigration was never again numerically significant.

There were several ironies in the ways that immigration and the furor against it worked themselves out. For example, the American Legion had been determined to exclude Germans and "alien slackers," which meant mostly Scandinavians; the quotas for Germany and the Scandinavian countries were better than for those countries that had been America's allies. (France had a smaller quota than Sweden.) Another irony was that the law did not impose quotas upon immigration from other American nations, and many in fact came from French Canada, Mexico, and Cuba who were just the kind of Catholic "new immigrants" the legislation was intended to eliminate. Nearly a million French-speaking immigrants from Canada entered the United States in the 1920's, largely into Calvin Coolidge's beloved Yankee New England. About a half-million Mexican immigrants were counted during the decade, and no one knows how many actually migrated. The census of 1930 showed about two million people in the United States who had been born in Mexico. But perhaps the biggest irony was that by the time the complicated final system went into effect in 1929, European immigration was almost a thing of the past anyway. This was true for several reasons. When the United States was burdened by the Great Depression few European families were eager to join the ranks of the American unemployed. Indeed, in some years in the 1930's more people emigrated from the United States than immigrated to it. Several European nations restricted emigration in the postwar years, particularly after Germany and Italy threatened the peace of the continent.

But the combination of the restrictive legislation, altered economic conditions, and changed European desires did certainly have the effect of reducing total immigration to a relative trickle. In the years from 1924 through 1947, years that saw the immigration of many refugees from fascism and of war-displaced persons, total immigration was only 2,718,006. After the number of aliens who left the United States is subtracted, the net increase for these twenty-three years was only 1,734,521, a few hundred thousand more than arrived in the peak immigration year of 1907.

The Fundamentalist Controversy

Since a society's religious beliefs are a distillation of its social and intellectual as well as its spiritual values, it was almost inevitable that many of the conflicts between urban and rural America in the 1920's should have had a religious aspect that sharpened and deepened the differences. The conflict between wets and drys had religious overtones. Al Smith's Catholicism was a major reason for the opposition to him within the Democratic party in 1924 and was to be a major factor in the election of 1928. The uproar over the biological theory of evolution was evidence that the urban-rural conflict was not simply between Protestants and Catholics. It was a difference between modernist and fundamentalist Protestants, largely between urban and rural Protestants.

Few books of the nineteenth century had a greater impact upon the thought of the Western world than Charles Darwin's *The Origin of Species* (1859). The religious implications of the Darwinian theory of evolution were clear. One could not accept both Darwin's theory and the literal truth of the Biblical account in

Genesis of the origin of man and life. Both in England and America there had been a sharp controversy over Darwinism in the late nineteenth century, but by the beginning of the present century most urban clergymen and their congregations had accommodated the new scientific theory into their theology. That rural America, especially the rural part of the South, should have waited until the 1920's before bringing the conflict between Darwin and Genesis to a dramatic climax is a measure of the insularity and resistance to change in rural America.

William Jennings Bryan, still the political idol of rural America, particularly of rural Democratic America, together with various fundamentalist church leaders, launched a crusade against Darwinism soon after World War I. Bryan lectured on what he considered the iniquity of Darwin's theory and charged that biologists who accepted Darwinism were evil heretics. Northern and western rural states failed to respond to Bryan's crusade, but his ideas caught fire in the South. As in many cases of resistance to new ideas, the schools became the focus of the fundamentalist crusade. Fundamentalists demanded that Darwinism be banned from consideration in high school biology classes and that the account of the origin of man and life related in Genesis be taught instead. State after state considered the matter solemnly. In Kentucky the anti-evolutionists came within one vote of enacting a law that would have banned Darwinism from the schools. The Texas legislature rejected such a proposal also, but Governor "Ma" Ferguson, a rural fundamentalist, personally inspected biology textbooks and refused to certify for state use those that presented Darwin's theory. Anti-evolutionists passed restrictive laws in Oklahoma, Florida, and North Carolina. The Tennessee legislature passed a law that was all the fundamentalists desired, making it illegal for teachers in the public schools "to teach any theory that denies the story of the divine creation of man as taught in the Bible." The legislatures of Arkansas and Mississippi soon thereafter enacted laws very much like Tennessee's.

Urban states paid little attention to the anti-evolutionist crusade until the famous Scopes case, or "monkey trial," at Dayton, Tennessee, in 1925. The American Civil Liberties Union, founded late in the Wilson administration, denounced the Tennessee law and stated that it would provide legal counsel for any teacher who might be indicted under it. John Scopes, young biology teacher of Dayton, was indicted under the law, and the ACLU sent two of its top lawyers to defend him. The case attracted national attention when Bryan volunteered his services as a special prosecuting attorney, and Clarence Darrow, the most famous criminal lawyer of the day, joined the ACLU attorneys as a defense counsel.

Dayton, a small county seat not far from Chattanooga, became the focus of national attention in July 1925. Fundamentalists, some of them bizarre characters indeed, poured into the town to erect revival tents and to sell hardshell religious tracts. Reporters, who were generally pro-Scopes and anti-Bryan, reported the circus atmosphere of the courthouse square. No reporter was more famous nor more avidly read than H. L. Mencken of the *Baltimore Sun* and *The American Mercury*. Mencken was the most widely acclaimed iconoclast of his day, and his comments about rural people, although clever, were brutal. With Bryan, Darrow, and Mencken on the scene, young Mr. Scopes became one of the least important figures in the trial and his guilt or innocence became less important in the courtroom than whether or not Genesis were literally true.

The trial itself was unusual, to say the least. Darrow got Bryan up on the stand, an unusual way to conduct a trial, and proceeded to cross-examine him ruthlessly about the Bible. Bryan insisted that the Bible was in all respects the literal truth, and Darrow goaded him into extreme statements. Soon Darrow had the Great Commoner immersed in a sea of contradictions. But the jury found Scopes guilty as charged, and the judge fined him $100, which the *Baltimore Sun* gladly paid. The state supreme court later reversed the Dayton court on a technicality without remarking upon the wisdom or the constitutionality of the anti-evolution law. Bryan died in his sleep a few days after the trial ended, and the question of teaching evolution in the schools faded from the national consciousness.

Perhaps the most striking feature of the whole Scopes case was the lack of understanding and tolerance in both city and country. The rural fundamentalists displayed no comprehension either of modern science, or of scientific and intellectual methods of thought. When the field secretary of the Anti-Evolution League, one T. T. Martin, shouted his slogan "Keep Hell out of the High Schools," he revealed an anti-intellectual assumption completely at variance with the drift of enlightened Western thought since the time of Galileo. To his and Bryan's untutored minds, evolutionary theory and Hell were inextricably part of the city—of city theological seminaries where professors taught the higher criticism, of modern and urban social values and mores which were slowly eroding the nineteenth-century Puritanism of the countryside—and they thought the way to prevent the spread of what they considered Hell was to ban the teaching of it in the schools. On the other hand, Mencken and his readers who hailed him as their intellectual hero did not do themselves any credit with their superior and smart-alecky attitude toward Bryan and his rustic supporters. Most people would agree that Bryan in 1925 was an anachronism, but was Mencken justified in calling him "a sweating anthropoid" with followers who were "morons" and "gaping primates"? The Dayton trial and its treatment in the press reflected in a dramatic but foolish way how far apart the nation's city and rural people were in their intellectual assumptions.

The Ku Klux Klan and Anti-Catholicism

Prohibition, opposition to immigrants, anti-Catholicism, fundamentalism—all these facets of rural and small-town America and more reached organizational form in the Ku Klux Klan. From about 1922 until about 1925 the KKK was a major force in American politics and rural life, and the United States had never had a stronger "hate organization."

The Klan's origins were innocent enough. One William J. Simmons, a teacher of history at Lanier College, Georgia, and a romantic soul who yearned for a South that never existed except in the imaginations of romantics who never really accepted the fact of Appomattox, wanted to start a new fraternal lodge. Fraternal lodges were a major feature of small-town life until the Great Depression, and they are still stronger than most urban people are aware. What could be a better form for a southern lodge than the Ku Klux Klan, which briefly during the reconstruction period had terrorized the newly freed Negro to prevent his exercising his newly achieved citizenship? Simmons, in typical lodge fashion, invented a wild terminology for the organization. He himself held the office of Imperial Wizard. Local chapters were called Klaverns. He also devised the lodge costume: a loose white robe topped by a peaked white hood and mask. As in most things, the KKK's founder was not very successful. Founded in 1915, by 1920 it was still a local affair with a few chapters in Georgia and Alabama.

Then a racist dentist from Texas, Hiram Wesley Evans, became Imperial Wizard and stirred the organization into activity. He hired a pair of professional fund-raisers and publicists, Edward Y. Clarke and Mrs. Elizabeth Tyler, who with appeals to prejudice, high-pressure tactics, and a recruiting scheme that allowed the sponsor of a new member to take a commission from the $10 initiation fee, soon had the organization growing rapidly. The

Klan first became strong in the South, where it worked to keep the Negro "in his place." It expanded into the Midwest and Far West with an anti-Catholic appeal. To the degree that the KKK penetrated the East—it never had much strength east of Pittsburgh —it was anti-Semitic. In sum, the Klan appealed to whatever prejudice was popular in an area. But in certain matters it was consistent: everywhere it was strongly anti-immigrant, prohibitionist, and disapproving of sexual immorality. An eminent historian of the 1920's, John D. Hicks, has written that fundamentalists constituted "the backbone for the Ku Klux Klan." The Klan preached the values of nineteenth-century, Protestant, white rural America, and it resorted to conspiratorial secrecy, bloc voting, political maneuvering, and sometimes terror and violence in its attempt to force its code on the population in general. Burning a cross at night near the home of a person it wanted to intimidate was usually sufficient for the Klan's purposes, but sometimes it beat its victims and in a few cases killed them. Its secrecy made it difficult to combat, although in some areas where the KKK was particularly strong it abandoned the anonymity of the mask and conducted parades in which the marchers threw back their hoods.

The Klan first went into politics in a major way in Texas, where in 1922 it endorsed candidates in the Democratic primary. The next year in Oklahoma it helped to impeach the governor, who had been an opponent of the Klan. In traditionally Republican Oregon the Klan in 1922 moved into both parties and won control of the governorship and each house of the legislature. The KKK was also bipartisan in Indiana, one of its strongholds, where it almost utterly controlled the Republican party and had considerable strength among rural Democrats.

It was in Indiana that the Klan reached its greatest strength and began to crumble. D. C. Stephenson, the leader of the Klan in the Midwest, was a vigorous organizer and rabble-rouser who made his organization a major political force, but in 1925 he was involved in an unsavory personal episode that discredited the whole Klan. At a party in Indianapolis he picked up a secretary who worked for the state, made her drunk on bootleg liquor, got her on a Pullman bound for Chicago, and assaulted her. The girl took poison and became extremely ill. Stephenson removed her from the train before it left Indiana—and thereby avoided a federal offense— and took her to a hotel. For several days Stephenson and his henchmen denied her medical attention for fear of discovery. A month later she died. Stephenson might have been able to escape justice if it had not been for the hostile attitude of several Indiana politicians who had unwillingly cooperated with the Klan. These politicians felt themselves on the hook, and Stephenson's misconduct afforded them the chance to get off. They saw to it that Stephenson was arrested and indicted and sentenced to the maximum imprisonment for manslaughter. With the Klan's most famous leader in the penitentiary serving time for an offense that was a gross violation of professed Klan principles, the KKK began to fall to pieces. It hung on here and there in the South, but after 1925 it ceased to be a powerful political force.

That the Klan had faded badly by 1928 was indicated by the Democrats' nomination of Al Smith, a Roman Catholic, for the presidency. But that the kind of prejudice that the Klan had exploited still existed was indicated by the nature of the campaign against Smith and the election results.

When the Democrats met at Houston in 1928 the Republicans had already nominated Secretary of Commerce Hoover. Perhaps President Coolidge could have been renominated, but in the summer of 1927 he had released an enigmatic statement to the press: "I do not choose to run for President in 1928." Whether he meant that he would not actively seek the nomination but would accept a draft or whether he really meant to withdraw he never made clear. In any case, Secretary Hoover soon thereafter began his campaign for the nomination and had it well assured before his party met at Kansas City. The McNary-Haugen forces in the GOP supported Frank O. Lowden of Illinois, but when the convention defeated a McNary-Haugen plank in the platform Lowden saw that he had no chance and withdrew from consideration. In an effort to placate disgruntled farmers, the Republicans went on to name Senator Charles Curtis of Kansas for the vice-presidency.

Urban Democrats had been angry ever since 1924 about their party's refusal to nominate Al Smith. It was clear to most Democrats that if the 1928 convention denied Smith again the city machines would be so alienated from the national party that it would be years before the wound could be healed. The anti-Smith elements in the party did not have a candidate they could agree upon, and Smith received the nomination on the first ballot. To mollify the rural-southern-dry-Protestant parts of the party, the convention named Senator Joseph T. Robinson of Arkansas for the second place on the ticket and the platform promised "an honest effort" to enforce the Eighteenth Amendment. Smith said that if he were elected he would enforce prohibition but at the same time work for its repeal.

Smith conducted a generally conservative campaign, realizing that the nation's political mood was not ripe for innovation and that Hoover had a great advantage in being able to claim that the nation's general prosperity was the handiwork of his party. Smith named John J. Raskob as his campaign manager. Raskob was from big business; he had been a top official of General Motors and a Republican. He had voted for Coolidge in 1924.

But Smith's efforts to appear to be "safe" had almost no effect in getting the campaign away from the personal level that Smith's Catholicism made almost certain. It was not only that Smith was a Catholic; in small-town and rural eyes he was almost the stereotype of the big city politician. His parents were Irish immigrants. He had once worked as a salesman and bookkeeper at the Fulton Fish Market in New York City. He had lived in a tenement. He opposed prohibition. He had a lower-class New York City accent. He even adopted "The Sidewalks of New York" as his campaign theme song. If Smith had been a Catholic from a small town, Yankee background and had been a dry, the anti-Catholic tide that ran against him might not have been so strong as it was. One can never know. It is clear that Smith's wet position afforded anti-Catholics an opportunity to attack him and use the liquor question as a shield for prejudice. Respectable Protestant clergymen dwelt long on the prohibition issue—"Shall Dry America Elect a Cocktail President?" was one of their slogans—and anti-Catholicism may have been their real motive. There was a considerable amount of outright anti-Catholic propaganda against Smith also. Scurrilous stories circulated about immorality in convents, stories that were at least as old as the 1840's. Some Hoover supporters asserted that if Smith were elected the Pope would be the actual ruler of the United States.

Hoover won in a landslide. He received 21,392,190 popular votes to Smith's 15,016,443 and 444 electoral votes to Smith's 87. Smith carried no states outside the traditionally Democratic South except Massachusetts and Rhode Island and lost in many states of the old Confederacy: Virginia, North Carolina, Tennessee, Florida, and Texas. Smith also lost in the border states of Delaware, Maryland, West Virginia, Kentucky, and Missouri. Republicans won easy majorities in each house of Congress.

After the election Smith said that the results indicated to him that a Catholic could not "move into the White House," and for years many politicians accepted his interpretation of the election. The election of 1960, of course, proved the theory false, but there was good reason to be doubtful of it long before that. So powerful was the Republican advantage in 1928 that probably the Democrats could not have won even with a candidate more appealing to rural voters. We must remember that the majority of registered voters in 1928 were Republican, that Hoover was an attractive candidate, and that the Republicans had prosperity on their side.

One feature of the 1928 election results was heartening to the Democratic party. Analysis of the vote showed that Smith had run better in the big cities of the East and North than any Democratic candidate of modern times. In the total vote of the nation's twelve largest cities Smith had a slight majority. Davis had lost in these same cities by a large margin in 1924, as had Cox in 1920, and Wilson had not carried them in 1916. Smith's candidacy—and the anti-Catholic antics of many Hoover voters—brought the city vote firmly into the Democratic camp, where it has remained with little deviation ever since.

4

American Society and Culture

in the 1920's

JOURNALISTS, SCENARIO WRITERS, even professional historians (usually a rather solemn bunch) who normally make a serious effort to deal with the problems that confront society and individuals in their relations with one another are prone to get a little giddy when they approach the social and cultural history of the 1920's and prattle joyously but aimlessly about "the jazz age." To judge from some accounts, Americans did little else from 1920 until 1929 but make millions in the stock market, dance the Charleston and the Black Bottom, dodge gangster bullets, wear raccoon coats, and carry hip flasks. "Flapper," "saxophone," "bathtub gin," and "speakeasy" are the key words in this special genre of popular historical writing, and the interpretation of the era, usually only implied, is that America went on a hedonistic binge for approximately a decade. Obviously, such a characterization of an epoch is shallow and exaggerated once one thinks about it critically and looks into the epoch more searchingly, but that style of social history for the postwar decade persists and thrives.

Probably the great change in the conditions of society and the mood of the people after 1929 is the root cause of this curious historiographical aberration. The grimness, despair, and drab-ness of America in the 1930's probably prompted writers to look back at the previous decade with a kind of nostalgia for a more carefree existence and led them to look too fondly and too long at what were actually superficialities. An extraordinarily skillful popular historian, Frederick Lewis Allen, set the style with his *Only Yesterday*, which appeared in 1931, a gray year indeed. The book was a delight to read and still is, and Allen's feat was all the more remarkable for having done it so soon after the fact. A careful reading of *Only Yesterday* reveals that Allen was often concerned with more than the superficialities of the 1920's, but he nevertheless put an unusual emphasis upon the bizarre and transi-tory aspects of the 1920's that contrasted sharply with the 1930's.

The thesis of this chapter is not to declaim that there were no flappers, no saxophones, no jazz age. The chapter will suggest that there were other aspects of the 1920's—as the previous two chap-ters have already indicated—that are more useful to examine if we wish to understand the era and the way that it helped to shape our own contemporary society. In other words, the flappers were not a myth, but we will do well to look beyond the flappers, which have already been written about more than sufficiently.

Prosperity and Economic Change

Prosperity was a basic fact of the 1920's, one that shaped and conditioned many aspects of life outside the economic realm. A generally expanding economy underlay a generally expansive view about life, as happened again in the generation after World War II. To say that the economy was healthy would be to ignore the almost fatal illness that struck it low in 1929, but it was clearly prosperous.

The path of the economy even during its boom years was not entirely smooth, however. Although relatively brief, the postwar depression that hit in mid-1920 was as steep and as sudden as any the American economy had ever experienced. The year 1921 was a hard one. Unemployment went up to 4,750,000, and national income was down 28 per cent from the previous year. Farm prices were far too low to enable most farmers to meet their costs of production. But in 1922 the economy came back strong, and by the end of the year it was buzzing along in better shape than it had been when the depression hit. There were minor dips in the business cycle in 1924 and 1927, but they were not serious.

Besides cyclical fluctuations there were other blemishes on prosperity's record. Some economic activities did not share in the general prosperity. Agriculture never really recovered from the postwar depression, and low farm prices were the root of farmer discontent that manifested itself in McNary-Haugenism. Some industries were in bad shape throughout the period. The world market for textiles declined when women's styles changed. A dress in 1928 required less than one-half the material that a seamstress needed to make a dress in 1918. Furthermore, many clothes in the 1920's were made of synthetic fibers. Rayon became very popular. Consequently the textile industry was unable to pay wages consistent with the rising standard of living. The industry continued its long-range shift of operations from New England to the South, particularly to the southern Appalachians, where wage rates were lower. Coal was another sick industry. As home owners shifted gradually to other fuels for space heating and as automobiles and trucks gradually displaced the railroads, once a major market for coal, the total coal market shrank slightly. There was approximately 10 per cent less coal mined at the end of the decade than there had been at the beginning. New mining technology enabled mine operators to get along with a smaller labor force. Almost one fourth of the nation's coal miners at work in 1923 were out of the pits by 1929, and since most miners lived in isolated communities where there were almost no other employment opportunities, the economic hardship in the mining towns was acute. Even employed miners worked at hourly wage rates that were 14 per cent lower in 1929 than they had been in 1923.

But despite cyclical downswings and generally depressed conditions in agriculture, textiles, and coal, prosperity was strong. One has only to look at the statistics. Real per-capita income increased almost one third from 1919 to 1929. (Real per-capita income is total national income divided by population and adjusted for price changes.) The mythical average person—not worker, but all people, men, women, and children—received $716 in 1929. In 1919 he had received just $543, measured in 1929 dollars. Manufacturing industries increased their output by almost two thirds, but because of a tremendous increase in labor productivity due to technological advances there were actually fewer people engaged in manufacturing in 1929 than there had been in 1919. A large number of these displaced production workers went into service industries, where many of the jobs were "white collar." Furthermore, there was a shift in the nature of industrial production that tended to improve the lot of the consumer. Since the early days of American industry a large part of production had been capital goods, that is, products that were used to produce further wealth rather than be consumed by the people. Much American production, for example, had gone into building a vast railroad network, the biggest and most intricate rail system that any nation in the world had found it necessary to develop. The number of miles of railroad track began actually to decrease slightly after 1920. When any industrial economy matures it reaches a point at which a significantly higher proportion of production may go to consumer goods, and the American economy reached this level in the postwar decade. This is not to say that capital production ceased, which would have been calamitous for long-range growth—indeed, it even increased in absolute terms—but a larger proportion of annual production was in the form of articles that ordinary people could use, such as washing machines, radios, and motor cars. The number of such durable consumer goods in use was small compared to what it would be by midcentury, but still more people than ever before enjoyed their convenience. In fact, because of increased national production, relatively stable price levels, and increased production of consumer goods, most Americans lived better in the 1920's than ever before.

To a considerable degree the prosperity of the 1920's was due to the vast expansion of a few relatively new industries and to increased construction, much of which was actually due to the new industries. Road building, for example, was a major enterprise during the decade, and the roads were necessary because of the relatively new automobile industry.

In 1915, soon after Henry Ford developed the Model T, there were about 2.5 million cars on the roads of America. By 1920 there were over 9 million and the industry's growth had only started. By 1925 there were nearly 20 million cars registered, and in 1929 there were 26.5 million. In that last year of the boom the industry produced 5,622,000 motor vehicles. Ford had made the big break-through with his mass-produced, inexpensive Model T, but later decisions of the industry similarly broadened the market. In 1923 the major car manufacturers abandoned open cars except for a few sports models and concentrated on closed vehicles. Many a family that had resisted getting one of the older and colder models succumbed to the lure of relatively comfortable transportation. The auto industry also soon discovered that to tap a really mass market it had to develop a credit system. It developed an auto financing system which remains largely the same today. By 1925 over two thirds of the new cars purchased each year were bought on credit. Installment buying, which became general in other fields as well, did not increase the purchasing power of any given family income. In fact, it reduced it by as much as the interest charges amounted to. But it did greatly stimulate new car purchases, and the purchases had a stimulating effect upon the economy in general.

The auto industry statistics were impressive. In 1929 automobiles accounted for over one eighth of the total dollar value of all manufacturing in the nation. Over 7 per cent of all wage earners engaged in manufacturing worked for automobile companies. The industry took 15 per cent of national steel production. When one considers the effect that auto production had on the manufacture and distribution of tires, oil and gasoline, and glass it has been estimated that the industry provided jobs for about 3.7 million workers, roughly one tenth of the nonagricultural labor force.

Motor vehicles were the most spectacular new industry, but chemicals and electric appliances also had a very large growth. Before World War I the American chemical industry had been rather small, unable to compete with German firms for most items. The war shut off German imports and the federal government confiscated German patents and sold them to domestic corporations. By the end of the 1920's the American chemical industry had grown roughly 50 per cent larger than it had been before the outbreak of the war in Europe. The electric appliance industry became economically significant as more and more American homes gained access to electric power. In 1912 roughly one sixth of America's families had electricity in their homes; by 1927 almost two thirds of them had electric power. The first use that families put the new power to was lighting, but they quickly began to use it to lighten their work. By 1925, 80 per cent of the homes with electricity had electric irons, 37 per cent had vacuum cleaners, and 25 per cent had washing machines. Most families continued to use ice for food storage. Radio was intimately connected with the electric industry, although especially in the early 1920's many of the sets manufactured were operated by storage batteries, big things that weighed over twenty-five pounds and were nothing like the dry cells that power today's transistor radios. The home radio industry was altogether new. The first commercial radio station was KDKA, operated by the Westinghouse Electric Company from East Pittsburgh, in 1920. By 1924 there were over five hundred commercial radio stations. By 1929 sales of radios amounted to over $400 million and roughly two fifths of the families of America owned one. Without these new industries, which were based primarily upon new inventions or improved technology, it is doubtful if the 1920's would have been any more prosperous than the prewar period.

Trade unions usually increase in membership strength during periods of prosperity. More workers are employed, thereby increasing trade-union potential, and employers, optimistic about the prospect of profits, usually want labor stability and are willing to make concessions to unions in order to prevent disruption of production. But trade unions in the 1920's departed from this general rule; they actually decreased in membership and influence during the decade. Total union membership in 1920 was roughly five million; by the end of the decade it had declined to about three and one-half million.

There were three main reasons for failure of trade unions in the 1920's: a strong counterattack against them by employers, in which government cooperated; cautious and complacent union leadership; and widespread lack of interest in unions among unorganized workers. During the postwar depression, an opportune time, many employers engaged in a fierce and somewhat successful anti-union drive. Their campaign was for the open shop, which they called "the American plan" in an effort to associate unionism with un-Americanism. (In an open shop no employee is under any compulsion to join a union. If a union exists in the shop, nonmembers receive whatever wages and hours union members have, which puts the union at a disadvantage in getting new members. In a closed shop the employer agrees to hire only union members. In a union shop the employer hires as he chooses but the employees must join the union.) The open-shop campaign was strong even in some industries where unionism had been well established, such as printing and building construction. Some building contractors were under pressure to break unions. The president of the Bethlehem Steel Company announced in late 1920 that his firm would not sell steel to contractors in New York and Philadelphia who consented to keep their established closed-shop policy. Also in the 1920's employers embarked upon a program to extend what came to be called welfare capitalism. A rather nebulous concept, welfare capitalism ran the gamut from employee stock-purchase plans (usually nonvoting stock) to athletic and social programs for employees and better toilets and locker rooms. Welfare capitalism programs tended to make employees identify their welfare with the company rather than a union and to remove some of the annoyances that sometimes erupt into union-management conflict.

Despite the intensity of the employers' attack it is likely that more vigorous and imaginative union leadership would have enabled the unions to hold their own. Samuel Gompers, the primary founder of the American Federation of Labor and its president for all but one year of its existence during his lifetime, was seventy years old in 1920, hardened in his approach to unionism, and lacking in the vigor which he had displayed at the beginning of the century. William Green, successor to the AFL presidency after Gompers' death in 1924, was depressingly cautious and almost completely without imagination. Whatever forward motion the labor movement made from Green's accession to the AFL presidency in 1924 to his death in the 1950's was made despite Green rather than because of him. The fundamental difficulty in union leadership from World War I until the early 1930's was that the AFL had no real interest in getting the unorganized into unions except for those in skilled trades. Not until labor leaders eager to organize unskilled workers in basic industry came to the fore in the 1930's did the unions get off the ground. There was one major exception that proved the generalization: in the needle trades David Dubinsky and Sidney Hillman adopted new techniques and ideas. Their innovations were successful, and their organizations thrived while the rest of labor stagnated and shriveled.

Many workers in basic industry in the 1920's were apathetic or hostile to unionism, not only because of their employers' attitudes and the failure of union leadership to excite them but because they lived better than ever they had before and because they had formed their social ideas in a preindustrial society. There is no question but that most industrial workers were better off materially in the 1920's than they had been earlier. Real wages (the relationship of money wages to the cost of living) in 1919 were at 105 on a scale in which 1914 was 100. By 1928 the figure stood at 132, a truly significant increase. Many an industrial worker's social ideas and assumptions earned him the unionist's contemptuous term "company man." Especially in the new industries like autos and electric appliances a large part of the labor force was composed of men who had begun their lives in small towns or on the farm, where there had been no big employers and where the terms of work were laid down by the employer on a take-it-or-leave-it basis or settled by each individual employee bargaining with the employer. Individualistic social attitudes formed in a rural society were difficult to shake, even when a man lived the anything but individualistic life of a city worker on a production line, the employee of a vast and complex corporation. It took the depression of the next decade to shock many workers from a rural background into modifying their views about the relationship of capital and labor sufficiently to join a union and make it a countervailing power to the corporation.

There are no statistics that reveal precisely how many industrial workers in the 1920's were originally from urban areas, but the population statistics reveal a vast growth of the cities during the decade. Many rural counties continued to grow, but urban counties grew much more rapidly. The general pattern of migration was from the farm or small town to the small city of the same region and thence to a big city, often out of the region. The biggest growths were in New York City, the industrial cities on or near the Great Lakes, the San Francisco area, and Los Angeles. California tended to draw its new population from the West and the Midwest. New York's growth came from all over the nation, but the bulk of it came from the East and the Southeast. The burgeoning cities of the Midwest grew from rural-to-urban movement within the region and from migration from the South.

Great numbers of the migrants from the South were Negro. Negro migration to the North first became numerically significant during World War I. In 1910 more than 90 per cent of the Negroes of the United States lived in states that had been slave areas in 1860. The census of that year showed only 850,000 Negroes living outside the South. The census of 1920 showed 1,400,000 in the North and West, most of them having migrated after 1917. The movement continued, even expanded, during the 1920's. In the 1930 census, 2,300,000 Negroes were living outside the South. The day was rapidly coming when the typical American Negro would not be a southern sharecropper but a northern or western urban wage earner.

This movement from rural to urban areas, for both Negroes and whites, came about for essentially economic reasons. Agriculture languished; industry flourished. Economic conditions pushed people off the farms and out of the small towns; better economic conditions in the cities pulled them into population clusters.

The Effects of Affluence

America in the 1920's was a relatively affluent society. Affluence made it possible for Americans to change significantly the way they lived, to buy a car and a radio, to go to movies, to improve their schools and send their children to school for more years than they themselves had attended. These effects of affluence in turn had their own effects, some of them very far-reaching.

Foreign visitors to the United States in the late 1920's who had not seen the nation for a decade or two were impressed most of all by the numbers of automobiles they saw and the changes that the automobile had wrought in society. In 1929 there were between one fifth and one sixth as many cars in the United States as there were people, a far higher proportion than that of any other country except Canada. It was physically possible for everyone in America to be rolling on automobile wheels simultaneously, and in some of the traffic jams of summer weekends it appeared that the nation had actually tried to perform the feat.

Any attempt to enumerate all the effects of widespread automobile ownership would bog down in superficial relationships, but some of the major effects are evident. The very appearance of the country changed. Merchants and manufacturers could not resist trying to profit from the captive audiences that traveled the main highways and erected billboards on the land that only a few generations back had been a wilderness. Short-order restaurants and gasoline stations lined the roads approaching towns and cities. Tourist cabins, the predecessors of motels, clustered around the main points of tourist interest. Towns and cities began their sprawl into the countryside as the automobile enabled workers to live a great distance from their employment. Cities such as Los Angeles, which experienced most of their growth after the coming of the automobile age, tended not to have the central business area traditional in older American and European cities.

The social effects of the automobile have been the subject of a great deal of speculation. Many observers have asserted that the car changed courtship patterns by making young people more mobile and removing them from the supervision of their elders. Certainly every community by the end of the 1920's had a secluded area known as "lovers' lane" where cars parked on summer nights, but this whole theory of changed courtship patterns tends to underestimate the ingenuity of young people of the pre-automobile age. "Lovers' lanes" once had buggies parked beside them, and because of the superiority of horse intelligence to that of an automobile a buggy driver could pay less attention to his driving than could a car driver. Still, there are other, more important, and better documented social effects of the automobile.

By the end of the 1920's thousands of families took long vacation trips by car and quite obviously the American public knew more of its nation's geography at first hand than had earlier and less mobile generations. In 1904 a Chicago lawyer made a trip by auto from New York to San Francisco, and his trip was so unusual that he wrote a book about his experiences. By 1929, however, families that had taken such trips found it difficult even to interest their neighbors in their tales of travel.

Perhaps one of the most far-reaching changes brought by the automobile, or the bus, was the change in rural schools. Before the day of cars each rural township operated a grade school, some of them through grade six, more often through grade eight. Most of these rural schools had one room and one teacher. Despite the sentimental nostalgia of some people in a later age, these schools did not offer good education. The teachers were poorly prepared; most of them had not been to college at all. With a room full of children of various sizes and ages, most teachers were able to do little more than maintain a degree of discipline. The products of these schools were ill equipped for living anywhere but on the farm and were not particularly well educated even for that. The school bus made consolidated rural schools possible, and farm youngsters of high-school age for the first time began to go beyond the eighth grade in significant numbers. Many of the new consolidated rural schools were a long way from being ideal educational institutions, but they were clearly an improvement over the ungraded one-room school. At last, rural children were receiving substantially the same kind of education as urban children.

Indeed, the automobile and the radio tended to blur the distinction between rural and urban life. The farmer went to town for his entertainment (usually the movies) and listened to the same radio programs as the city dweller. His children attended schools like those in urban centers. He read a city newspaper. The farmer frequently even took a job in the city, at least for part of the year, and continued to live on the land. Because of the generally depressed conditions of agriculture during the 1920's and the greater amount of capital necessary to begin profitable farming that came as a result of farm mechanization, most of the farmer's children became wage earners in town or city. There still remained a great difference in the ways of life of the small town and the big city, but no longer, except in the most primitive, poorest, and most isolated parts of the nation, did the farmer live significantly differently from the small-town dweller.

Affluence changed the education of the city youngster just as it and the automobile had changed rural schooling. The greatest change was in the number of students in high school. High-school enrollments in 1920 totaled 2.2 million; by 1930 almost exactly twice as many students were in the nation's secondary schools. An increase in the population was part of the reason for the increased enrollments, but more important was an increase in the percentage of high-school-age boys and girls who went on past the eighth grade. In 1930 roughly one half of the population between the ages of fourteen and eighteen was in school.

The main reason why more young people stayed in school instead of dropping out to go to work was that their families, for the first time, could afford to continue without the youngsters' wages. Failure to recognize the fact that children's wages were needed at home was the chief flaw in the reasoning of earlier opponents of child labor. In the first Wilson administration reformers had put a law through Congress prohibiting child labor, and the Supreme Court had in 1918 declared the act unconstitutional. The reformers then set about amending the Constitution, getting an amendment through Congress but never getting it ratified by a sufficient number of states. Enforcement of compulsory school-attendance laws in the 1920's (usually to age fifteen or sixteen) succeeded in accomplishing most of what the reformers had desired, but not even the school laws could be enforced well when public opinion opposed them. When employers wanted to hire children, when parents wanted children to go to work to help on the family income, and when the children themselves wanted to leave school—and this was the situation in many of the textile towns of the Appalachian South throughout the decade—truant officers were unable really to enforce the law. But the attendance laws were enforced where public opinion supported them. Affluence rather than law kept children in school and off the labor market. By 1929 most urban young people at least started to high school. Finishing high school became almost universal in the middle classes, and most of the children from working-class homes finished high school if they had at least average academic ability.

The great number of high-school students had a profound effect on the nature of the high school. At one time, secondary education had been primarily preparation for the college and university. Now in the 1920's the high schools were filled with young people who had no intention whatsoever of going on to college. Furthermore, many of the students lacked the intelligence or the desire or both to cope with the conventional high-school curriculum of literature, mathematics, science, and foreign language. A number of educators argued that trigonometry and Latin did not have much relevance for students who were going to stop their formal education after high school to go to work and that the schools should provide these young people with other training. Many schools never solved the problem in a satisfactory manner; most of them watered down the conventional curriculum to accommodate the new kind of student and created vocational courses which often had little more relevance than did Latin. But despite educational deficiencies—and we must not assume that the secondary schools of the era before World War I were paragons of intellectual virtue—increasing numbers of young people insisted upon a high-school education and they probably profited from their high-school years.

Colleges and universities also were swollen during the 1920's, their enrollments increasing from about 600,000 in 1920 (larger than usual with soldiers returning from World War I) to about 1,200,000 in 1930. The greatest increase in college enrollments came in the vocational fields, teacher preparation, engineering, and business administration. Undergraduate schools of business were something new in higher education, but it was not surprising that in the business civilization of the 1920's hundreds of young men studied such vocational subjects as salesmanship and advertising.

The Culture of the 1920's: Literature

In considering such a vast subject as the culture of the 1920's we need to make some distinctions. On the one hand, there was one stream of culture (used here in the usual sense, as the works of artists and intellectuals, rather than in the broader anthropological sense) that merited the admiration of intelligent and well-educated people and that broke new ground in the development of art forms; on the other hand there was a stream that was conventional in form and that catered to the tastes of the great mass of people rather than to the most intelligent and best educated. Perhaps the most striking thing about the culture of the 1920's was the degree to which the artists and intellectuals of the first and less popular stream felt alienated from the American business civilization, rejected it as an acceptable framework for the human mind and spirit, and either attacked it directly or fled from it.

The story of Harold Stearns is a good example of this alienation from and rejection of American civilization. Stearns, a literary critic, was the editor of a volume entitled *Civilization in the United States,* for which thirty artists and intellectuals in all fields contributed articles about their specialties and the environment in which they worked. The articles were without exception gloomy about America. The thirty writers agreed that the United States was an unlikely place for a renaissance, that it was disgustingly materialistic, that it was artistically and intellectually barren, and that its dominant mood was repressive. Stearns agreed. He read the publisher's proof, returned it, and departed for France. Thousands of other artists also expatriated themselves for what they considered more congenial intellectual climates, and even more of them gathered in Greenwich Village and other artistic islands in the sea of the business civilization. Many of them lashed out at the civilization they criticized; others did not make their criticism explicit and only pursued their muse and tried not to think about popular American values.

The two most effective critics of American culture in the years of boom, H. L. Mencken and Sinclair Lewis, were not innovators artistically and did not produce works that have endured. Henry Louis Mencken, a Baltimore newspaperman of German-American bourgeois background, became a founder of *The American Mercury* in 1924 and edited the journal for the rest of the decade. Iconoclasm was the *Mercury*'s watchword. Nothing was sacred to Mencken. He denounced everything about America except the beer he got from his bootlegger. Politicians were hypocritical "beaters of breasts." "A good politician is quite as unthinkable as an honest burglar." He declared that what America needed was a wave of suicides among college presidents and volunteered to provide the weapons. The Statue of Liberty, he said, should be sunk. Mencken exuberantly laid about him with a meat axe. There was no subtlety in his attacks on the "booboisie," as he called the vast bulk of Americans. The surprising thing was how seriously Americans regarded him. Pious ministers and presidents of Rotary clubs denounced him passionately, but rebels, particularly young ones, acclaimed him as a hero and quoted him as an oracle.

Sinclair Lewis, creator of Babbitt, was equally popular in *American Mercury* circles, equally denounced by many, and equally crude in his attacks. He put the American small town through the wringer with *Main Street* in 1920 and the medium-sized city two years later with *Babbitt. Arrowsmith* (1925) let fly at American physicians and *Elmer Gantry* (1927) did a similar job on ministers. That Lewis, and Mencken as well, aimed their hatchets at targets deserving to be deflated is a proposition with which most people today would agree, but that Lewis should have received the Nobel Prize for Literature in 1930 seems inconceivable to one who tries to read his novels years later. Nevertheless, Lewis' and Mencken's wide readership and degree of acclamation indicate that there was indeed a great deal of sham in American society and that it bothered a significant number of people.

Mencken and Lewis stayed in America during the boom years and attacked what they believed needed criticism. Those literati who escaped to Europe were no less critical but most of them refrained from direct assaults. The giants of American letters among the expatriates were Ernest Hemingway and F. Scott Fitzgerald. Through both men's novels written during the decade ran a thread of rejection of dominant American values. Their books were peopled by characters who were lost and despairing, who found no meaning in life beyond animal pleasures, who rejected the world as it was but had no solution and no theory about what had gone wrong. They reflected the feeling that the war had overturned Western civilization and left the world upside down. To the next generation, which saw even greater dislocations, even wilder insanities, and even more tragedy, the note of self-pity in the writings of the "lost generation" was not very attractive. But for catching the mood of their generation of intellectual rebels Hemingway and Fitzgerald were superb, and Hemingway, at least, profoundly affected the form of the American novel.

Hemingway's lean, hard style had a tremendous impact upon his era. His short sentences, shorn of all traditional niceties, and his use of vigorous seldom-printed words as well as his choice of themes represented a sharp break with the tradition of gentility that had dominated American literature until World War I. To a considerable extent, the intellectuals' revolt in the 1920's was a reaction against a style of life that had been honored before the war. Even Hemingway's style of writing was a harsh and blatant comment upon that prewar style of life, and his generation, which above all wanted not to be old-fashioned, lionized him as few American generations have lionized their authors. Where Hemingway was the literary hero of his generation, Scott Fitzgerald was its darling. Fitzgerald *was* flaming youth. He tried to live like a character from one of his own novels, and if to us today he seems rather self-consciously and determinedly dissolute, his own generation loved him because he was that which they wanted to be. Many young people whose lives revolved around the real Main Streets of the nation longed to be Dick Diver or to go to Jay Gatsby's parties.

Perhaps in time the playwright Eugene O'Neill will be widely accepted as America's greatest literary talent of the 1920's. A brooding, tormented man personally, O'Neill focused upon what was dark and violent and latent in mankind generally. Through his plays of the 1920's—*The Emperor Jones* (1920), *The Hairy Ape* (1922), *Desire under the Elms* (1924), and *The Great God Brown* (1926)—ran a theme of violence or tension from potential violence, of a subterranean stream of irrationality in men only a little below the surface veneer of civilization. O'Neill was even more of an innovator in form than Hemingway. Even though his plays enjoyed a great vogue both in America and abroad after his death in 1953, many of his stage devices were still rejected as too great a departure from the conventional theater.

Looking back upon the literature of the United States in the 1920's one can see that the pessimistic appraisal of Stearns and his colleagues was not entirely correct: America was the scene of a literary renaissance of considerable importance. Besides the writers mentioned here, there were dozens of others who should be considered in a more comprehensive account: T. S. Eliot, Elmer Rice, Maxwell Anderson, Theodore Dreiser, Willa Cather, Ring Lardner. But for all the writers of stature who were active during the dollar decade and who are recognized today as the giants they were, we must remember that during the decade itself most of the honors and most of the royalties went to popular writers who today lie all but forgotten. This was the second stream of culture, the more popular and conventional one.

Just as rejection of America's business civilization was a feature of the first stream of literature, acceptance of that civilization and even glorification of it was a primary feature of the second stream. Sampling the short stories and articles in the popular magazines of the day is a revealing if not very exciting exercise. Although *The Saturday Evening Post* and the slick magazines designed for women did occasionally carry some of the second-rate work of the first-rate authors, they were generally characterized by light stuff that was artistically trite, intellectually puerile, and socially conventional. The heroes of the stories were often little more than modernized versions of Horatio Alger's paragons of Social Darwinistic virtues. Optimism, boosterism, conformity, the hope of getting rich quick—in sum, the qualities of Sinclair Lewis's Babbitt—were the values expressed in these articles and stories, and we must remember that while thousands read Lewis millions read the *Post*.

Perhaps the best illustration of this kind of thinking was Bruce Barton's *The Man Nobody Knows: A Biography of Jesus*, published in 1925 and a best seller for two years. Barton, a partner in the advertising agency of Batton, Barton, Durstine and Osborn, and the son of a Protestant minister, strove to reinterpret Jesus of Nazareth in a way consistent with business values of the 1920's. Indeed, Barton's final chapter called Him "The Founder of Modern Business." Jesus was also, Barton asserted, an advertising genius, the greatest salesman of His age, and a "forceful executive." The manner in which He gathered His disciples indicated that He was a bold and daring personnel officer. Further, He was "an outdoor man," a regular fellow who might under other circumstances have fitted in well with Rotary members. So thoroughly had Babbittry permeated American society that Barton's book was not regarded as sacrilege; it was even praised. On the dust jacket the publishers printed glowing endorsements from prominent clergymen.

The Culture of the 1920's: Art and Architecture

America's affluence during the 1920's underlay the more widespread interest in art. Original paintings of merit, with relatively few exceptions, hung only on the walls of the homes of the very rich before World War I. Some of the millionaires bought widely, it is true, and they caused some consternation in Europe lest they deplete the continent of its art masterpieces. But not until the 1920's did any significant number of people of only moderate wealth purchase art for their homes beyond perhaps a portrait of a family member or prints of sentimental subjects. Affluence also made possible the establishment of more art museums. Sixty new museums opened in American cities during the 1920's.

Interest in American art, and even contemporary painting, however, was still relatively slight. In 1927 the Irish-American collector John Quinn sold his magnificent collection of recent French and American painting for $700,000. By midcentury, the Quinn collection would have brought millions. But there was some market for the products of contemporary painters. At least several serious painters managed to make a living throughout the decade. Not all Americans were as ignorant of American art as President Coolidge who, when asked by the French government in 1925 to send an exhibit of contemporary American painting to an international show in Paris, replied that the United States would have to pass up the affair because it did not have any painters.

Actually, American painting was in something of a ferment and had been for almost a decade before the United States entered the war. The United States, of course, like any society, had always had a certain number of professional painters, and some of them were artists of distinction. By the early twentieth century, however, a group of painters in New York known collectively as the Academy had managed to get almost a monopoly on exhibitions of American painting. Some members of the Academy were able technicians, but their work was seldom exciting and was thoroughly conventional. Two groups, one a small set of realists led by Robert Henri and another of modernists who might be said to have been led by the photographer Alfred Stieglitz, broke the grip that the Academy had on art and set the art world aflame.

In 1908 Henri and seven of his friends and students, who came to be known as The Eight or the Ash Can School, managed to present an exhibition in New York at a private gallery. Not strikingly different from Academy painters in technique, The Eight departed from convention primarily in their subject matter, which usually was ordinary people and ordinary sights of city life. They did not often actually paint ash cans, but the term did suggest their emphasis. Of The Eight, John Sloan became the best known, although George Bellows, who was in the same tradition but not of the original group, became even more widely known and respected.

The Armory Art Show of 1913, which appeared in New York, Chicago, and Boston and which had been organized by the group of painters who made Stieglitz's studio on Fifth Avenue their headquarters, had an impact greater than The Eight. A huge exhibition, the Armory Show included works by French modernists of various kinds, all of whom took considerable liberties with surface reality or appearances in their painting and some of whom, the cubists for example, came close to abstraction. The Armory Show caused a tremendous furor. Conventional art critics even asserted that the artists' purpose was to overturn morality and Christianity. Former President Theodore Roosevelt denounced the exhibition. But to artists, especially young ones, the show had an enormously stimulating effect. Many young painters adopted the techniques and styles of the French *avant-garde*, a few art patrons became interested, and American art was never again the same.

During the dollar decade the American modernists were more in the limelight than the realists, just as in literary circles Proust and Joyce enjoyed a greater vogue than the "slice of life" school that derived from Zola. It would be difficult to get unanimity about a list of the outstanding modernist American painters of the 1920's, but John Marin, Georgia O'Keeffe, Max Weber, and the "cubist-realist" group, Charles Demuth, Charles Sheeler, and Jo-

Woodrow Wilson. His lofty idealism and dedication to the cause of peace appealed to the masses, and made his name a household word throughout Europe as well as America.

"Fighting Bob" LaFollette, the champion of the Progressives.

Hooded figures on the march. The Ku Klux Klan, Tulsa, Oklahoma, 1923.

Familiar Scenes of the Great Depression:
A typical "Hooverville" in New York, and a
farm family, dispossessed and on the move.

Communist Party Parade, May Day, 1930, New York City.

Huey Pierce Long, perhaps the most brilliant of the demagogic messiahs of the 30's.

A Sit Down Strike. Auto workers in the Fisher Body Plant, Flint, Michigan, 1937.

President Franklin Delano Roosevelt, the most loved — and hated — American of his times.

Collection of Lawrence A. Fleischman.

"Eyes Tested," by Reginald Marsh.

F. Scott Fitzgerald

**H. L. Mencken and
George Jean Nathan.**

Sinclair Lewis

**A scene from Eugene O'Neill's
"The Emperor Jones."**

seph Stella, were certainly painters of top quality and representative of modernist painting of the decade. Marin, who became very well known before his death in 1953, was in his most abstract stage of development in the 1920's. Best known for his water colors, Marin painted New York City and Maine coastal scenes that were recognizable but distorted. Weber, who likewise had his greatest following after World War II, painted in a variety of styles, usually drawing strongly upon contemporary trends in Paris. Miss O'Keeffe, who married Stieglitz, employed a hard, clean line that was almost photographic, even when she was at her most abstract. Demuth, Sheeler, and Stella were midway between the kind of cubism that was popular in Paris before the war and realism. Their paintings were representational, but they emphasized the geometric forms of their subject matter, which often was a building or a machine or a bridge, distorting appearances to give their work a greater impression of reality. Some of their work, in fact, resembled the "art photography" of those who sought out intricate and geometric interplays of light and shadow.

Although the modernists attracted more attention, the realists continued to work in their tradition throughout the decade. Bellows became quite well known before his death in 1925, when he was still in his early forties, because of the subjects of his canvases and his own background. He had been an athlete, one of the star infielders of the Ohio State baseball team, before he began to study with Henri, and he frequently painted athletes. His boxing pictures especially were popular.

When one says that Bellows was popular it must be remembered that the term is relative. He was more popular than most serious painters, but to the great majority of Americans he was entirely unknown. Art in the formal sense was unimportant to most people. Most people lived out their days without ever seeing a great picture, little knowing or caring about the gap in their lives. To most people art was something you bought at a furniture store when you refurnished a room or the covers of *The Saturday Evening Post*, homey, sentimental things designed to evoke a chuckle or a sigh.

There was far more imagination, ferment, and modernism in painting than there was in architecture during the 1920's. Late in the nineteenth and early in the twentieth centuries American architects had pioneered in the design of the tall building, what came to be known popularly as the skyscraper, by developing the steel skeleton system of construction rather than using supporting walls of masonry. Skyscrapers continued to be built in the 1920's,

to be sure—the economics of urban real estate demanded them—
but their design was no longer unusual. Often it was not even sensible. Architects frequently decorated their skyscrapers with all
sorts of unfunctional gingerbread. Many architects went over-
board in efforts to reproduce Gothic cathedrals in twentieth-century America. College campuses were especially cursed with these
dark, unfunctional, and very expensive designs. Designs of family
residences were especially weak and puerile during the decade.
There were a few more ambitious efforts, of course, but the ro-
mantically conceived cute little Cape Cods and Dutch Colonials
that cluttered George Babbitt's Floral Heights and the English
manor-house imitations and Spanish castles that went up in the
more expensive suburbs and resorts were far from architectural
excellence. The most encouraging development architecturally
was the bringing of more imaginative and unconventional de-
signers into the schools of architecture. Within just a few years
the work of these men and their students would again put the
United States at the forefront architecturally.

Mass Culture

The brief discussions in the previous sections of popular literature and art raise the complex and subtle matter of mass culture,
a problem that began to assume considerable proportions during
the dollar decade and was to become even more difficult later.
The problem fundamentally was—and is—a conflict between economic motive and cultural aspiration: should the communications
and cultural media that were dependent upon mass consumption
for their economic well-being play down to the tastes of the great
majority of people to insure themselves of a market or should they
attempt to improve the tastes of their audience?

The problem was by no means new in the 1920's. The situation
certainly existed as early as when William Randolph Hearst began
publishing his newspapers in the late nineteenth century. In the
1920's the matter only became more acute, as some newspapers
reached new depths of sensationalism and as radio and Hollywood came into being. Publishers, radio company executives and
advertising sponsors, and movie companies were in business primarily to make profits, and especially when their overhead expenses were high they found it necessary to attract as wide an
audience as possible. Only with a big circulation could they get
fat advertising contracts; only with millions of listeners could
broadcasters sell their time and services to sponsors; only with

big box-office receipts could Hollywood pay for the extravagant and always increasing cost of producing films. But publishers, broadcasters, and picture producers were engaged also in a cultural enterprise, and they had a responsibility to society, which they too frequently shirked, to keep the public well informed and to enrich it culturally. It was obvious that Hearst and Bernarr Macfadden were far more concerned with circulation than with disseminating information. If an "advice to the lovelorn" column in the newspaper increased circulation, it little mattered to them that the columns often contained the worst kind of trash and took the place of news stories. That their newspapers had notorious reputations as low-brow made no difference to their bank accounts. Macfadden's difficulty was that he underestimated popular taste and pitched his product too low on the scale of respectability. His New York *Daily Graphic,* one of the first tabloids, was so smutty that it was popularly called the "Daily Pornographic," and it went under in a few years. Macfadden then turned to magazines and published *Liberty,* which likewise failed after several years because again Macfadden thought the public was more low-brow than it actually was. Radio programming in the 1920's was not as banal as it was to become later, but then the broadcasting companies were new at the game. It would be difficult to say whether Hollywood's products were any worse in the 1920's than they were in succeeding decades, but most of them were poor enough to warrant the disrespect of people with any reasonable cultural standards. Too many Hollywood people agreed with the producer who went on record with the statement: "The picture industry is no different from the underwear business, for example. It is completely governed by the law of supply and demand."

A few entrepreneurs in the mass media discovered partial solutions during the 1920's. In the mid-1920's a group of magazine journalists established *The New Yorker Magazine,* which deliberately and forcefully emphasized that it was a class rather than a mass periodical. (Its early slogan was "Not for the old lady from Dubuque," which made it irresistible to those who were in rebellion against Dubuque old ladies.) Economically *The New Yorker* did very well indeed with only a relatively small circulation. It carried a great deal of advertising for expensive and "quality" merchandise, frequently with a certain snob appeal. That the magazine catered to a sophisticated audience did not necessarily mean that its content was always of a high quality, but it did contain many articles and stories of recognized worth. Henry Luce gradually came forth with another formula during the decade after he started *Time*. Luce's scheme was to publish a smorgasbord, a little bit of a lot of things for a wide variety of tastes. Nothing was to be taxingly high-brow and nothing was to be extravagantly low-brow; he aimed at the middle spectrum of brows with a scattergun —a little news, a little science, a bit of religion and art, a soupçon of gossip and sex, all in a sprightly, lively, and easily understood but somewhat jagged and jarring style. Mass middle-brow publishing had its own cultural problems and handicaps, as later generations of intellectuals would assert forcefully, but it clearly was an improvement over the New York *Daily News* and the Hearst chain.

By 1929 the typical American had become a mass man. He worked for a huge industrial corporation; he bought mass-produced articles made by the large corporation; he more than likely lived in an apartment house or in a small residence that differed little from thousands of others; he read a mass newspaper; he attended Metro-Goldwyn-Mayer movies and listened to national radio programs; he avidly followed the athletic exploits of Babe Ruth and Red Grange—and, wondrously, he voted for Herbert Hoover because the Great Engineer praised "rugged individualism." He was the new mass man of the New Era and all seemed rosy. But he and the New Era were soon to receive a jolt of unprecedented force and power.

Part Two

Bust Years

5

The Great Depression

MARCH 4, 1929. Former Secretary of Commerce Herbert Hoover took the presidential oath of office administered by the dignified Chief Justice Charles Evans Hughes. If ever fortune seemed to smile upon the United States it was on that day. Surely Hoover would be the perfect president. It was an age of technology, and Hoover was an engineer—"the Great Engineer" was the way Republican campaign literature had emphasized the point. It was a year of peace, no war clouds were on the horizon, and American wealth was actively expanding overseas and changing conditions in less economically fortunate parts of the world. President Hoover was also the Great Humanitarian, a title earned as relief administrator in Belgium after the German invasion in 1914. Most of all, the new President was the chief builder of the New Era. As Secretary of Commerce under Presidents Harding and Coolidge he had been in effect a special vice-president for economic affairs, and during those years when he had been the chief government economic official the national economy had boomed as never before.

More than Hoover's background prompted the great majority of citizens to breathe easily with his inauguration. If Hoover had lost the election to Governor Smith many people would have been seriously concerned. As Roger Babson, a stock market analyst and adviser, had put it in September 1928: "If Smith should be elected with a Democratic Congress, we are almost certain to have a resulting business depression in 1929." The forces of respectability, the honored people of American society, had supported Hoover strongly. Not since the last time Bryan lost a presidential election in 1908 had respectable people been so solidly behind a presidential candidate as they were behind Hoover in 1928. They saw no sign, no warning to discourage optimism on inaugural day of 1929. The only discordant note was the retiring president. The sour and tight-fisted Coolidge made a small scene as he left the White House and turned it over to the Hoovers, insisting all the while that the servants find his other overshoe.

With the knowledge that comes with hindsight, knowing what the future actually held for the United States, one can smile ironically at this optimism of the spring of 1929. Yet one cannot condemn Americans of that day for not seeing the future. Hoover's credentials for the nation's highest office seemed superb. No other president of the century had brought such qualifications to the White House. The only aspect of Hoover's career that one might have criticized was his lack of electoral and political experience. The first time he had ever been a candidate for elected public office was when he ran for the presidency. But, thought many people, that he was not a professional politician was to his credit rather than his detriment. Politics, they thought, was inherently distasteful, perhaps even dishonest, and Hoover was "above politics." Actually, a lack of sensitivity to public opinion, which most professional politicians develop to a high degree, a personal aloofness that successful politicians seldom display, and a distaste for the rough and tumble of partisan politics were to cause Hoover a great many headaches in the next four years.

March 3, 1933, was Hoover's last full day in the White House. The national mood had utterly reversed. Instead of optimism there was pessimism, desperation, a heavy measure of despair. Except for the darkest days of the Civil War the nation had never had a lower moment, and during the great and bloody war the enemy had been tangible. Now the adversary was invisible but no less real. Over three years of economic depression had made the nation hungry, listless, rebellious, and cynical. Fighting the Great Depression was a great deal more trying intellectually and psychologically than struggling against a foe on the battlefield. If, as Professor David Potter has argued cogently and persuasively, the key to American national character is material abundance, the very foundation of American beliefs had disappeared for millions and left them bewildered and deeply resentful.

A most highly respected and admired figure in 1929, President Hoover by 1933 had become an object of contempt, ridicule, and hatred. Homeless families had built shack towns at the edges of almost every industrial city of America, and these jerry-built, ramshackle communities built of discarded packing crates and flattened tin cans were known almost universally as Hoovervilles. The newspapers that unemployed men put under their clothes on cold nights in a futile effort to be comfortable were called Hoover blankets. The hungry—and there were millions whose diet was appallingly meager—cynically remembered a Republican slogan in 1928, "a chicken in every pot and two cars in every garage."

The profound change in the national temper as well as the deterioration of the objective conditions of life were attributable solely to the Great Depression, the greatest economic calamity in the nation's history. A survey of the extent of the calamity is necessary to any understanding of the politics, the foreign relations, and social-cultural developments of the 1930's.

The Descent in Statistical Terms

Any series of economic indices shows a sharp deterioration in the nation's economic health from the fall of 1929 until the spring of 1933. The depression began with the stock market crash in October 1929, and the general direction of all economic indicators from then until Hoover left office was downward. The year after the crash saw only a gradual curve toward the bottom of the chart. The curve dropped more steeply in 1931 and 1932, and conditions were serious indeed. But the worst was yet to come. The period between Hoover's defeat for re-election in November 1932 and Franklin D. Roosevelt's inauguration on March 4, 1933, saw the bottom drop out. Many have said that during those four terrible months "capitalism almost failed." It "almost" failed only if one defines failure as the economy's grinding to an utter stop. If however, one defines failure as inability to provide a minimum standard of living for a large part of the population, an opportunity for profitable investment of capital, and security for savings and other funds already invested, then the economy did not "almost" fail; it did fail.

The best single indicator of a nation's economic health is the gross national product. The GNP, as it is commonly called, is the total of all goods and services produced. In 1929 GNP was $104.4

billion. In 1933 it had fallen to $74.2 billion, expressed in 1929 prices. The per-capita GNP of 1929 (GNP divided by the total population) was $857. The figure for 1933 was $590: lower than the average for the years 1907 through 1911. That is to say, by 1933 all the national economic progress made since the Taft administration and more had been wiped away. Actually, since these figures are for the whole calendar year of 1933 and since conditions improved appreciably but by no means satisfactorily in the spring and summer of that year, these statistics do not accurately reveal the situation of the first three months of 1933.

Unemployment statistics constitute the best index of economic privation. One must remember that unemployment insurance did not exist then and that public relief was woefully inadequate. In 1929, according to the Bureau of Labor Statistics (BLS) of the Department of Labor, there were 1,499,000 unemployed workers, 3.1 per cent of the total labor force. For 1930 the BLS reported 4,248,000 unemployed, or 8.8 per cent; for 1931, 7,911,000 and 16.1 per cent; for 1932, 11,901,000 and 24 per cent; for 1933, 12,-634,000 unemployed, over one fourth the labor force. Again, the figures represent entire calendar years. But statisticians of unemployment differed considerably in their estimates. The National Industrial Conference Board, which represented the business community, placed unemployment in 1933 at just 11,842,000. The American Federation of Labor reported it as 13,271,000. The left-wing Labor Research Association placed the figure at 16,138,-000. Which if any of these statistics was correct we can never know. None of them indicates how long people were unemployed. None of them indicates how many workers had jobs that were below their demonstrated capacity and earning power, how many tool-and-die workers were driving garbage trucks, how many accountants were clerking in grocery stores. We do know that in March 1933 more than every fourth worker—perhaps as many as one out of three—had no job whatsoever.

Nor do these figures cited here tell us anything about farmers, who worked as much as ever but frequently came out in the red after a year's labor. Farm prices, which were low enough even in 1929 to cause considerable agricultural unrest, fell 61 per cent from 1929 to 1933. Total farm income declined from approximately $13 billion in 1929 to only $5.5 billion in 1932, the last full year before farmers began to receive direct subsidies from the federal government. In the fall of 1932 many farmers found that to transport their products to market and sell them would only put them more in the red than ever. Consequently, while starvation was a real possibility in cities, some farmers used their corn for fuel.

Bank failures caused more distress among the middle classes than among industrial workers because few workers had significant bank accounts. When a bank failed depositors simply lost their money since there was no deposit insurance at that time. Many banks that went under reorganized and paid off their creditors in part and some in full, but even in these circumstances depositors went for months or years before they regained their funds. Not infrequently people who lost their savings in a bank failure had to continue to pay on a loan from the same bank. Banks frequently sold some of their assets, including notes that were due to the bank, to other banking institutions in a futile effort to remain solvent. The notes were still valid and payable.

Bank failures were nothing new to the American people. Banks had failed by the hundreds in the economic crises of the nineteenth century, and there had even been many failures during the generally prosperous 1920's. From mid-1928 until mid-1929, at the height of the boom, 549 American banks closed their doors, most of them in the agriculturally depressed regions. But failures became much more frequent after the stock-market crash, because banks had part of their assets in corporation stocks. As the market value of these stocks declined, the general assets of the banks diminished. Banks also had accepted millions of shares of stock as collateral on loans, and this stock shrank in value as well. In the year beginning July 1, 1929, 640 banks were forced to close. The following year 1,553 banks failed, losing over $1 billion in depositors' funds. In the first ten months of 1932, 1,199 banks went out of business.

One could pile gloomy statistic upon gloomy statistic. Only a few more will suffice. The total income that labor received fell 42.3 per cent from 1929 to 1933, from $5.1 billion to $29.5 billion. Income from salaries, a part of the previous figures, declined 40 per cent during the four years. Total exports declined 68 per cent from 1929 through 1932. Imports fell off a little more. In 1932 there were roughly 30 per cent more business failures than there had been in 1929. A fairly useful economic indicator, the weekly index of business activity compiled by *The New York Times*, told the same dreary story. This index was calculated upon the amount of electric power consumed, freight cars loaded, and steel, lumber, cotton textiles, and automobiles produced. The index was at its peak in late June 1929, when it stood at 114.8. In mid-March 1933 this index was at only 63.7, almost half-way to the bottom.

The Descent in Human Terms

Statistics provide the only way to tell the national story of the first years of the depression. But they tell us nothing about the depression in human terms, and it was people, not numbers, that suffered through the era. There are no words to describe the whole calamity adequately. One can only describe certain aspects or effects of the depression and multiply what happened to individuals by thousands or millions. One can only take samples from the stories of approximately 125 million American people.

Among those who were hardest hit by the depression, getting food was a major problem. People who were more comfortably established sometimes try to shrug off the problem and say, "No one has starved." This was not quite true. Some people actually starved to death in the United States during the depression. An article in *Fortune* magazine with the title "No One Has Starved" documented cases of death from malnutrition. Hospitals, particularly those in big cities, reported receiving patients whose primary illness was starvation. The director of relief of Philadelphia described for a Senate committee some of the things that happened in his city when relief funds were utterly exhausted for eleven days in the spring of 1932. One family had no food whatsoever for two days before the father pulled dandelions from a city park for the dinner table. Several families existed only on stale bread, which was available for 3½ cents a loaf. The American Friends Service Committee endeavored to feed hungry children in the coal-mining regions of West Virginia, Kentucky, and Illinois. The Friends provided lunches at schools in communities where the mines were working less than two days a week. The organization reported that most of the children in these schools were underweight. In one school 99 per cent of the children were underweight when the Friends started their lunch program. In New York City, where relief for the unemployed was closer to being adequate than any other major American city, the Health Department reported that slightly more than one fifth of the children in the schools in 1932 were suffering from malnutrition. Diseases related directly to malnutrition such as pellagra increased significantly, especially in the South. Not everyone, of course, was hungry. Food prices were fantastically low by today's standards—ordinary hamburger was available for ten to fifteen cents a pound throughout the 1930's—and those who were fortunate enough to have no cut in income actually spent a smaller part of the family budget for food than they had in the 1920's. But one should remember that in the late winter of 1932-1933 over one fourth the wage earners were unemployed, others were only partially employed, and still others were working at reduced wages.

The nation's housing standards deteriorated badly during the Great Depression, particularly until about 1937. New residential construction all but stopped in the first years of the depression. In fact, it had slowed down significantly in the two years just before the crash. Yet there was no housing shortage. On the contrary, vacant rental apartments and houses were abundant in all cities. This quantity of available housing, despite an absence of new construction and a slowly increasing population, was simply because there were many families who could not afford to rent or buy housing they wanted and needed. When husbands and fathers lost their jobs they frequently moved their families in with relatives to save rent; "doubling up" became very common. Visiting nurses in the New York City Department of Health reported that to find twelve or more people living in a three-room apartment was not at all unusual. Just how many people who had lived alone were forced to give up all semblance of maintaining a home will never be known, but it was quite apparent that there were significant numbers of homeless people in the big cities. Most of the inhabitants of the Hoovervilles were men without families, although often families with children lived in these places. Some people slept in the New York subways; the police seldom bothered them. In the summer of 1931 the commissioner of public welfare in Chicago reported that "several hundred" homeless women were sleeping in the city parks. Railroads reported a sharp increase in vagrants who roamed the country in empty box cars, and motorists noticed an increased number of down-and-out hitchhikers.

Evictions for nonpayment of rent and foreclosures of mortgages on residences occurred, but there were not nearly as many enforced removals as one might have anticipated. Most people made a great effort to keep up their rent or mortgage payments, although landlords sometimes encountered families who "beat the rent" by moving away in the night without leaving a forwarding address. When families did get behind on the rent or were unable to meet their mortgage obligations, landlords and creditors often calculated that it was a better financial risk for them to allow the families to continue to live in the property and hope they would be able to pay soon than to evict them or foreclose. The rental and selling market being what it was, the property was likely to be vacant for a long time if the families were forcibly removed.

Urban renewal or slum clearance programs did not become numerically important until late in the 1930's—and even then were miniscule as compared with post-World War II efforts—and urban slums, already unhealthy and unsightly in 1929, further deteriorated during the depression. "Doubling up" intensified slum problems, landlords were financially unable to remodel and refurbish, and city governments often reduced such services as garbage removal and street cleaning as their tax problems became acute.

The precise number of people who had to accept substandard housing because of economic want can never be known. Even families with a fair degree of security postponed needed housing maintenance. But when President Roosevelt said in his second inaugural address in January 1937, that "one-third of the nation" was "ill-fed, ill-housed, and ill-clad" he was probably not far off in his estimate. And conditions in 1937 were better than they had been in 1932 and 1933.

There was considerable anxiety during the depression about what effects economic hardship would ultimately have on the family, the basic social unit. If the traditional family unit became shattered for millions of people, the consequences for society at large would be staggering. There was reasonable cause for anxiety. Especially early in the depression, when relief was so inadequate as to make keeping a family's roots in the home community of little or no economic advantage, many families took to the roads, sometimes in old automobiles, sometimes by freight cars, in a usually fruitless search for work. The National Association of Travelers' Aid Societies calculated in 1932 that there were 25,000 such nomadic families. In the mid-1930's, dust storms ruined agriculture in parts of the southern Great Plains and the Agricultural Adjustment Act had an unfortunate side effect on southern share-croppers, which will be described in the chapter on the New Deal, so that thousands of other families took to the highways, usually bound for California's Imperial Valley. In many ways these "Okies" were twentieth-century counterparts of earlier westward-moving pioneers, but they were driven away by desperation more than they were attracted by a promise of better life in the Far West. On the constant move, struggling with woefully inadequate funds, these families underwent terrible strains in their efforts to keep together as family units. Some of them failed to do so; the older children sometimes drifted away from the family to pursue their own chances.

Indeed, the number of young nomads—boy and girl tramps—

was estimated to be at least 200,000 in 1932. Most of them were in their late teens, but some of them were younger, and most of them had left an intolerable home situation in the hope that life for them would be better elsewhere. For these youngsters the family as the basic social unit had disappeared at least temporarily. Most families were able to stick together and stick it out, but "doubling up" and going on short rations undoubtedly increased family strife.

Statistics indicate that there were fewer new families in the 1930's and that they were smaller. Because of unemployment, many young people put off marriage until they could afford to establish a separate household. The birth rate declined significantly. Many families simply could not afford another mouth to feed. The national birth rate in the 1930's was only 18 per thousand population. In 1933 maternity wards were far from full; in that year there were only 6.5 births per thousand population. (Some figures for comparison: in 1915 and 1957 there were 25 births per thousand; in 1960, 23.6.) Some optimists pointed to the decline in the number of divorces, but it appears that this was more a result of inability to pay legal fees than evidence of marital harmony. Social workers reported an increase in the incidence of desertion, the "poor man's divorce."

The family as a social institution, of course, did survive the depression, in substantially the same form. But its endurance during the 1930's—and during World War II, at least an equally disruptive force—is testimony to the inherent strength of the institution and not of wholesome conditions for it.

It is mistaken to think that the only people hard hit by the depression were those who were marginal members of society before the calamity struck. Although it was certainly true that people who were poorly trained and in the lower strata of the economy before the crash suffered more and longer than those more comfortably placed, still many people of considerable training and ability who had been economically well off became destitute. The depression affected all classes of American society in greater or lesser degree. More than a few small businessmen were forced to give up their businesses and take whatever employment they could get; some former independent businessmen were on WPA in the late 1930's. A 1933 survey of college and university alumni officers showed that unemployment among graduates, while certainly less than among those who had only high-school educations, was serious. Ohio State University's alumni office reported that it knew of over 2,000 cases of unemployment among its graduates, and even Princeton, which drew mostly from economically comfortable homes for its new students, reported 450 unemployed alumni. In the spring of 1932 an association of chemists and chemical engineers opened a placement office for unemployed men with this kind of specialty. Over 455 unemployed chemists and chemical engineers, one fourth of whom were destitute, registered with the office for jobs. One chemist, who formerly had held a position of responsibility in his profession, had been sleeping in subways.

Many college graduates who kept their jobs suffered from salary cuts. Teachers especially suffered in this respect since local units of government were sometimes unable to support their school systems as well as in the past. Some communities drastically shortened the school year to save money. In Arkansas in 1932-1933 more than three hundred schools had classes for only sixty days during the year. Many cities in relatively wealthy Ohio cut their school term to seven months. The most publicized school affair was in Chicago. The schools there remained open as usual but the teachers received only "tax anticipation warrants" rather than cash for their salaries. These IOU's were eventually paid off—during World War II—but by that time most Chicago teachers had sold them to bankers to get much needed cash and had found it necessary to sell them at a 10 to 12 per cent discount.

How much unhappiness did the Great Depression cause? How many lives did it frustrate and warp? How much stronger as a nation would the United States have been if it had not suffered the depression? These questions can not be fully and satisfactorily answered. But it is clear that the depression's impact on human beings was vast and horrible.

Why the Crash?

An important and legitimate question, one which people in the depression years pondered often and which is still relevant today, was why did the Great Depression occur. The balance of this chapter is devoted to consideration of that question.

The stock-market crash of October 1929 triggered the depression. It was not a fundamental cause of the more general economic blight, but since the Wall Street crash started the downswing it is worth investigation.

Basically, the crash was the inevitable puncturing of a vast speculative bubble. It was not the first time in the history of mankind that a speculative bubble had broken and left speculators, or many of them, in a bad position, nor was it the last. In the early and mid-1920's there had been a speculative boom in Florida real estate. Florida land had exchanged hands for ridiculously high prices, the purchasers buying only because they were confident that they could sell for a higher price than they had bought. A well-publicized hurricane shocked the public back to reality, and Florida land prices quickly dropped to more realistic levels. The bubble collapsed. The last owners of the speculative land were left with deeds that they could sell for only a fraction of what they had paid for them. The Wall Street crash was psychologically the same phenomenon. The awakening to reality, the psychological panic that developed when stock prices began to fall to realistic levels, came in the autumn of 1929. The Wall Street crash involved more people and far more money than the Florida bubble, however, and it was more complicated.

For roughly five years before the stock-market crash there had been an enormous bull market. (In Wall Street parlance, those who speculate upon an assumption of a rise in stock prices are called bulls; those who anticipate a decline in market quotations are called bears.) The bull market got started in the latter part of 1924 and carried throughout 1925. *The New York Times* index of twenty-five industrial stocks was 106 in May 1924 and had risen to 181 in December 1925. (A stock index, of which there were several, is a method of measuring the general strength of the stock market rather than just of a single issue. Some indices measure only industrial stocks, others only utilities or railroads, still others the whole range of stock-market prices.) In 1926 the market slumped; there was a small bear market for a few months. But by the end of 1926 the market reversed itself again and became bullish. In fact, it became the biggest bull market in Wall Street history.

The *Times* index of industrial stocks stood at 245 at the end of 1927, up 35 per cent in the preceding two years. It went up to 331 by the end of 1928, up another 35 per cent in one year and 83 per cent higher than it had been three years earlier. By Labor Day of 1929 the *Times* industrial index had risen to 452, which was 36 per cent higher in eight months and 149 per cent higher than it had been at the end of 1925. In other words, if a person had invested equally in the twenty-five industrial stocks used in the *Times* index at the end of 1925 and sold this block of stocks at the beginning of September 1929, he would have realized a capital gain of approximately one and one-half times, or $2.50 for every $1.00 he had invested. Some individual stocks had much more spectacular increases. Radio Corporation of America common stock sold for $85 a share in early 1928; its quotation was $505 a share by Labor Day of 1929.

Anticipation of good dividends had little to do with the bull market. Whatever dividends stock speculators received were just extra bonus. Prices of stocks had gone so high that the ratio of dividends to market prices was very low indeed. Some popular stocks paid no dividends at all during the months of their greatest popularity. Radio Corporation of America, for example, paid no dividends while its market price soared. In other words, this big bull market was a capital gains or speculative market. Corporate earnings had little to do with the attractiveness of a stock; anticipated increase in market value was almost the only consideration.

The reason stock prices soared was that more people wanted to buy more stocks than ever before, and there were two basic reasons for the increased demand: the market attracted a great many newcomers; and more capital for investment (or rather, for speculation) was available than ever before. There are many myths about who the newcomers to stock speculation were. Frederick Lewis Allen told the story in *Only Yesterday* of a chauffeur who overheard the conversation of his corporation executive passengers and played the market on the basis of information learned by such eavesdropping. There is no reason to doubt the validity of the story, but one should not draw the conclusion that chauffeurs and others with similar incomes were widely involved in speculation. It was impossible for them to speculate on the market because they did not have the capital necessary to do so even if they bought stocks on margin. Most of the new market players were from the middle classes, usually the upper reaches of that rather ill-defined social-economic stratum. Brokerage firms made a major effort to establish accounts in cities and towns where there had never been much stock-buying, and as the word spread of fat gains to be made in the market, more and more people began to speculate. Market events became front-page news. Even fairly small cities had customers' rooms with a ticker and a blackboard with the latest prices. But even with all the new speculators, the amateurs, relatively few people were involved directly with the stock market boom. One estimate, based upon income-tax returns, put the maximum number of people who owned corporation stocks at 9 million, roughly 7 per cent of the total population.

The reasons for additional capital in the stock market were more complex. First we must understand the operation of the so-called call-money market and the use of brokers' loans. To buy stock it was not necessary to pay cash for the entire amount. One could buy on margin and borrow the rest from the broker—a brokers' loan—with the stock he had just bought as collateral. The margin required in 1929 was 45 and then 50 per cent. That is, one could purchase stock with as little as 50 per cent down payment. Brokers' loans were a quite safe kind of credit. If the value of the stock held as collateral should decline in the market, the broker had only to demand of the debtor that he put up "more margin," that he supply more collateral. Brokers received the funds for their loans from the call-money market, most of which came from banks. Interest rates in the call-money market were quite high, as much as 12 per cent, and they too were considered a good risk because again the lender could always demand more margin as collateral.

The amount of money available in the call-money market expanded enormously from 1927 to 1929. One reason for the expansion was the easy-money policies pursued by the Federal Reserve System. In 1927 there appeared to be a slow-down in economic activity outside the stock market, to be described in greater detail a few pages later. In view of this economic prospect, the Federal Reserve lowered the rediscount rate, or, in effect, the interest rate that Federal Reserve System member banks paid for loans from their regional Reserve banks. This policy normally was a wise one. When conditions seem to warrant an economic stimulus, lowering the rediscount rate serves to stimulate credit and thereby increase economic activity. The trouble in 1927, however, was that the additional credit thus created went into stock speculation rather than into more solid economic investment; it went into the call-money market to a greater extent than into housing construction, machinery modernization, and the like. A reason for this sluicing of credit away from traditional markets was that corporations had made such handsome profits that they were able to do their own financing from their reserves rather than borrow from bankers. In 1928 the Federal Reserve reversed itself and raised the rediscount rate, as it did again in August 1929. Both actions failed significantly to check the expansion of the call-money market because the interest that creditors received for such loans was still much higher than what they paid through rediscounting. Another reason for the expansion of call money was that some large corporations found they could make more money from lending in that market than they could from their ordinary economic activities. For example, in 1929 the Standard Oil Company of New Jersey lent money in the call-money market at the rate of $69 million a day. There was more money to be made there than in selling gasoline.

By early 1929 stock prices were so unrealistic in terms of corporate assets and earnings that some professional speculators began to sell short. (To sell short is to wager that the price of a stock will go down. A hypothetical case: the short seller contracts to deliver one hundred shares of Stock X, selling at the time of the contract at 105, in thirty days for 103. At the end of the period the short seller buys one hundred shares of Stock X and delivers them. If the price dropped below 103 he has made a profit; if the price went up, he must pay more for the stocks than he has contracted to sell them for.) But prices continued to rise in the great speculative bubble. The number of professionals selling short—and losing money—indicated that there was a certain lack of confidence that the bubble would go on forever.

The market began to act peculiarly after Labor Day 1929, rising and dropping in an unusual manner. Then on Black Thursday, October 24, sell orders came onto the market floor in such volume that prices dropped precipitously. As this happened, many calculated that it was time to get out and placed sell orders. Prices went down even further. The ticker was hours behind the actual situation on the exchange floor. Early in the afternoon, representatives of four big New York banks met in the offices of the House of Morgan, decided to pool some of their resources and conspicuously buy above the quoted price. They hoped this dramatic move would end the panic that was developing and that the trend would reverse itself. When they bought higher than the market the effect was as they had expected. Speculators figured that the banks were pegging the price in order to prevent the market's bottom from dropping out, regained confidence, and began to buy. By the end of the trading day prices recovered considerably. The *Times* industrial index dropped only $12 for the day. The next two trading days saw relatively steady markets.

But when the market opened on Monday, October 28, sell orders flooded the floor. Prices dropped sharply. The next day was even worse. This time no banker pool came to the rescue, and the decline was devastating. The *Times* industrials fell $92 in those two days. Thereafter the market continued to fall, not every day to be sure, but its trend was generally downward. Within two weeks after the crash the total value of all stocks traded on the exchange had fallen 40 per cent. Still they went down. By January 1933, the Dow-Jones index of thirty industrial stocks had fallen 83 per cent below the price at the end of September 1929. Other kinds of stocks dropped accordingly but not quite so disastrously. The big bull market had come to a dramatic and calamitous end and had triggered the Great Depression.

Why Did the Crash Become a Depression?

How, it might be asked, did the Wall Street crash bring such havoc to the economy in general? After all, speculation in stock had little directly to do with the production and distribution of real wealth and real services. The answer is that possibly if the "real economy" had been healthy it might have rolled with the punch of the stock debacle, adjusted itself, and been relatively little affected. But the "real economy" was not healthy. There were several aspects of the economic structure that today would be considered inherent weaknesses, and conditions even within that structure were not what they should have been. In 1927, as we have seen, the Federal Reserve System was concerned enough about the softness in the "real economy" to adopt an easier credit policy. The GNP had increased only a little over the previous year, not as much as it should have. Residential construction had absolutely declined, as had consumer outlay for durable goods. The bull market's profits for speculators stimulated the economy for roughly another eighteen months and kept it going, but there were several economic indicators even at the peak of the boom that would alarm later economists. Residential construction declined even more. Business inventories approximately doubled in 1929, an indication that consumers were unable to purchase enough to keep production at top capacity.

The stock-market crash spread into the "real economy" through the banks and through its adverse psychological effects on investors. These psychological effects are impossible to measure, but quite obviously the times did not seem propitious for expansion or establishment of new and expensive enterprises. The rate of investment in new productive or distributive capacity declined. The effect on the banks was more tangible. Banks had many of their assets in stocks and held stocks as collateral on loans. As the value of stocks declined, so their assets and loan collateral declined. At the same time that businessmen were gloomy about the economic future and not inclined to borrow funds for expansion or new enterprises, banks were less well equipped to extend credit. Some banks were in a rather shaky condition, and when depositors suspected their accounts were not safe they hurried to withdraw them. In many cities "bank runs" developed; long lines formed outside banks as depositors waited to get their money out before the bank closed. This made the already shaky bank even worse, and, as we have seen, over three thousand banks closed in the three years after the crash.

By the late winter of 1932-1933 the economy had all but ceased to function. What was the basic difficulty? Why were farm prices well below the farmers' costs of production, why were factories shut, and why were millions of wage earners unemployed? We must remember that the basic equipment still remained. The capacity to produce and distribute was relatively unimpaired. The factories were still there, raw materials had not disappeared, transportation facilities existed. Businessmen certainly wanted to produce and distribute goods or services at a profit, and consumers certainly wanted their products. But the economic wheels had either ceased to turn or were turning exceedingly slowly. Why?

These were questions that perplexed the whole American people, for only through discovery of the reason or reasons for the depression could society make a rational attack on the problem of recovery. Until the root of the illness was diagnosed, it could not intelligently be treated.

Quite naturally, in a large and diverse population with assorted and often conflicting economic interests, there was no unanimity about the source of the trouble or the means of rectifying it. Opinions ranged from the highly sophisticated to the bizarre and ignorant. A few people even blamed the calamity on sun spots. Others said it was fate and dug into their copies of Nostradamus. Still others said the depression was the inevitable aftermath of the World War. A great many Puritan souls attributed the hardship to retribution for the good times of the 1920's and thought of the whole situation as a "hangover" or "the morning after." Marxists argued that the depression was inherent in the nature of capitalism and that the only cure was socialism. President Hoover believed that America's hardship was only part of a general world malaise, that the United States had been dragged down by economic failure in Europe. From his point of view this was a comforting theory; it shifted the blame away from his administration and those of Harding and Coolidge and relieved American business leadership from the responsibility. That the American and European depressions were related there can be no doubt. But one could build a good case for the opposite point of view, that the American slump dragged down Europe. Hard-shell advocates of laissez faire blamed government "meddling." Their argument was that the Federal Reserve System's action in raising the rediscount rate in August 1929 had destroyed "confidence," one of their favorite words, in the stock market and had thereby precipitated the crash.

Even today there is no unanimously endorsed opinion on what was the cause or causes of the Great Depression. One can only abstract the thinking of a majority of contemporary professional economists. First, today's economists reason, a capitalistic economy must be constantly expanding in order to be healthy. If it stands still, it in effect retreats. The rate of capital investment in the "real economy" as opposed to stock or some other kind of speculation must expand, as must the level of consumption. If either capital investment or consumer spending declines or tends to become stagnant, there should be a compensating increase in the other, which in turn will stimulate the weak factor. Let us therefore look briefly at capital expansion and then at consumer spending.

There was an enormous capital expansion during most of the 1920's, largely in the form of new industries such as radio or rapidly expanding recently founded industries such as automobiles and related fields. By late in the decade, however, industrial consumption approached saturation. But the market approached saturation in terms of consumer purchasing power rather than in terms of consumer desires or needs. The consuming public would have liked to have purchased more, but it did not have the funds to do so. Thus we come back to consumer spending.

The basic trouble with consumer spending was an inadequate distribution of income. Although the number of gainfully employed workers rose 11 per cent from 1923 to 1929, hourly wage rates increased an average of 8 per cent in manufacturing during the same period, and the cost of living remained remarkably stable, distribution of income became inadequate to support enough purchasing power to keep the economic wheels turning fast enough. The main difficulty was that labor and consumers received too small a share of the benefits of increased labor productivity. Labor productivity, mostly from better machinery and industrial organization, increased 43 per cent from 1919 until the depression. In other words, any given number of man-hours of work produced roughly two fifths more in 1929 than it had in 1919. But wages and salaries did not increase this much and prices did not decline. Further, workers in depressed industries, such as coal, and farmers in general had less purchasing power in the 1920's than they previously enjoyed. The share of total income payments received by the rich increased significantly during the decade, while the share (but not the absolute amount) received by the poor shrank in the same amount. In 1923 the richest 5 per cent of income receivers had 22.9 per cent of the total income; in 1929 this 5 per cent had 26.1 per cent of the total, an increase of 14 per cent. The share going to the richest one per cent grew even more rapidly, from 12.3 per cent in 1923 to 14.5 per cent in 1929, an increase of 19 per cent. If everyone spent all the money he received, distribution of income would have no effect on total consumer purchasing, but materially comfortable receivers of income put part of their money into speculation. An increase in income at the lower levels would have resulted in greater consumer spending, because the poor or relatively poor necessarily would spend almost all the money they received; the increase at the other end of the scale, however, while it stimulated the sale of some luxuries, did not get back into the "real economy" as quickly.

After the stock-market crash, capital expansion cut back and there was no compensatory increase in consumer spending. Indeed, there was some decrease, since those who lost a great deal of money in the stock market cut back their expenditures. With less of a market for their products, manufacturers and others decreased their production. This meant laying off workers or reducing work weeks or both, which brought further decrease in consumer spending, which brought further production cutbacks, and so on down and around the spiral. An enormous spurt of consumer spending might have stopped the downward spiral, but how could unemployed consumers spend more? An enormous expenditure for capital expansion might have stopped it also, but shrinking markets did not encourage businessmen to sink more money in what appeared to be a losing proposition.

Besides the imbalance of consumer spending and capital expansion, there were other faults in the economy. In banking, for example, an unhealthy proportion of the total funds of the nation's banks were tied up in speculation, and, without any assurance that their funds were safe after the crash, depositors' anxiety led to bank failures and hoarding. Jerry-built holding-company empires were another structural weakness. In Insull's pyramid of public utilities, for example, when power generating companies at the bottom of the pyramid were unable over a long period of time to pay dividends, the holding companies piled on top of them were unable to pay on their bonds. More capital than was necessary or healthy was dependent upon the profitable operation of the bottom of the pyramid.

Oligopolistic or monopolistic industries hastened the economic decline and braked recovery through "administered prices." In Adam Smith's model of a properly working capitalist economy, whenever there is a reduction in demand competition brings about a reduction in prices, which thereby restores effective demand. But this was not the way prices were set in monopolistic and oligopolistic industries. Instead of reducing prices enough to stimulate sales, these industries cut their production—that is, laid off workers and reduced hours. In economic fields characterized by sharp competition there was a steep decline in prices. Agricultural prices went down by 86 per cent from 1929 to 1933, but agricultural production declined only 6 per cent. On the other hand, prices of the twenty most important agricultural implements, which were produced by an oligopolistic industry, fell only 6 per cent between 1929 and 1934 while production of these implements fell off 80 per cent. Prices in general declined after 1929. The cost of living was less in 1933 than it had been in 1929. But the decline in prices was not commensurate with the decline of consumers' incomes, and there was certainly no automatically self-correcting adjustment of prices such as Adam Smith had envisioned.

Still another defect in the economy is obvious with hindsight: the inadequacy of economic thought. Although there were conditions all over the economy in 1928 and 1929 that would signal danger to today's economists, the eminent economists and business leaders of the New Era saw nothing to disturb their optimism. On the day that the stock market first began to crumble, the president of the National City Bank was quoted in a newspaper, "I see no reason for the end-of-the-year slump which some people are predicting." Only a few days before the crash, Irving Fisher, a Yale economist and one of the most respected men in his field, said that stock prices were at "what looks like a permanently high plateau." In 1930 he wrote that "the outlook is bright." A month after the crash the Harvard Economic Society announced that "a serious depression ... is outside the range of probability." President Hoover was equally reassuring—and equally wrong. The day after the crash he declared for the press, "The fundamental business of the country—that is, the production and distribution of goods and services—is on a sound and prosperous basis." The President was not being hypocritical. His faith in the New Era was so profound that he was unable to see that it had failed.

6

The Ordeal of Herbert Hoover

THE MYTHS ABOUT THE HOOVER ADMINISTRATION are the products of partisan politics and ideology. They were created, not by historians years after the event, but by politicians and newspaper editors and columnists almost as the events happened. These myths in recent years have faded from popular consciousness as the Hoover years have receded in time and new issues and problems have occupied the national attention, but for several years after World War II many Democratic candidates continued to run against the Republican record of 1929 to 1933 and many Republican candidates appeared to believe that their opponent was really the ghost of Franklin D. Roosevelt.

The Republican myth is that Hoover was well on his way to conquering the depression when the elections of 1932 intervened. The villain in the myth is Roosevelt, who demagogically pitted class against class in the campaign and destroyed the public's faith in the business community. Business then, so the myth goes, became alarmed by the drift of events, lost confidence that the new administration would be cooperative, and held back from new investments that would have raised the economy to normal. The myth had a sequel: Roosevelt's antagonism to business throughout his first two terms prevented a real recovery and the depression did not end until FDR became friendly to business desires, under pressure, in order to gain industrial support for the defense and war effort. For the first part of the myth Republican publicists cite the course of the economy as measured by the *Times* weekly index of business activity. The index went up from 66.2 in early August 1932 to 73.8 in early January 1933. Then in two months it fell below the August figure. The difficulty with this theory when one looks at it hard and critically is that the rise was hardly spectacular and that it was the downward course of the economy in general and such things as bank failures, low farm prices, factory closings, and the 1932 Bonus Army disgrace in particular that caused widespread disillusionment with the Hoover administration and the businessman. Roosevelt was the political beneficiary of popular disgust with the New Era, but his campaign in 1932 was actually quite mild and ambivalent. As for the ultimate recovery as the war approached, this was more the result of vastly increased federal spending than of hands across the directors' table.

The Democratic myth is that Hoover was an American Nero who ineffectually fretted rather than fiddled while the nation rusted rather than burned. According to Democratic publicists, Hoover was so committed to laissez faire that he did nothing to combat the depression other than to issue press statements designed to restore business confidence, statements that were no more than a necromancer's incantations. As evidence for their argument the supporters of this myth point to the contrast between Hoover's administration and the pace and style of his successor. But the trouble with their interpretation is that, first, Hoover's political-economic philosophy quite obviously was not laissez faire. He was pro-business, suspicious of organized labor and agriculture, and fearful of government compulsion in economic affairs, but as Secretary of Commerce and as president he clearly was not an advocate of Adam Smith's vision of capitalism with its unrestrained competition and a government role restricted to keeping the public peace and enforcing contracts. Hoover was a neomercantilist in his general objectives, but a century of business propaganda had made him gun-shy about using strong government methods to advance toward his objectives. Second, the record indicates that Hoover did in fact use the power of government to try to fight the depression and bring about economic recovery. President Hoover was more ambitious in his antidepression program than any previous president confronted with a similar economic problem. Wilson had done nothing to counteract the brief postwar depression. Grover Cleveland watched his party split during the depression that followed the panic of 1893 rather than launch a frontal attack on the economic crisis and relieve the plight of those who suffered from it.

But, although Hoover did seek to combat the depression through government action, he did so rather cautiously and with some misgivings. He was cold to the idea of direct federal relief and he seemed to those people to be unsympathetic and uninterested in their welfare. What Hoover did appeared not so important to most people as what he failed to do. He failed to defeat the depression, he failed to leave the impression with voters that he was fighting it vigorously, he failed to lead decisively and forcefully. This failure of leadership was the result partly of his personality and style, partly of inexperience in the rough give-and-take of electoral office, and partly of ideological anxiety about strong government action lest it lead to a loss of "liberty." At any rate, despite his positive actions, Hoover let the actual political and economic situation get the psychological offensive against him; he was on the defensive for over three years. Hoover looked poor in retrospect because his successor had the personality and the will to act boldly that Hoover lacked. But it must be added, as we shall see in detail in the next chapter, that Roosevelt did not defeat the depression either. It was World War II that ended the depression in the United States.

The Farmer and the Tariff

Two aspects of Hoover's economic policies were conceived in the predepression months of his administration. During the campaign against Smith, Hoover had recognized that something had to be done to improve farm prices. At Senator Borah's urging, he had promised to call a special session of Congress early in his administration and request it to raise tariffs on agricultural products. The special session met in mid-April 1929. (A special session was necessary because under the Constitution at that time a newly elected Congress did not meet until December of the year following its election, thirteen months after the polling. The Twentieth Amendment, submitted to the states March 2, 1932, and ratified February 6, 1933, moved the convocation date for a newly elected Congress forward to January 3, just two months after election, and moved the presidential inauguration day forward from March 4 to January 20. FDR was the first to be inaugurated on the new date at the beginning of his second term.) Hoover's message to Congress called not only for a "limited" increase in the tariff but for the creation of a new "great instrumentality" to deal with the farm problem.

The Agricultural Market Act of June 1929 created the Federal Farm Board, which turned out to be something less than a "great instrumentality" and a total failure at solving the problem of low farm prices. When the administration measure came before Congress several representatives in the farm bloc tried to amend it to include the "export debenture" plan, a method, similar in some ways to the McNary-Haugen idea, for subsidizing agriculture through funds gained from the collection of customs duties. Hoover was adamantly opposed to the plan, and the administration farm bill passed without it.

The Federal Farm Board, which was headed by Alexander Legge, president of the International Harvester Company, had a fund of $500 million to lend to agricultural marketing associations and to commodity stabilization corporations. There was to be a separate corporation for each commodity—wheat, corn, cotton, and so on—and these corporations were to have no direct connection with the federal government. They would be public corporations chartered by the states. Each of these corporations was empowered, if necessary, to buy its commodity on the open market and store it for possible future sale. In other words, these corporations could buy commodity surpluses in an effort to peg prices.

The whole system went into operation just as the stock market broke. Prices fell so disastrously that government money going into the market had relatively little effect. Wheat dropped from $1.05 a bushel in 1929 to 68 cents in 1930 despite the government-financed purchase program. It fell to 39 cents the following year. Rather than to continue to spend more funds that were not accomplishing the purpose of pegging prices, the Federal Farm Board, having already used most of its capital, switched to urging farmers to grow less. They would work at the problem of the surplus at the other end, by reducing its size rather than buying it. But the Board's campaign to reduce production was doomed to fail since it did not have any leverage behind it, no way to enforce less production. It could only plead with farmers to produce less. The individual farmer was in a box. If he reduced his production by one half and all other producers of his commodity did the same, then the surplus would be eliminated and the price per bushel would improve. But if the individual farmer cut his production and other farmers did not, thereby creating a surplus again, the farmer who cut back would not only be getting a low price again but would have fewer bushels to sell. Farmers in fact did not limit their production. Agricultural production in 1932 was greater than it had been in 1929—and prices were well below the farmers' costs of production.

The "limited" upward revision of the tariff turned out to be a major tariff increase and to be more of an industrial than an agricultural boon. The course of the bill through Congress was characterized by intense lobbying and log-rolling of the kind that had always accompanied major tariff legislation. The original bill submitted by Representative Willis C. Hawley of Oregon was mild; the House increased the tariff levels and extended them to more industrial products. But the major amendments came in the Senate. The bill's managers there were Reed Smoot of Utah, chairman of the Finance Committee and a representative of sugar-beet interests, and Joseph R. Grundy of Pennsylvania, president of his state manufacturers' association. Farm-bloc members of Congress who opposed a further increase in duties on industrial products were numerous enough to present Smoot and Grundy with an intricate and delicate problem. Their task was to bargain with senators from agricultural states, roll an agricultural log their way in exchange for acceptance of industrial increases. Senators from grain and cotton states put forward their demand for the export debenture plan again, but the administration and industrial protectionists still opposed the scheme. Senators from Florida (citrus fruit), Wyoming (wool), and Louisiana (sugar) voted for the Hawley-Smoot bill's industrial duties in exchange for increased duties for their states' agricultural products. This log-rolling put the bill over. It passed the Senate with a two-vote margin.

Representative Hawley had introduced the measure in its original form in May 1929, months before the depression began. By the time all the log-rolling and bargaining was finished, the Wall Street crash had occurred and the general economic decline was well under way. Sound economic sense indicated that the impact of the law when Hoover signed it on June 17, 1930, would not be what its sponsors believed it would be when they started the bill through the congressional mill thirteen months earlier. Professional economists were alarmed by the tariff increases—up to an average of 40 per cent from the old tariff's average of 33 per cent —in the face of the beginnings of the world depression. Over one thousand members of the American Economics Association signed a statement in May 1930 that urged Congress to reject the measure and Hoover to veto it if Congress declined the advice, but the bill became law. Senator James E. Watson of Indiana in rejecting the economists' advice even argued that if the bill were passed, "within a year . . .we shall have regained the peak of prosperity."

Senator Watson was obviously wrong in his economic prediction, but it is impossible to measure precisely how much the Hawley-Smoot Tariff harmed the economy. Imports declined considerably, and one would anticipate a decline in exports as other nations, because of the higher tariff, became less able to purchase American goods. But there were many other forces operating to reduce international trade, and the whole decline was not attributable solely to the higher American tariff wall.

Hoover and the Depression

The month after the Wall Street crash President Hoover called a conference of business leaders at the White House. He urged them to maintain their present wage rates, thereby preventing a further shrinkage of consumer purchasing power. The businessmen agreed, if labor would assure them that it would not strike or seek higher wages. Officials of the AFL gave the necessary assurances.

Most industrial employers kept wage rates at their 1929 level until 1931, but in the spring and summer of 1930 they began to make important production cutbacks, laying some workers off altogether and putting others on reduced hours. When the United States Steel Company announced a pay cut of 10 to 15 per cent for salaried employees in August 1931 and followed the next month with a 10 per cent cut for its almost a quarter-million employees on hourly wages, it set off a wave of wage cuts in industry, particularly by big corporations with large numbers of employees. By the end of 1932, wage earners in Ohio manufacturing had suffered income cuts of about 36 per cent because of lower wage rates and reduced hours—and these were employed workers. The incomes of the unemployed were far lower.

Quite obviously Hoover's policy of maintaining purchasing power by requesting employers to cooperate was a failure. The reason was not that employers wanted to violate White House wishes. They were simply driven to it by economic conditions. With shrinking markets, they had to cut production volume and costs or go broke, even though production cutbacks only further shrank purchasing power or markets. Some other way out of the box had to be found. Many people thought they had solutions. Congressmen came forward with several proposals to alleviate distress and stimulate the economy, but the President seldom agreed with the proposals and Washington settled down to a war between the White House and Capitol Hill. Some businessmen came forward with vast schemes of national planning to be designed and administered by business rather than government. "Industrial self-government," the general idea was called. Gerard Swope, president of the General Electric Company, presented one such scheme, and the United States Chamber of Commerce approved another. In these plans individual corporations within an industry would agree to divide the market among themselves, would refrain from undercutting one another's prices, and would maintain standard wage rates. The proposals, in effect, were to rationalize the whole economy under corporation control, to extend the scope of industrial rationalization that had been under way for decades but especially in the 1920's. To be effective any such plan would necessitate government cooperation. For one thing, the antitrust laws could not be applied if the schemes were to function and government power would be necessary to enforce compliance with the industrial plan.

President Hoover never approved the idea of industrial self-government with federal enforcement. In view of his record of stimulating industrial rationalization while he was Secretary of Commerce his opposition is a little puzzling. The President did not spell out the grounds for his opposition in the public record, and his private papers are not yet fully open to researchers. One may only deduce from his public statements while in the White House and the character of his subsequent criticism of the New Deal—the National Recovery Administration, as we shall see, had similarities to the industrial self-government proposals—that Hoover feared that such schemes would destroy individual liberties. He feared that the proposed cures would be worse than the economic disease, and he rejected moving in the direction of a formal corporate state.

But he also rejected, sometimes in most vigorous language, the proposals from Congress that would have enlarged the functions of the federal government in the economy by moving into relief of the destitute and into greatly expanded public works. Hoover went along with some congressional proposals of relatively small scale that only indirectly involved the federal government—and in the case of the Reconstruction Finance Corporation even came forward with a proposal of his own—but he steadfastly refused to use the power of the government of the United States in an all-out frontal assault on the depression. Part of the conflict between Hoover and Congress was due to partisan political rivalry but by no means all of it. A considerable number of members of Congress from both parties was acutely aware of the extent of suffering among their constituents and determined that the government should take action. Ideological difference with the President ran deep.

The Republicans had good majorities in both houses of the Congress elected in 1928, and although they lost control of the House of Representatives in the 1930 elections the old Congress sat in "lame-duck" session after the election because the Twentieth Amendment was not yet on the books. In the new Senate the Republicans had a majority of one, but several Republican senators from the upper Mississippi Valley, such as George Norris and Robert M. La Follette, Jr., were more at odds with the President than were some of the more conservative Democratic members.

Indeed, some of the congressional measures that Hoover opposed came from maverick Republicans. Senator Norris, who had preserved federal ownership of Muscle Shoals almost single-handedly during the 1920's, got Congress in 1931 to pass a bill that would have had the federal government operate the dam's electric generating potential and manufacture fertilizer. Hoover vetoed the bill. His veto message asserted that for him to sign the bill would mean the end of "the initiative and enterprise of the American people" as well as "the negation of the ideals upon which our civilization has been based." After the new Congress convened, Capitol Hill abounded with projects for public works and relief. These proposals, said Hoover, were the result of "playing politics at the expense of human misery." John N. Garner of Texas, the new Speaker of the House, and the Democratic senator from New York, Robert F. Wagner, jointly sponsored a measure calling for a two-billion-dollar public works program. Their argument was that government spending on such a scale would help the economy and put men back to work. Hoover vetoed it. The bill, he said, was filled with danger. "Never before" in the nation's entire history had anyone made "so dangerous a suggestion." Senator Wagner got through another bill to establish a system of federal employment offices to more efficiently get the unemployed to what few jobs existed. The President vetoed the idea, saying that it went beyond the acceptable functions of government.

The President and Congress differed most sharply on the question of relief. Hoover was not utterly opposed to the idea of indirect federal government involvement with relief, but he opposed any kind of direct relief. Just before the elections of 1930 Hoover established the President's Committee for Unemployment Relief and named a former police commissioner of New York City, Colonel Arthur Woods, as its head. The Woods committee had almost no funds—it spent only $157,000 during its entire existence—and did no more than give encouragement to city and state relief organizations. This was an almost entirely superfluous kind of enterprise. Local relief organizations knew very well how serious the economic distress was and were constantly crying for more funds. In the summer of 1931 Hoover established another committee to replace the defunct Woods group. This President's Organization on Unemployment Relief (POUR), headed by Walter S. Gifford, president of the American Telephone and Telegraph Company, proved equally ineffective. Apparently, Hoover's basic purpose was for the committee to stimulate giving to private charity in the hope that more effective local community chests and the like would take off the pressure for federal relief. POUR restricted itself to advertising and public relations campaigns designed to increase private contributions, but the volume of relief necessary was far more than private organizations could ever supply. A senate committee looking into relief needs, headed by Senators La Follette and Edward P. Costigan of Colorado, asked Gifford in a committee hearing if he could tell them what was the total amount of relief necessary in the nation. The witness did not know. Further questioning revealed that he did not even know how many communities did not have community chests. Congress thereafter ceased to appropriate funds for POUR and concentrated on getting through some kind of federal relief that Hoover would approve.

But there was not very much. La Follette and Costigan pushed a bill that would have granted $375 million to the states to be used for relief. They hoped that Hoover would approve this indirect kind of federal assistance. But the administration mustered its strength on Capitol Hill and defeated the bill. A bill to provide relief to drought-stricken farmers in Arkansas clearly revealed Hoover's position. He did not object to loans from the federal government to farmers to save their livestock, to protect their property, but to grant funds to aid the human victims of the drought would, he said, injure "the spiritual responses of the American people." Hoover did not approve any kind of helpful federal relief measure until July 1932, when he approved a compromise scheme, the Emergency Relief and Construction Act. This act established a special Reconstruction Finance Corporation fund of $300 million to be lent to the states for relief. No state could borrow more than 15 per cent of the total fund and would have to begin repayment of the loan in 1935 at 3 per cent interest. The relief thus provided was grossly inadequate. As Republican Governor of Pennsylvania Gifford Pinchot pointed out, if his state could get the maximum loan allowable—and it actually received only one fourth of the maximum—there would be only a few pennies a day available for each Pennsylvania relief family. The act also appropriated $322.2 million for public works.

That President Hoover was not opposed to government aid to depression-struck business was indicated by his sponsoring the establishment of the Reconstruction Finance Corporation (RFC). But he moved to establish the RFC only under pressure and administered it in such a way as to create major political opposition. In 1931, as more and more banks began to close, Hoover suggested to the bankers that they form a pool of capital among themselves to be lent to banks that were on the verge of going under. The resulting National Credit Association was a help, but it was inadequate to cope with the whole banking crisis. When its inadequacy became apparent Hoover asked Congress for the RFC. Created in January 1932, the RFC was a federally chartered and owned corporation with an original capital of $500 million. It was authorized to borrow three times its capitalization through tax-exempt bonds guaranteed by the federal government. The RFC's function was to lend money to businesses of various kinds. For most of its loans it selected the business areas whose survival was critically necessary for the whole economy. Banks and other credit institutions received most of the RFC loans during the Hoover years. Railroads were next on the loan list, partly because many banks and insurance companies had a large part of their assets in railroad stocks and bonds. Insurance companies were third in priority. The RFC's loans to federal agricultural credit institutions such as the Federal Land Banks amounted to much less than those to insurance companies.

To the degree that the RFC saved banks from failure, kept railroads operating, and enabled insurance companies to pay off their beneficiaries it clearly worked to the economy's advantage. But because the Hoover administration was willing through the RFC to extend aid to business but at best reluctant to extend it to poverty-stricken families, it was vulnerable to the criticism that the government was willing to help only business. Every bank saved helped hundreds or thousands of depositors and helped stave off further trouble for thousands more, but this kind of government aid was at best a prop. As a means of reviving the economy it had little utility. The RFC has many times been cited as an example of the "trickle down" theory of government economic aid. Government funds going into the top or near the top of the economic pyramid provide benefits to all to the degree that the benefits trickle down from the top. Funds put into the bottom or near bottom of the pyramid, however, through relief and public works circulate throughout the economy much faster and have a much faster effect.

But the way the RFC in the Hoover administration distributed its loans within even this business-aiding framework caused widespread criticism. For the first several months of its operation the RFC was not required by law to make public what loans it had made. Press releases by the RFC were designed to leave the impression that small business was its primary beneficiary. Suspecting there was political hay to be made, congressional Democrats maneuvered the administration into reporting on its loans to Congress. There was indeed political advantage thus gained. The best-publicized case involved Charles G. Dawes. When the former Vice-President left office at the end of the Coolidge administration he went back to banking in Chicago, where he was an officer in the Central Republic Bank. Hoover named him to be the first president of the RFC. In June 1932 Dawes resigned from the RFC, saying that it was necessary for him to devote full time to the affairs of his bank. A few weeks later the RFC reported that it lent $92 million to the Central Republic Bank. The loan was entirely legal; Dawes had not been with the RFC when the loan was made. But the political uproar was enormous. After all, the Dawes bank received a loan almost one third as big as the total that was about to be made available to all the states for relief. (Incidentally, the loan did not save the bank. It later went under and the RFC had to go to the courts to collect the loan.) Atlee Pomerene, former Republican Senator from Ohio and one of the authors of the Webb-Pomerene Act of the late Wilson administration, succeeded Dawes as RFC president. He authorized a loan of $12 million to a Cleveland bank of which he was a director. With loans to individual banks that were greater than the funds large industrial states like Pennsylvania received for public relief, it is small wonder that progressives of all kinds were in open rebellion against the Hoover administration.

The only satisfaction that progressives could find in the President was his consent to the Norris-La Guardia Anti-Injunction Act of March 1932. This law greatly restricted the power of federal courts to issue injunctions involving labor unions. The main value of the law from labor's point of view was that for all practical purposes it made "yellow-dog" contracts ineffective. A "yellow-dog" contract was an agreement between employer and employee, which sometimes consisted of no more than a poster in the hiring office, that the employee would not join a union. Employees who violated "yellow dogs" were not sued for breach of contract. That was not their purpose. Their purpose was to provide a pretext for labor injunctions to prevent attempts to organize employees into unions. When a "yellow-dog" contract existed, a union organizer necessarily endangered the contract and could therefore be enjoined from doing anything that would cause a contractual breach. Hoover was not enthusiastic about the new law. There is evidence that members of his administration worked behind the scenes in Congress to prevent its passage, but he did not veto it.

Hoover's acceptance of the Norris-La Guardia Act did not reverse the steadily growing popular dissatisfaction with him and his administration. In the summer of 1932 his prestige slumped to a new low when some farmers began to resort to force or the threat of force to raise farm prices in a "farm holiday" movement and when Hoover ordered the dispersal of the war veterans' Bonus Army. The first farm "holiday," or strike, occurred in western Iowa in August. In the hope of raising prices on the Sioux City market by refusing to sell there until they got better prices, farmers encircled the city with a series of road blocks. The pickets turned back cargoes of farm products and dumped perishable commodities such as milk into the ditches. The action had no appreciable effect on prices; it only served to dramatize the desperation of farmers.

The Bonus Army affair caused widespread disgust with the administration. The story of a bonus for World War veterans goes back to soon after the Armistice. After considerable agitation by veterans' organizations for a bonus equal to the servicemen's wartime loss of income, Congress in 1924 passed a law that provided for "adjusted compensation certificates" to be issued to veterans. The certificates were to be redeemable for cash in 1945, a date that, as it developed, had a certain irony. With the advent of large-scale unemployment veterans began to demand payment of the bonus immediately. In 1931 Congress overrode Hoover's veto of a bill to pay half the bonus, but veterans continued to clamor for the whole payment. Late in 1931 Senator Wright Patman of Texas introduced a measure to pay the balance of the bonus with fiat money. The proposal was frankly inflationary, but given the degree of deflation that already existed such a law would not have hurt the economy and probably would have stimulated it slightly. Certainly, to the extent that the bonus would have increased mass purchasing power, its general economic effects would have been beneficial—as well as humanitarian. But Hoover vigorously opposed the Patman bill.

Veterans on the West Coast began to organize a "Bonus Expeditionary Force" to march on Washington and remain there until their demands were met. In May 1932 they moved toward the capital by freight trains and other makeshift transportation. Some governors recognized the danger inherent in a horde of desperate unemployed transients in their states and used National Guard trucks to move them across their states toward Washington as quickly as possible. By mid-June there were from twelve to fifteen thousand bonus marchers in Washington, some of them with their families. Some of them moved into abandoned temporary buildings left over from the war; many more built a "Hooverville" on the Anacostia Flats. The marchers were well disciplined and caused a minimum of trouble, thanks largely to the firm but generous supervision of the Washington police force. The House passed the Patman bill on June 15. Two days later the Senate defeated it. The marchers were massed on the Capitol grounds as the Senate rejected the proposal, but there was no riot. Most of the marchers remained in Washington.

Trouble erupted in late July. The administration ordered the police to clear marchers from some abandoned buildings. A policeman panicked during the process and fired into a crowd of marchers, killing two veterans. Fearful of riots, the administration then ordered the army to clear out the marchers altogether. Chief of Staff General Douglas MacArthur went about the task in no uncertain terms. Cavalry, infantrymen with bayonets fixed, and tanks herded the marchers out of the city and burned the shack town. Administration officials asserted that Communists and criminals were prevalent in the Bonus Army and that their dispersal was necessary to prevent possible revolutionary action, but most people were not impressed. The spectacle of unarmed unemployed men who had been victorious heroes only fourteen years before being driven from the nation's capital at bayonet point was not encouraging.

Hoover and Foreign Affairs

President Hoover's ordeal in the White House was not restricted to domestic affairs. The early years of the depression brought events both in Europe and in Asia that caused headaches in Washington. In neither the European international financial crisis nor the threat to the Open Door that the Japanese presented in northern China was the Hoover administration conspicuously successful in bringing about a solution consistent with the American national interest as most people understood that interest. But even if Hoover had been able in each of these situations to have maneuvered a complete American victory, which was probably impossible, it is doubtful that his prestige in the population at large would have improved greatly. Quite understandably, people were far more concerned with unemployment and low farm prices than with European and Asian problems even if those problems did have relevance to their own lives.

Europe, particularly Germany and Austria, faced a severe financial crisis in the spring of 1931. Hoping to stimulate their economies, Germany and Austria had announced their intentions of forming a customs union. France objected vehemently, arguing that such an arrangement was contrary to the Treaty of Versailles, and French banks began to recall their loans from central Europe. The largest bank of Austria nearly failed—it was saved only by the action of the Austrian government—and a big bank of northern Germany closed its doors. Besides threatening the economic welfare and political stability of Europe, the crisis jeopardized the continuation of reparations payments to Great Britain and France.

On June 20, 1931, President Hoover made an announcement that made headlines all over the Western world. He proposed a moratorium, or postponement, for one year of all international reparations and government debt payments. Congress was not in session, but Hoover had conferred with its leaders and announced that if Congress approved when it met later in the year, the United States would not expect payment on the Allied war debt for the year beginning in July. Hoover's hope was that the moratorium would permit Europe to stabilize its finances. The European nations consented to the proposal.

When Congress met it consented to the one-year waiver of debt collections, but it balked at Hoover's further proposal to re-establish the World War Foreign Debt Commission and authorize it to negotiate on foreign debts. The commission a few years earlier had consented to amended terms of payment and interest for the Allies, but after the beginning of the depression the thought of further reduction of the debts due the United States government was quite unpopular. Understanding little of international economics, most voters and most congressmen thought the situation identical with an ordinary business debt. Now that the creditor too was in economic difficulty, they thought, the payment of the debt had a new importance. As far as Congress was concerned, the Allies should begin to pay the debt again at the end of the moratorium.

The European nations worked for another arrangement. Representatives of the European powers met at Lausanne, Switzerland, over the summer of 1932 and reached a new agreement among themselves. Germany's reparation bill would be reduced by nine tenths if the Allies could get a similar reduction from their creditors. For all practical purposes, this meant that if the United States would scale down the debt due from the Allies, then the Allies would reduce their reparations bill to the former Central Powers. But Congress would not consent to such an arrangement, and the Lausanne agreements fell through. Hoover had no alternative but to send out notices of debt payments due on December 15, 1932. Most of the debtor nations met that payment, but except for some further token payments the 1932 debt payments were the last received. (Finland, which had a favorable trade balance with America, continued to pay.) Germany ceased even to try to pay reparations after Adolf Hitler's advent to power in early 1933, and without reparations coming in, the Allies could not meet their American debt payments.

The Asian problem facing Hoover was far more serious. Indeed, in 1931 and 1932 Japan embarked upon a militaristic and expansionist policy of colonial imperialism that was in sharp conflict with the American Open Door policy. Japan's policy ultimately brought the United States into World War II.

Chinese nationalists, led by the Kuomintang of Sun Yat-sen until his death in 1925 and then by Chiang Kai-shek, had considerable success in the 1920's in their campaign to strengthen the Chinese government and reassert its powers in the northern part of the country. Japanese militarists, fearful that China would become a more formidable foe in the future, struck quickly in Manchuria. Without orders from the Japanese government, Japanese troops captured the Chinese garrison at Mukden, Manchuria, in September 1931 and seized control of the South Manchurian Railway. The Japanese commanding officer asserted the action was a reprisal for an explosion on the railroad. If there was an explosion at all, it was a minor one. The explosion story, in any event, was only a pretext for the Manchurian aggression. The Chinese government protested to the League of Nations and to the United

States. The League's only immediate reaction was to request both Japan and China to do nothing to further complicate the problem.

At first, Secretary of State Henry L. Stimson pursued a quiet wait-and-see policy. Since the Japanese adventures had been the policy of Japanese field commanders rather than of the government, which contained many moderates, Stimson feared that a more belligerent attitude by the United States would strengthen the hand of the militarists in Japan. But his forbearance did not have the anticipated effect of strengthening Japanese moderates. The Japanese army gradually extended its power in southern Manchuria and at home. In December 1931 the Japanese government fell and was replaced with a more militaristic one. The next month the Japanese army practically completed its conquest of Manchuria.

Seeing that his first policy had not been a success, Stimson wanted to try stiffer measures. He advocated a policy of non-recognition of Japanese conquests and economic sanctions against Japan—either a refusal to sell to or buy from that country or, at the least, a ban on some items. Secretary of War Patrick Hurley suggested even more active measures, such as threatening Japan with armed force. President Hoover was greatly concerned about the Japanese efforts to close the open door, but he was not willing to go as far as Hurley, or even Stimson. Probably Hoover recognized better than his cabinet members that public opinion would not support risky ventures abroad. Stimson modified his policies in view of his chief's caution.

On January 7, 1932, Secretary Stimson sent identical notes to Japan and China. The position taken in these notes was at the time called the Stimson Doctrine, and many historians have also used that term. But since the notes served notice only of nonrecognition, rather than of nonrecognition plus economic sanctions, it would be more accurate to call the position the Hoover-Stimson Doctrine. The critical parts of the notes were: ". . . The American Government . . . cannot admit the legality of any situation *de facto* nor does it intend to recognize any treaty or agreement . . . which may impair the treaty rights of the United States or its citizens in China, including those which relate to the sovereignty, the independence, or the territorial and administrative integrity of the Republic of China, or to the international policy relative to China, commonly known as the open-door policy." In these notes Stimson cited as the standard of international conduct the Kellogg-Briand Pact, which China, Japan, and the United States had signed.

Japan defied the note. It replied that the Chinese in Manchuria had a right to self-determination, and in February 1932 it arranged for a puppet prince to declare the independence of the state of Manchuria, or Manchukuo as the Japanese called it. In September the Japanese government officially recognized the Manchukuo government it had itself established in power, and thereafter the open door in Manchuria no longer existed. The area was Japan's private preserve.

Secretary Stimson modified the doctrine slightly after the Japanese created the Manchukuo puppet state. He shifted the basis for judging Japan's action from the Kellogg-Briand Pact to the Nine-Power Naval Treaty that had been written at the Washington Conference. This opened the possibility of more leverage for the American position. The naval treaties agreed to at the Washington Conference, said Stimson, were dependent upon one another and neither Japan nor any other signatory power could ignore the obligations of one of the treaties and continue to enjoy the advantages of the other treaties. This was a legalistic way of saying that when Japan slammed the open door in Manchuria, in violation of the Nine-Power Treaty, the United States was no longer bound to honor the naval limitations agreed to in the Five-Power Treaty. The United States did move its fleet, or most of it, from the Atlantic to the Pacific in 1932, but Japan hardly felt threatened. The United States did not in fact embark upon a major naval building program until the late 1930's.

By the end of the Hoover administration the Chinese-Japanese conflict had quieted down, not to erupt again for about five years. The Japanese were really only taking some time to digest their last bites of China. In the absence of an exercised public opinion, the Hoover administration had been able to do no more than protest Japanese aggression, refuse to recognize officially the results of it, and establish a legalistic basis for further action against Japan. Perhaps American diplomacy also strengthened the League of Nation's policy on Japan. The other great Western powers were more cautious than the United States at first, but in time the League came around to the American policy of nonrecognition of Manchukuo. When the League advised its members against recognition, Japan began the two-year process of quitting the world organization.

The Election of 1932

Not having any spectacular success in foreign policy which

might compensate in the electorate's mind for the failure of the Hoover administration to prevent or ameliorate the depression, the Republican party was understandably gloomy about its chances of victory in the 1932 elections. Further, the leaders of Republican organizations in some states, particularly in the agricultural states of the upper Mississippi Valley, were in almost open rebellion against the administration. But the Republicans had no real alternative but to renominate Hoover and hope the Democrats would blunder. When the party met in national convention Hoover's renomination was a foregone conclusion. The GOP also renominated Vice-President Charles Curtis, a former senator from Kansas who was better known for being part Kaw Indian than for his political philosophy.

Because the Democratic nomination more than likely meant the presidency, Democratic intramural fighting for the top place on the ticket was more than usually spirited. When the Democrats met at Chicago at the end of June, Governor Franklin D. Roosevelt of New York was the front runner, but Al Smith and Speaker of the House John N. Garner of Texas were also serious contenders. Roosevelt's political advisor, James A. Farley, had begun the process of lining up delegates a year before the convention and he had done a remarkable job, but Roosevelt was still about one hundred votes short of the two-thirds majority that until 1936 was necessary for a Democratic nomination. Garner's candidacy was not entirely serious. Southern delegates at Democratic conventions often put forward a southern candidate more in the hope of gaining something else than in the hope of actually nominating a son of Dixie. Smith's effort, however, was serious indeed.

Farley managed to head off a stop-Roosevelt drive on the first three ballots, after which the convention at last recessed from an almost twenty-four-hour session. During the recess Farley persuaded the California delegation, largely controlled by the newspaper publisher William Randolph Hearst, to enlist in the Roosevelt cause and got Garner to release his pledged delegates. Roosevelt then received the nomination on the fourth ballot. Smith refused to make the nomination unanimous and left Chicago before Roosevelt arrived rather than extend the usual courtesies. Garner received the second place on the ticket. Roosevelt, or FDR as headline writers soon dubbed him, demonstrated his capacity for the dramatic when he went to the convention to give his acceptance speech instead of waiting several days, as was then the custom. In his speech FDR said, "I pledge you—I pledge myself to a new deal for the American people." A new political term had been born.

If one examines the campaign and election of 1932 only in terms of Democratic-Republican rivalry it was not a very exciting or even an interesting race. Hoover was not an effective campaigner, and his campaign was noteworthy chiefly for its contrast to the race against Smith four years earlier. In 1928 Hoover had taken a lofty position, never criticized his opponent, and had not even mentioned his name in a public address; in 1932 Hoover became increasingly bitter and denounced Roosevelt with some heat. But if one examines the Roosevelt campaign in terms of internal struggles within the Democratic party it acquires an additional dimension. One must always remember in examining politics and political history that the major parties in the United States are by no means unified organizations of identical interest or ideology. Each party ranges widely on the political spectrum from left to right, each party has regional peculiarities, and each party contains elements with different and sometimes opposing political and economic interests.

FDR's tactic in 1932 was to try to keep the various elements within his party working in a degree of harmony, to refrain from taking strong positions which might only lose him votes without gaining him many that he would not get anyway, and to capitalize on Hoover's unpopularity. The task as he saw it was to let Hoover defeat himself and try to avoid losing votes. At first FDR was fearful that the convention had alienated too many of the northern Democratic conservatives who had supported Smith. To offset anxieties on the right, he held a series of well-publicized conferences with business leaders and refrained from further references to "the forgotten man" and pleas for a "more equitable opportunity to share in the distribution of national wealth." When he began to appear too safe and cautious to other elements of the party, he turned his campaign a little more to the left, particularly when he visited the western states. In late September in San Francisco he again mentioned the distribution of wealth; he said there was a need for "distributing wealth and products more equitably, of adapting existing economic organizations to the service of the people." Then, fearful that such statements might result in a loss of strength among more conservative parts of the coalition, he swung toward the right again. At Pittsburgh in October he condemned the Hoover administration for failing to balance the federal budget, described Hoover's spending as "most reckless and extravagant," and promised to carry out the Democratic platform plank of reducing federal expenditures by 25 per cent. On several matters that were to occupy the consciousness of Americans in the next few years FDR was altogether silent. He said nothing during the campaign, for example, about foreign policy, and one could not detect what his attitude was toward trade unions.

Since one could not be sure of just what the Democratic candidate stood for, the election results could only be interpreted as a repudiation of Hoover and the Republican party. Roosevelt received 22,821,857 popular votes to Hoover's 15,761,841; 472 electoral votes to 59. Hoover carried only six states: Maine, Vermont, New Hampshire, Connecticut, Pennsylvania, and Delaware. In the new House of Representatives would be 313 Democrats, 117 Republicans, and 5 independents and in the Senate 59 Democrats, 36 Republicans, and one Farmer-Laborite.

What sort of man was the president-elect? He had been born in 1882 to a wealthy family of Hudson valley squires, had been educated at Groton, Harvard, and Columbia Law School, and had gone into politics in 1910 when he won election to the New York State Senate. He had supported Wilson for the Democratic nomination in 1912 against the wishes of Tammany Hall, and Wilson had rewarded him with an offer to be an assistant secretary in the Department of the Treasury. FDR had declined but accepted a subsequent offer to be Assistant Secretary of the Navy. Probably he thought of himself as following in the footsteps of his distant relative, former president Theodore Roosevelt. In 1920 he had received the vice-presidential nomination and gone down to defeat with Cox. The next year he had suffered an attack of polio that left him with almost useless legs, but he had refused to retire from an active life as he could have afforded to do. Al Smith had asked him to run for governor in 1928, thinking that he would strengthen the ticket. Smith's estimate of FDR's polling power had been correct: Roosevelt won by about 25,000 votes while Smith lost his own state by about 100,000. In 1930 Roosevelt won re-election by a huge margin. As governor he had been moderately progressive, although perhaps no more so than political conditions of New York require a governor to be, had been extremely popular, and had established the best state relief program in the nation. On the basis of FDR's record an acute political observer at the end of 1932 would not have been confident about pinning an ideological label on the president-elect or about predicting what he would do in the White House. All that was clear was that he was a Democrat, sensitive to the major economic problems of the day, flexible enough to depart from convention, and a masterful political leader and campaigner.

Roosevelt's personality and character were to be important in the life of the nation. He was a man who stood out in any collection of people. He had in abundance the personal qualities necessary for political success in the United States: magnetic charm, intelligence, physical and spiritual toughness, a superb speaking voice, and a flair for the dramatic. Perhaps the outstanding aspect of his personality was self-confidence, which his admirers found warming and his detractors found irritating. In his youth he had had the assurance that comes from secure social position and superior education. As a young man he had demonstrated to himself as well as to others that he was a capable government administrator. The bout with polio had established that he had the inner resources necessary to take personal tragedy in his stride. His career after 1928 had assured him that he had the qualities necessary to operate successfully at top levels of government and politics. And in March 1933, surely, confidence both in one's self and in the future of the nation was a quality sorely needed in the White House.

7

Franklin D. Roosevelt
and the New Deal

ALTHOUGH THE NEW DEAL and Franklin D. Roosevelt were realities so recently that many living Americans' knowledge of them is based upon personal memory of the 1930's rather than upon written historical accounts, the political and economic history of the decade has quickly become one of the most myth-laden aspects of the nation's past. Indeed, myths about FDR became so widespread even before he died in office in 1945 that they constituted political forces to be reckoned with, and misinterpretations of the New Deal were prevalent well before it passed from the scene.

Most of the myths about Roosevelt and the New Deal arose from political partisanship. He was both the best loved and the most hated president of the twentieth century, and it is easy for people to believe about him what they want to believe rather than what is objectively true. Many of his admirers regard him as a knight in gleaming armor, an American St. George who slayed the dragon of economic royalism, rescued the nation from economic disaster, restored control of the country to its people, and then alerted them to the danger of fascism and saved them from Tojo, Hitler, and Mussolini. From the oratory at AFL-CIO picnics one would gather that it was Roosevelt himself who created modern

147

labor unions. Negroes regard him as the best white friend of their race in their long and troubled history, with the single exception of Abraham Lincoln. Most American voters who think of themselves as liberals look back upon the New Deal as the high point of their political lives and consciously or unconsciously measure contemporary presidents and would-be presidents by an FDR yardstick.

On the other side of the political fence is the legend that Roosevelt was primarily responsible for all that is distasteful and wrong in contemporary America. It was he, one hears in the locker rooms of elite country clubs, who started the nation along the road to "socialism," destroyed initiative, and created what some people call a "welfare state." There are still some people who can not bring themselves to say Roosevelt's name and refer to him as "that man." In the late 1940's there was even a Chicagoan who tried to start a movement among consumers to refuse to accept dimes that bore FDR's image. The Roosevelt haters also measure contemporary presidents and would-be presidents of the Democratic party by an FDR yardstick. Those who are moderate in their domestic policies are "better than FDR"; those who speak in a militant rhetoric are "as bad."

Aside from the facts that the contemporary American economy is clearly capitalistic rather than socialistic and that the federal and state governments offer fewer "welfare state" services than any major, economically developed nation in the world, the primary difficulty with these interpretations of Roosevelt, both by his admirers and detractors, is that they overemphasize his personal role and assume that he had more power than he or any other president ever had. Whether approving or disapproving of the New Deal, the myths make Roosevelt an all-powerful giant who performed the New Deal single-handedly. Granted that FDR was the most powerful president in the nation's history, that he exercised the leverage of the White House as had never been done before, that he was a consummate molder of public opinion and manipulator of political forces, and that he was the most important political figure of his age, one must still remember that Roosevelt by no means personally brought about all the changes in American life, even the political and economic changes, that occurred in the 1930's.

Because the United States is a political democracy and a vast and complex nation and because the major political parties are coalitions of state and regional organizations with diverse interests and ideologies, any president, including Franklin Roosevelt, must to a very great extent play the role of a political broker. Presidents, and congressmen too, are subjected to pressures from business, agriculture, and labor, from producers and consumers, from exporters and importers, from debtors and creditors, from militarists and pacifists, from the ideological left and right. The chief executive must play the broker with the various pressures exerted upon him because it is true that politics *is* the art of the possible. (Political middle-roaders often quote this adage as justification for inaction, but if one defines *possible* realistically it is a basic fact of political life.) It is not going too far to say that government in the United States is a wonderfully complex kind of collective bargaining among all the various interests and pressures and that the occupant of the White House is the chairman of the continuous, interminable bargaining session as well as the administrator of the resulting policy.

FDR was an extraordinarily gifted political broker. To a greater degree than any other president of this century he was able to play off one pressure against another, to yield to one kind of pressure and minimize the opposition to it, and to use his power over public opinion to strengthen those pressures he wanted strengthened. But the point is that he harmonized diverse interests in such a way as to build the most successful national political coalition in recent American history. He did not design the New Deal; he "brokered" it. In the nature of things, the New Deal was a complex set of compromises. Roosevelt was the most important of the political figures bringing about the compromises, to be sure, but the New Deal did not spring from his mind. He was most instrumental in molding the New Deal, but the clay from which it was molded was the pressures exerted upon him.

Now, if we accept this general view of government and politics in the United States, it follows that an historian of the era will not find an unfolding of a grand plan. Indeed, if one looks in the political record for a blueprint of the New Deal, for the doctrine that guided Roosevelt and the New Dealers' actions, one can only conclude that if there was a blueprint it changed from season to season, almost from month to month. There was much in the New Deal that was contradictory. Roosevelt zigged and zagged, ran to the left and to the right and stood in the middle. For example, Roosevelt, as we have seen, criticized Hoover for having spent too much government money. In his first days in office FDR tried seriously to reduce federal spending. Later he resorted to vast government spending and deficit financing, then tried to balance the budget again in 1937, and later still returned to annual deficits.

Another example: the early New Deal in effect suspended the anti-trust laws, but in 1938 the federal government became concerned with enforcing these laws and investigating the extent of monopoly and its abuses. As building the military and naval potential of the nation became paramount after the outbreak of war in Europe in 1939, White House concern about vigorous enforcement of the Sherman and Clayton acts shriveled almost to nothing. Roosevelt quite obviously accepted Emerson's dictum that a foolish consistency was the hobgoblin of small minds.

This is not to say that Roosevelt was an unprincipled opportunist; it is to say that he most certainly was not doctrinaire. Roosevelt's basic principles were widely shared ones. He believed in democracy, and he was humanitarian. He believed in employing the power of the federal government to combat the depression and to relieve those most sorely injured by it. He was willing to modify traditional relationships between government and privately owned economic enterprise in the interest of the general welfare, but he clearly was no opponent of capitalism as such. And as for the means to be employed in working toward these general ends of recovery, relief, and reform, his were within the framework of the Constitution and representative democracy even though much that government did while he was in office was novel.

An anecdote about Roosevelt reveals both his basic principles and his lack of doctrine. Early in his first year in office a bewildered and apparently callow and brash reporter asked, "Mr. President, are you a Communist?" Roosevelt replied that he was not. "Are you a fascist then?" Again Roosevelt replied that he was not. "What then are you, Mr. President?" Roosevelt seemed puzzled and a little amused. "Why," he said after a moment, "I'm a Christian—and a Democrat."

The Banking Crisis

Roosevelt took the presidential oath of office in the midst of the worst financial crisis the nation had ever known. A sense of panic gripped the nation, which FDR tried to subdue with the statement in his inaugural address that "the only thing we have to fear is fear itself," and customary political tugging and hauling all but ceased. Never before during peacetime had the nation abdicated its political prerogatives to such a degree and placed governmental responsibility and power in the hands of one man.

Practically all the nation's banks were closed on Inauguration Day, and the banks were to the economy what the heart is to the body. Business was at a standstill. One could not cash a check, make a deposit, or withdraw deposited funds. The "bank holidays" had begun in Nevada in October 1932, when the governor of the state closed the banks in order to prevent several imminent failures. Midwestern governors took similar action in February 1933, and in the first three days of March Treasury Department officials of both the old and new administrations urged other governors to declare bank holidays. The primary reason for the Treasury's request was the alarming decline of the nation's gold reserves, the primary basis for currency. The flow of gold from the nation's banking center in New York to interior banks and to countries abroad had reduced the reserve over 71 per cent since the first of the year. Roosevelt's first task was to surmount this banking and financial crisis. Nothing more could be done until it was past.

Roosevelt's first official actions were to call a special session of Congress for March 9 and to issue an executive order declaring a national bank holiday. For his statutory authority Roosevelt cited a World War I measure that was not directly relevant. Treasury officials began drafting a banking bill to be introduced into the new Congress as soon as it met. They completed the drafting of the bill at 2:00 A.M. on March 9, Congress convened at noon, and Roosevelt signed the bill into law at 9:00 P.M.

This Emergency Banking Act, besides granting the President the statutory power for the executive order he already had issued, created a means to aid banks in danger of failure and provided for the reopening of only those banks that seemed in reasonably healthy condition. The measure empowered the Reconstruction Finance Corporation to purchase preferred stock of banks and the Federal Reserve Banks to lend funds to state-chartered banks outside the Federal Reserve System. It also authorized the issue of additional Federal Reserve bank notes. The Act divided the closed banks into four categories, depending upon their degree of soundness. The strongest of them, after inspection by examiners, were allowed to begin operations quickly . . . the weakest of them, about one thousand in all, were closed permanently. By March 15 about half the banks in the country were again open for business. They were the bigger banks and held about 90 per cent of the total banking deposits. The banking crisis had passed. On Sunday evening, March 12, in a national radio address from the White House, Roosevelt explained the banking crisis and the action that had been taken. These "fireside chats," as he called them, proved a potent method of influencing public opinion.

The sense of urgency which gripped the country during FDR's first days in office was such that the new President could have done almost anything he wished with the nation's banks. At one extreme, he could have nationalized them or at least nationalized the important ones; at the other extreme, he could have done nothing and let the crisis run its natural course. The way actually chosen was a middle course that preserved the traditional arrangement with only minor modifications. Raymond Moley, one of FDR's early economic advisers who later parted company with the New Deal because he considered it too radical, wrote of the banking crisis and Roosevelt's actions, "If ever there was a moment when things hung in the balance, it was on March 5, 1933 —when unorthodoxy would have drained the last remaining strength of the capitalistic system. Capitalism was saved in eight days."

At the end of the Hoover administration and in the first months of FDR's presidency a Senate investigation of banking and the stock market—often called the Pecora investigation after the committee's chief counsel, Ferdinand Pecora—revealed widespread abuses. Public opinion demanded reform after the March 1933 crisis was surmounted. The Glass-Steagall Banking Act of June 1933 had features designed to prevent the kind of banking malpractices the Pecora committee had discovered. This law increased the power of the Federal Reserve Banks to regulate its members, especially with respect to lending for speculative purposes. It also required that banks utterly divorce themselves from affiliated investment companies, for the Pecora committee had demonstrated that banks sometimes operated in such a way as to advance the interest of their affiliated investment firms at the risk of their depositors' security. Perhaps most important for future banking stability, the law created the Federal Deposit Insurance Corporation (FDIC), a federally owned corporation, which insured deposits up to $2,500. Banks were required to take insurance policies on their deposits, for which they paid a small premium. If the bank failed, all deposits up to $2,500 would be paid off by the insurer, the FDIC. (The limit of insurance on each account went up to $5,000 in 1935 and to $10,000 in 1950.) Knowing that their accounts were insured, depositors were unlikely to cause a bank run. Bank failures declined to insignificance. In the rest of the decade less than one tenth as many banks failed as had done so in 1933. As in several other New Deal measures, the beneficiaries of the new law, the banks, fought the measure and argued that it was "government interference." The American Bankers Association tried to prevent the bill's passage, even though it had the effect of greatly stabilizing their enterprise.

The Pecora committee also turned up evidence of stock-market rigging and of false representation of new stock issues. The Truth-in-Securities Act of May 1933 required that prospective purchasers of new stock issues be fully informed about the financial condition of the firm issuing the stock, but it failed to establish an agency to enforce the law. A year later Congress established the Securities and Exchange Commission and granted it power to regulate the sale of all securities, whether new issues or not. Wall Street objected to the SEC. To soften the blow, Roosevelt appointed a Boston millionaire with Wall Street connections, Joseph P. Kennedy, to be the first SEC chairman.

With the immediate banking crisis over by about ten days after Roosevelt's inauguration, the new administration and Congress were ready to move on to the broader problem of combatting the depression. New laws creating new agencies came with great speed in the next several weeks, and the burst of legislation seemed to assure the population that Washington had at last taken decisive action. It is necessary for us to examine these new measures of the early New Deal in a logical presentation rather than in chronological order, but we should remember that newspaper readers of 1933 were seldom able to see the contemporary events in such coherent fashion.

The First New Deal

The early New Deal was no unified, systematic, and articulated attack on the depression. It was a shotgun approach precisely because the pressures upon Congress, of Congress upon the White House, and from the citizenry directly upon the White House were not to be denied and the objects of these pressures were diverse. Some parts of the population wanted inflationary policies, and there was great support for inflation in Congress, especially among those congressmen with largely agricultural constituencies. Some wanted massive federal spending, both to relieve poverty through federal relief and to stimulate the economy by expanding the total market. Others wanted just the reverse: minimum spending and balanced budgets. Some wanted an over-all industrial plan. Some wanted a plan for only certain parts of the economy. In general, FDR compromised among these several demands, and the resulting first New Deal actions represented a variety of purposes and theories.

The closest thing to a systematic governmental attack on the problem of recovery was the National Industrial Recovery Act of June 16, 1933, but even this measure was a blend of several ideas, and the administrators of the National Recovery Administration (NRA) established by the act were never agreed in their economic philosophies. The central idea of NRA arose from the "industrial self-government" plans that had come to the fore in the last two years of the Hoover administration. But the idea of "industrial self-government," under the demands of those who urged government rather than corporation planning, of those who urged large-scale government spending for public works, and of labor pressures for the right to organize and for minimum wages, was considerably modified in the resulting legislation.

The law had a curious legislative origin. At the end of the Hoover administration Senator Hugo Black of Alabama had introduced a bill sponsored by the AFL that would have prohibited interstate commerce of goods produced by labor that worked more than thirty hours a week. The idea of the proposal was to spread the number of jobs available to a greater number of workers. Support for the scheme was widespread. On April 6, 1933, the Black bill passed the Senate. FDR and his "brain trust," as the newspapers tagged his advisers who came from university faculties, wanted a more comprehensive approach to industrial stagnation. He sent Secretary of Labor Frances Perkins to the House Labor Committee to head off the Black bill. Miss Perkins succeeded in her mission and proposed instead of maximum hours a scheme of minimum wages and governmentally controlled industrial production quotas. Businessmen objected vigorously to this idea. The administration then set about finding a plan that business would accept and came forward in May with a draft of the National Industrial Recovery Act.

The bill had something for the many pressures exerted on the government. For business it had a rather heavy dose of "industrial self-government"; for those who advocated national planning there was a scheme of government approval of the codes that industry would write; for labor there was Section 7 (a), which guranteed the right to bargain collectively and to form unions of the workers' own choosing; for those demanding a large public works program there was Title II of the bill, which created the Public Works Administration (PWA) and appropriated the huge sum of $3.3 billion.

The codes were the heart of the NRA. There was to be a special code written for each industry, some employing thousands of workers, such as the cotton textile industry, and some, such as the kosher poultry business, which was to bring about NRA's ultimate constitutional downfall, employing only a few hundred. Representatives from each business of an industry, as well as representatives from labor, the consuming public, and government, met and wrote a code for the industry which, after it had been approved by the NRA administrators, had the force of law. As it worked out with but few exceptions, business representatives actually wrote the codes, and they were usually from the biggest firms in the industry. Labor was usually almost voiceless, the consumer always had inadequate representation, and government representatives were without the special knowledge of the industry's detailed operations that might have made them effective. Writing the codes took time, and NRA approval of them was an enormous administrative task if they were to be reviewed carefully and effectively.

Taking advantage of the delay in getting the codes written and into operation, some manufacturers began to produce at full scale while wages and other costs were still unregulated so as to build inventories to be sold after the codes went into effect and better prices were guaranteed. To head off this self-defeating action, Roosevelt in late July urged all employers to sign up under what was popularly called the "blanket code," to be effective until the regular code was written and approved. The blanket code prohibited the employment of children, provided for a minimum wage of forty cents an hour, and set a maximum work week of thirty-six hours for production workers and forty for clerical personnel. Firms signed the blanket code so as to be able to display the blue eagle emblem that signified cooperation with NRA, which was thought to be necessary for the consuming public's acceptance. But the "chiseling," to use the popular term of the day, had already done its damage. Industrial production in July rose to a little more than the 1923-1928 average, only to fall by 35 per cent by October when the blanket code became almost universal.

A great many people were unhappy with the way NRA worked. Labor gained less than it had anticipated and said that NRA stood for "National Run Around." Small businessmen resented the domination of big business in the writing of the codes. Big businessmen complained of the concessions they had to make to labor. Consumers were unhappy about the higher prices they had to pay for goods. And there was considerable unrest among those who feared the power of concentrated big business because NRA suspended the antitrust laws. Congress had created NRA for only a two-year period, and it remained to be seen what Congress would do when asked to renew the legislation. But the Supreme Court intervened on May 25, 1935, and in *Schechter* v. *United States* unanimously declared NRA unconstitutional. The Court's primary objection was that the Constitution invested only Congress with the power to legislate and that the codes were actually legislation. Some New Dealers thought that the Court in the Schechter case had saved the administration from further embarrassment, but Roosevelt was greatly disappointed. As he anticipated after the Court's decision, child labor increased, as did unemployment, while wages declined. Yet NRA obviously had not effected full recovery, and many people were concerned lest it lead to development of the kind of formal corporate state then in force in Mussolini's Italy. After adjusting to the idea of the death of NRA, Roosevelt abandoned the idea of industrial self-government and never returned to it.

Three other kinds of measures or programs of the early New Deal must be considered: monetary manipulation to bring a degree of inflation, federal spending for public works and relief, and special agricultural recovery legislation. The political pressures for all three were overwhelming.

Inflation through monetary manipulation had been a demand of agricultural America during depressions from the colonial period forward and had been especially strong in the late nineteenth century. Roosevelt did not agree altogether with the inflationists in Congress—he was happy that Senator Burton K. Wheeler's bill putting forward the 1896 Bryanite demand for free and unlimited coinage of silver at a ratio of 16 to 1 with gold was defeated in the Senate, although by only ten votes—but he recognized that the depression had brought a severe deflation and he was willing to resort to a degree of inflation to offset it. Roosevelt was further bothered by the international implications of an inflationary program. He had pledged support of the World Economic Conference which was to meet in London in June 1933 and which, among other things, would endeavor to stabilize the world's currencies. This put FDR in just the kind of position he hated: he had to decide between support of the conference or a degree of inflation. He could not have both. After vacillating until the last minute, he decided for inflation and scuttled the conference.

There were two main aspects of New Deal monetary manipulation: changing the gold content of the dollar and a silver purchase program. Through a series of executive orders and laws in the first two months of the administration the United States in effect abandoned the gold standard. An executive order prohibited the hoarding of gold, prohibited the redemption of currency for gold, and forbade the export of gold without Treasury permission. Then in October 1933 FDR instructed the Reconstruction Finance Corporation to begin buying gold on the world market above the world price. This meant that the gold content of the dollar was reduced by as much as the government paid above the world price. In January 1934 FDR requested Congress to pass the Gold Reserve Act, which became effective at the end of the month and authorized the chief executive to fix the gold content of the dollar between fifty and sixty cents. Roosevelt fixed the gold price at which the United States would buy at an even $35 an ounce. The price of gold when he took office had been $20.67. In other words, the dollar had been devalued roughly 40 per cent in terms of gold, thus making it 40 per cent easier for foreigners to purchase American products.

The Silver Purchase Act of June 1934 also had an inflationary purpose, but it was largely a raid by the nation's silver interests. The law required the Treasury to buy silver until its supply of the metal equaled one fourth of its total metallic reserve, or until the price of silver reached $1.29 an ounce, and to issue silver certificates and silver dollars on the purchased metal. The stated purpose of the act was to increase prices until they reached 1926 levels, but despite the law and all the other New Deal measures prices did not rise to that level until after Pearl Harbor.

Expanded federal budgets probably did more to bring about recovery than did monetary manipulation. Federal spending for relief of the indigent was not only humanitarian, it was also economically stimulating because it directly increased total purchasing power. This kind of government stimulation of the economy was the reverse of the "trickle down" aid that the RFC had employed under Hoover and continued to practice under Roosevelt. The first New Deal relief act was the creation of the Civilian Conservation Corps in late March 1933. The CCC took 250,000 young men from relief families, put them to work under War Department supervision at reforestation and other conservation projects, and paid them $30 a month, of which $25 went directly home to their families. When the CCC stopped in 1940 two and a quarter million young men had served in the organization. For relief of others Congress created the Federal Emergency Relief Administration (FERA) in May 1933 with an appropriation of

$500 million, but in the fall of that year it became apparent that a larger program would be necessary to get relief families through the winter.

The administration had hoped that the Public Works Administration, headed by Secretary of the Interior Harold L. Ickes and created under Title II of NIRA, would be in full operation by the winter of 1933-1934, enough to employ thousands of men on public works such as new schools and highways. Ickes, however, was so determined that the money be spent wisely and carefully that PWA did not quickly put large numbers of men to work. Consequently in November 1933 FDR took some of the PWA funds, created the Civil Works Administration (CWA), installed Harry Hopkins as its head, and instructed him to spend the funds as quickly as possible so that men on relief could be put to work. Within two months Hopkins had four million people working on CWA projects. Many of the projects were ill conceived, but CWA did get dollars into the hands of families that needed it badly and thereby stimulated the whole economy as well. When the winter was over FDR closed down CWA, and Congress reinvigorated FERA with another large appropriation. Undoubtedly, federal relief in 1933 and 1934 greatly helped poor families, but the whole relief program was makeshift and temporary until 1935 when Congress created the Works Progress Administration.

Public works, as distinct from make-work projects primarily for relief purposes, made a lasting contribution to the country's welfare. The PWA ultimately created over four million man-hours of work and built millions of dollars' worth of roads, schools, post offices, courthouses, and other public buildings. The most ambitious New Deal public work was the Tennessee Valley Authority (TVA), the brain-child of Senator Norris. TVA expanded from the Muscle Shoals installation into a huge and complex system of dams that not only provided millions of kilowatt hours of electricity but made possible for the first time a systematic way to control floods in the valley and to help control them downstream in the Mississippi system. As inexpensive electric power became available the Tennessee valley increasingly became industrialized, and the living standards of the region, once near the lowest in the nation, significantly improved.

Even with a degree of inflation and federal relief, it was apparent that special legislation for agriculture was essential just as the NRA was special legislation for industry. Increasing the amount of agricultural credit available was one necessary action—this was accomplished by the Emergency Farm Mortgage Act and the

Farm Credit Act in the spring of 1933 and the Frazier-Lemke Farm Bankruptcy Act a year later—but the essential problem was to increase the prices of farm products so that farming would once again become a profitable enterprise. The scheme adopted by the New Deal, as embodied in the Agricultural Adjustment Act of May 12, 1933, set the pattern of farm policy that the federal government has followed with some modifications ever since. The AAA was not a new idea. It was the culmination of various agricultural proposals going as far back as those of the Populists of the 1890's, and in some respects it was the logical next step after the Federal Farm Board experiment of the Hoover administration.

The object of the AAA was to bring about a better balance between the prices of agricultural and industrial products, to bring them to the same ratio that had existed from 1909 to 1914. This ratio, or parity as it was generally called, was to be achieved, it was hoped, by restricting agricultural production. In other words, the method was to increase prices by reducing supply. Individual farmers of basic crops made agreements with the AAA in which they agreed to take some of their land out of production and receive a subsidy from the AAA for the land thus left fallow. The AAA also had authority to buy up surplus agricultural commodities, or to lend funds to producers with the crops as collateral, to peg farm prices. A special tax on processors of agricultural products financed the whole AAA program. The processors, of course, passed the tax on to the consumer. In 1936 the Supreme Court declared AAA unconstitutional because of this special tax, and Congress subsequently rewrote the law in a manner that met the constitutional objection.

In a narrow sense, AAA was successful. Helped along by droughts that also lowered production, AAA succeeded in approximately doubling the price of wheat, corn, and cotton by 1935. Total farm income increased by about 53 per cent. But on the other hand the program had deep-rooted difficulties. Crop restriction by putting some land out of production was less than fully effective because farmers could use more fertilizer on the land actually being used and thereby increase their yields. The system also had an unfortunate side effect on cotton-farming sharecroppers. Landlords sometimes failed to share AAA benefits with their tenants and often used their government checks to buy tractors and other equipment which tended to make sharecroppers obsolete. Forced off the land and having no other vocational skills, displaced sharecroppers were a serious social problem until full employment during the war alleviated their plight.

But the most distressing feature of the program was that it reduced the amount of food and fiber available when people were hungry and ragged, and the idea of calculated wasted potential went against the grain. Yet in more than a generation no one has come forth with a better proposal that is acceptable to both farmer and consumer.

The Second New Deal

In the late winter of 1934-1935 any objective observer would have had to recognize that in Roosevelt's first two years there had been an improvement in the nation's economic condition. Most importantly, the banks were open and functioning normally and the panic that had characterized Hoover's last and Roosevelt's first weeks had disappeared. There was less unemployment than there had been in March 1933, the farmers were not in as desperate a condition, and the poor were not so close to utter disaster as they had been when Roosevelt took office. Yet the observer would also have noted that the depression was by no means over. Unemployment stood at about ten million, and the number of those who had jobs was only at about the level of 1932. Young people coming into the labor market still went for months, even years, before they were able to find even a poor job. Businessmen, or most of them, did not face annual deficits as they had just two or three years before, but none of them was so foolish as to describe business conditions as good. And reformers, those who had hoped that the New Deal would be the triumph of progressivism, could point to little in the New Deal record that warmed their hearts. The banking legislation, the tax act of 1934 which closed some income-tax loopholes permitting men such as J. P. Morgan, Jr. to escape paying income taxes altogether, the SEC, and the TVA were about all the New Deal measures so far that clearly had reform as their primary intent.

The political situation had changed drastically since FDR's inauguration. The urgency of the economic crisis had been so severe in the New Deal's earliest weeks and many Republicans had been so demoralized by recent events that Roosevelt enjoyed something close to a political honeymoon at first. For example, when the Emergency Banking Act was before the House of Representatives on March 9, 1933, the Republican floor leader told his colleagues, "The house is burning down, and the President of the United States says this is the way to put out the fire." The House went on to approve the measure after only forty minutes' debate. The Republican press was usually gentle with the new President. The New York *Daily News,* part of the Patterson-Mc-Cormick group of newspapers, even organized a campaign for raising funds to build a swimming pool in the White House. Roosevelt enjoyed swimming, and it was about the only exercise that his paralyzed legs permitted. The Hearst newspapers, nominally Democratic because of their owner's adventures in that party, supported Roosevelt in 1933. Soon they would become shrill critics of the White House editorially.

In 1934, conservative newspaper attacks on the New Deal and the organization of the American Liberty League in August of that year indicated that the right wing had recovered from its depression shell-shock and was prepared for counterattack. The honeymoon was obviously over. Wealthy men, most of them in the Du Pont family or officials in the Du Pont-controlled General Motors Corporation, financed the Liberty League, but a group of conservative Democrats who had once led their party got most of the publicity. Al Smith was the prize speaker for the Liberty League, and he categorically described the New Deal's laws as "socialism." The Liberty League pulled out all the stops for Republican candidates in the 1934 elections but was unable to bring the party through. Republicans lost fourteen more House seats in that election and won only eleven of the disputed senatorships. There were only seven Republican governors after the 1934 elections.

Roosevelt regretted the end of the truce by the political right although he probably anticipated it. He was more seriously concerned with what was happening within his own coalition. Democratic members of Congress, under pressure from home, were pushing for reform of the economy as well as greater relief and bolder recovery policies. Significant numbers of voters who had been for FDR in 1932 believed that the New Deal had not yet done enough and they were increasingly following new leaders, some of them with odd programs, who demanded more radical departures. In the upper Mississippi Valley progressive Democrats and La Follette Republicans kept talking of a new national Farmer-Labor party although they always stopped short of forming one and deserting the Roosevelt coalition. Labor-union leaders, not yet as strong as they would be after the great organizing campaigns of 1936 and 1937 but still influential, frequently expressed disillusionment with FDR. Most alarming to FDR were Upton Sinclair's capture of the Democratic party in California, the growing strength of Senator Huey Long's Share Our Wealth organization, and the immense popularity of the Townsend plan.

Sinclair, a well-known novelist and a member of the Socialist party for most of his life, entered the Democratic primary for governor in 1934 and ran on a program he called EPIC, End Poverty in California. EPIC proposed a $50-a-month pension for the indigent over age sixty and a system of "production for use" workshops for the unemployed, partly producer-cooperative, partly socialistic in scope. Despite great opposition from the party machine, Sinclair won the primary rather easily. In the general election, the campaign against Sinclair was intense, heavily financed by Hollywood figures, and low in its tactics. FDR refused to support Sinclair, and prominent Golden State Democrats worked for the Republican candidate. Although he lost to the Republican, Sinclair still ran a strong race. Huey Long was the epitome of the back-country demagogic politician, but in the mid-1930's political demagogues found economic radicalism rather than anti-Bolshevism or racism the best way to attract followers. Long's slogan was "Every Man a King," and he promised everyone a homestead worth $5,000 and a $2,500 annual income to be derived from the confiscation of large fortunes. Francis E. Townsend, a retired physician of Long Beach, California, proposed the Old Age Revolving Pension. The plan called for a $200 pension to be paid to all unemployed people over sixty, with the requirement that the recipients spend the entire amount within a month in order to be eligible for the next payment. Townsend thought a 2 per cent tax on all financial transactions would be sufficient to finance the scheme. The plan was very popular among the aged all over the country, and in 1934 the Townsendites succeeded in electing a congressman from southern California. That some of these proposals were odd, perhaps even dangerous, only more sharply delineated the widespread dissatisfaction many voters felt toward the accomplishments of the New Deal.

With the political right having come back to life and with apparently large sections of Roosevelt's electoral support deserting toward the left or the pseudo-left, it was obvious that the administration must change direction if it were to remain politically strong. Recovering the right was probably impossible, but if it could be accomplished it could be only at the expense of greater defections to the left. The only thing to do was for the administration to shift toward the left and take the wind out of the sails that had been bearing men such as Sinclair, Long, and Townsend with such vigor. FDR debated with himself for weeks in the late winter, but in the spring of 1935 he began to accept, even began to urge, proposals that had been advocated by the more progressive members of Congress for many months. The result was that in 1935 Congress passed and the President signed a most unusual slate of progressive legislation. The year 1935 may be said to have been progressivism's high tide.

The shift in the way the White House was leaning was indicated by word passed to Congress that the President was for a great increase in spending for public works and relief. One of the conservative arguments against the New Deal was that it cost too much and failed to balance the federal budget. Many New Dealers argued that large-scale government spending was necessary "to prime the pump." Economists who followed the theories of Britain's John Maynard Keynes argued that government dollars spent had a "multiplier effect," that for every dollar spent by the government there would be an increase in GNP between two and three dollars. They also argued that federal deficits were at least in the short run beneficial during depressions because through bank-purchased government bonds they increased money in circulation and loosened credit.

In early April 1935, Congress passed the Emergency Relief Appropriation Act with an appropriation of $4,888,000,000, a new high for public works and relief. The following month FDR established the Works Progress Administration (WPA) under the act and put Harry Hopkins in charge. Most of the money went for construction and conservation. Before the end of 1936, 1,497 new water-works had been completed, hundreds of new roads and sewage-disposal plants, and scores of bridges, levees, and airports. About one fifth of the funds went for community-service projects of all kinds, some of which employed jobless artists, musicians, and actors. In the six years that the WPA was active it employed over eight million different individuals (about one sixth of the labor force) and spent $11.4 billion. WPA wages varied according to degree of skill required and from region to region, but the average monthly wage in 1936 was $52.14.

The same law that created the WPA also provided for the National Youth Administration (NYA). NYA's main purpose was to provide part-time employment for students in high school and college, but it also had a small program for young people who were not in school. Huge numbers of students were thus enabled to continue their education and remain off the labor market. In 1940, 100,000 college undergraduates and over 1,500 graduate students were on NYA rolls. Congress in 1935 also doubled its appropriation for the CCC.

A 1935 law that had far-reaching implications for the operation of the economy was the National Labor Relations Act, often called the Wagner Act for its sponsor, Senator Robert F. Wagner of New York. At first trade unionists had been elated by the labor provisions of NRA, but the law in practice fell far short of their expectations. There were two difficulties with Section 7(a) from the unions' point of view: a company union (not a genuine union, but one dominated and financed by the employer) enabled companies to circumvent the purpose of the law, and such unions more than doubled in number during the NRA years; and the law permitted more than one collective-bargaining agent for men in the same shop, even those doing the same work, which enabled employers to play off one union against another. Labor unions grew in strength under NRA, but the basic labor law was a continual frustration.

Throughout 1934 Senator Wagner worked for a new labor law more conducive to union growth and strength. He got no support from the White House and was unable to get his bill through without the President's help. He reintroduced his bill in the new Congress. After he had successfully fought off amendments to the bill that would have weakened it considerably, the Senate passed the proposal on May 16 with only twelve dissenting votes. Still FDR offered the measure no support. On May 24, three days before the Supreme Court voided NRA, Roosevelt at last gave the Wagner bill encouragement, probably because he thought it would pass Congress anyway. Less than a month later the House passed the bill. Although businessmen were almost unanimously opposed to it, the House approved it overwhelmingly without even a roll call.

The Wagner Act created the National Labor Relations Board and asserted that all employees had a right to join or form a union and through the union to bargain collectively with their employers. A union that won a majority of employee votes in a NLRB-conducted secret-ballot election became the workers' sole bargaining agent, and the law required employers to bargain with the union in good faith. The law also enumerated and prohibited employer "unfair practices," among them firing men for union activity and subsidizing company unions. For the first time, federal law was favorable to trade-union growth, and unions quickly capitalized on the opportunity and organized basic industries such as automobiles and steel.

Another 1935 law at least equal to the Wagner Act in its modification of the economy was the Social Security Act, which became law in August. The idea behind social security was by no means new. Theodore Roosevelt had advocated old-age pensions in

1912, and by the 1930's about half the states had some kind of a pension or unemployment-compensation system. Very few of the state laws even approached adequacy, and most were of little help at all. Popular demand for a social security system was strong, particularly after the Townsend plan caught the imagination of aged people. In 1934 Congress could not decide between two social security bills, and Roosevelt proposed a special committee to study the problem and report back to Congress. The committee made its report in January 1935. That Congress would pass some kind of legislation soon was a foregone conclusion; the only real disagreement was over details. In the final votes only six senators and thirty-three representatives opposed the law.

A very complex law, the Social Security Act primarily provided for old-age pensions and compensations for the unemployed. Through a payroll tax on both employers and employees—at first only 1 per cent on the first $3,000 of employee income, but to be gradually increased—the act created a fund from which retired workers aged sixty-five or more would receive monthly pensions. The first payments were to begin in 1942 and would be $10 at a minimum and $85 at a maximum, depending upon how much the retired worker and his employer had contributed. For those who had already retired and were at least sixty-five, the federal government would share the costs of pensions with the states. The unemployment-compensation provisions also involved federal-state cooperation, but the law established a minimum weekly compensation and the minimum number of weeks during which those who lost jobs could receive payments.

The original law was far from satisfactory to everyone. Farm laborers, domestic and casual workers, public employees, and those on the payrolls of educational and religious institutions did not come under the provisions of the act, and the old-age pensions were inadequate for a decent living standard if the beneficiary had no other income. The unemployment-compensation provisions were of no help to those who were already unemployed. One had first to get a job and then lose it to receive compensation. But, clearly, once the basic idea of federal social security was enacted the benefits could be increased and extended to further categories of employees, and the law has since been amended several times.

The new labor and social security laws were the later New Deal's most basic reform legislation, but there were other reforms as well. Marriner S. Eccles, whom FDR had appointed chairman of the Federal Reserve Board, urged passage of a law to enlarge the powers of the Board so that it could more readily and more effectively take compensatory action against fluctuations in the business cycle. The Banking Act of 1935 did not contain all that Eccles wished, but it was the most important revision of the Federal Reserve System since it had been established in the early Wilson administration. The law transferred from the twelve regional Reserve Banks to the central Board the power to raise or lower the discount rate and gave the Board additional power to determine the reserve requirements of all banks in the system and to conduct its open-market operations. The law also extended the kinds of commercial paper against which Federal Reserve notes could be issued and raised the maximum FDIC-insured account to $5,000. The law has since been used many times to offset cyclical tendencies, to raise the discount rate when undesired inflation seemed likely, for example, and to lower it and thereby make credit easier when a downswing in the cycle seemed imminent.

A new tax law in 1935, passed after FDR sent Congress a message in which he urged tax revision "encouraging a wider distribution of wealth," earned the vigorous opposition of conservatives who called it a "soak the rich" measure. The new law by no means made it impossible to amass great wealth nor to pass it on to heirs, but it did increase inheritance taxes sharply and established a new surtax on net incomes of over $50,000 a year.

The reform measure of 1935 that had the most difficult road to passage was a law passed in August forbidding further development of holding-company empires in public utilities, such as the Insull system, and providing for the gradual breakup of holding-company pyramids that already existed in public utilities. Lobbyists for power companies were extremely active in resisting the law, but when Senator Black brought forward the information that the flood of telegrams against the bill received by members of Congress were actually from lobbyists and not from those whose names appeared on them, the lobbyists received a setback. The law empowered the SEC to limit holding companies to a single integrated system with no more than one layer of holding company.

The Rural Electrification Authority (REA) created by executive order in May 1935 with already appropriated funds did much to improve living conditions and lighten work loads on the nation's farms. At that time, only 10 per cent of American farms had electricity, less than most European countries. Within a few years REA electric cooperatives and privately owned electric companies, spurred at last to action, brought electricity to all but the most remote farm areas. Electric automatic pumps on farm wells made running water feasible—no inconsiderable aspect of the narrowing differences between urban and rural life.

The New Deal's shift toward the left brought the results anticipated. The electorate, it became obvious in the next elections, overwhelmingly approved the measures and ceased to follow left-of-New Deal leaders in significant numbers. Sinclair's EPIC faded to complete obscurity. The Townsend movement continued but with less steam. Long's movement failed to survive his assassination in September 1935. Roosevelt's conservative opposition was more vigorous than ever, despite FDR's announcement in the fall of 1935 of a "breathing spell" for business, but the President well understood that he and his party would have received few votes from conservatives in any case. But before considering the 1936 elections let us look briefly at the methods the New Deal took to alleviate the depression through foreign policy.

New Deal Foreign Policy

Remarkably seldom do those who study the past recognize that certain foreign policies of the Roosevelt administration were part of its program to effect economic recovery. A nation's foreign affairs, one must remember, are not conducted in a vacuum; domestic conditions and pressures play a major role in determining a country's policies with other nations.

Until at least the late 1930's, when questions of war and peace came to dominate the New Deal's conduct of foreign affairs, the administration's main concern in foreign policy was to increase markets for American products abroad. Actually, in one way of looking at it, the whole attack on the Great Depression was one of increasing markets, both domestic and foreign. If the United States could sell wheat or steel or automobiles abroad, American investors got a better return and labor had jobs. With the advent of the depression American exports had shrunk very badly. Exports had amounted to $5,240,995 in 1929; they fell to $1,611,016 in 1932, the lowest year, a decline of roughly two thirds. (Imports declined similarly. The United States had an excess of exports over imports throughout the depression, although in some years the excess was quite small.) Both the administration and business leaders recognized that regaining these foreign markets would have a stimulating effect upon the domestic economy. The Roosevelt administration's means to achieve this goal were many, among others recognition of theretofore unrecognized foreign regimes so as to facilitate commercial relations, loans with which to purchase American products, and, most important, a new scheme of tariffs.

President Wilson had refused to extend diplomatic recognition to the new regime in Russia after the Bolshevik revolution in 1917, and each of his successors in the 1920's had continued the non-recognition policy. Hoover had been under some pressure to recognize the Soviet Union because there were some businessmen who wanted to sell their products to the Communists and thought that regular diplomatic relations would facilitate commerce, but Hoover had committed himself against recognition and would do no more than arrange for the RFC to underwrite some cotton exports to Russia. Roosevelt had made no commitment against recognition, and a few weeks after his inauguration he began correspondence looking toward formal recognition. FDR, of course, had more than commercial considerations in mind, but hoped-for sales to the Soviets were no minor motivating factor. Formal recognition came on November 16, 1933. Early the next year the administration created the Export-Import Bank, under authority of the National Industrial Recovery Act and financed originally with RFC funds. Ex-Im, as it is commonly called, began to underwrite the financing for sales to the Soviets. Despite the expectations of 1933 and 1934, however, the Russian market did not develop significantly. The Russians were balky in the negotiations over the bonds owned by Americans that the Czarist government had issued, the USSR refusing to honor the prerevolutionary debt, and relatively little American production went to Russia until the Lend-Lease exports of World War II.

Ex-Im lay dormant after the Russian debt negotiations fell through, but Congress revived it in 1935 on a two-year basis. Congress subsequently extended its life periodically, and Ex-Im has grown into a major international credit agency that today materially stimulates American sales abroad. It became a permanent agency in 1945. It is important to realize that Ex-Im foreign loans are not sums that the receiving nation is free to spend indiscriminately and wherever it chooses. The purposes of the loans are spelled out in detail, and all, or practically all, of the loan is in the form of credits from American firms. Thus loans extended by an agency of the federal government are used to purchase American production. In 1938 Ex-Im began to make development loans to economically underdeveloped nations, which to the degree that the loans led to an increase in the borrowing nation's GNP made further exports possible. Some Ex-Im loans were for military strategic purposes; a 1938 loan to China of $25 million was for the Burma Road, which was essential in the war against Japan. Ex-Im was not the only federal agency engaged in foreign loans designed to stimulate American foreign sales. In 1934, for example, the RFC lent China $15 million with which to purchase United States cotton, wheat, and flour. By the end of 1941 the RFC had authorized the spending of $47,301,000 for financing exports of agricultural surpluses.

The reciprocal trade agreement program was the New Deal's most ambitious effort to increase American foreign markets. The enabling law, passed in June 1934, expressly stated in its preamble that its purpose was to expand "foreign markets for the products of the United States." Reciprocity, an old idea, was a pet project of Secretary of State Cordell Hull, who was long an advocate of low tariffs. To lower tariffs across the board while jobs were scarce would have been political dynamite, but the more selective tariff reduction of reciprocal agreements was less likely to arouse domestic opposition, and shrewdly bargained agreements were often a considerable boon to American exports. Even so, those who advocated traditionally high tariffs objected strenuously. The Republican platform of 1936 singled out, of all the New Deal's measures, only the reciprocity program for repeal.

The Reciprocal Trade Agreements Act of 1934 granted the executive branch the power to negotiate arrangements with other countries in which American customs duties could be lowered by as much as 50 per cent in exchange for reciprocal reductions by the other powers. Such agreements were not treaties, did not require ratification by the Senate, and could go into effect immediately upon their signing. The original act of 1934 authorized such agreements for a period of three years, and Congress thereafter extended the measure for two or three years at a time. The problem in negotiating the agreements was to persuade the other nation to reduce its duties on products that the United States had in abundance and for which it needed a bigger market and, in exchange, to lower American duties on articles that would not be in competition with domestic production. Of course, the same problem presented itself to the other power at the negotiating table, and the negotiations were slow and difficult. Nevertheless, by 1942 the United States had signed reciprocal trade agreements with twenty-three nations, largely with Latin American countries but also with Canada (1936 and 1940), Sweden (1935), France (1936), and Great Britain (1939).

One feature of the Reciprocal Trade Agreements Act led to a

general lowering of the tariff: the law provided that agreements contain a "most favored nation" clause. Thus, any lowering of duties arrived at by an agreement between the United States and any second power would automatically be extended, for the products covered in the agreement, to all other powers of the world except those that the chief executive stated were discriminatory in their commercial relations with the United States. An example: the 1936 agreement with Brazil lowered the American duty on coffee; it thereby decreased the American duty on coffee imported from all other nations that had "most-favored-nation" status. Roosevelt excepted only Nazi Germany (and Australia very briefly) from the general decrease in tariff rates emanating from trade agreements, and the agreements therefore worked to bring about a significant scaling down of the United States tariff wall. Calculating how much precisely the trade agreements reduced the general tariff level was a formidable mathematical exercise, but in 1942 the government estimated that the agreements, together with the generalizing effect for "most favored nations," had reduced the tariff level by 29 per cent since 1933.

It is impossible to say exactly how much reciprocal trade agreements extended American markets because there were too many variables, too many other forces operating which also extended the export market. But the market did increase. Exports increased to $3,349,167 in 1937, fell off a little in the recession of 1938, and then climbed again to $4,021,146 in 1940, the last full year before the beginning of Lend-Lease. Exports of most nations increased simultaneously, of course, as the world depression became less serious, but it is significant that until the recession American exports increased more rapidly than did those of other nations. In other words, the United States increased its share of the world's markets, and the increase probably was due to advantages bargained for in the trade agreements.

Although much that has been written about Roosevelt's well-publicized Good Neighbor policy toward Latin America has emphasized United States diplomatic maturity and its growing sense of international responsibility, an emphasis that is valid, those who developed and directed the policy nevertheless had a strong concern for American economic interest. United States trade with Latin American nations declined approximately 70 per cent between 1929 and 1932. Growing anti-Yanqui sentiment in Latin America threatened North American investments and discouraged them for the future. Quite obviously, if the United States during the Great Depression had continued Theodore

Rooseveltian, interventionist, and high-handed Latin American policies, it would not have been doing itself an economic favor.

The Hoover administration moved in the direction of the Good Neighbor policy with its publication of the Clark memorandum on the Monroe Doctrine in 1930. This memorandum omitted reference to the Theodore Roosevelt corollary to the doctrine. But the United States still had not renounced armed intervention in Latin American nations on other grounds until the Montevideo Conference of American States in December 1933, where Secretary of State Hull explicitly renounced the right to intervene. Immediately after the end of the conference, FDR said publicly that opposition to armed intervention was ". . . the definite policy of the United States from now on." In 1936 the State Department agreed to a protocol that forbade intervention "directly or indirectly, and for whatever reason," and the Senate approved the action.

Actions accompanied words. Washington refrained from armed intervention in Cuba in that island's troubles in 1933 and abrogated the Platt Amendment the following year. Also in 1933 the Roosevelt administration agreed to withdraw American marines from Haiti, and when the last unit left the following summer it was the first time in decades that marines had not been garrisoned somewhere in a Latin American republic. The biggest test of the Good Neighbor policy came with Mexico in 1938 and thereafter. The Mexican government in early 1938 expropriated oil lands owned by American and other foreign firms. Although the pressures on the White House were intense, the administration stuck to its announced Latin American policy and countenanced the expropriation, which was entirely legal.

The Good Neighbor policy was a success both in terms of the general national interest and of economic interest. After Pearl Harbor the Latin American republics, with the exception of Argentina, stood by the United States and helped in the war against the Axis. If there had been a lack of Latin American cooperation or if that area had been actually hostile, the American war effort would have been severely handicapped and complicated. Sales to and investments in Latin America did not significantly help the United States to emerge from the depression, but trade with the Latins did increase. Exports to the Latin American nations more than quadrupled between 1932 and 1941, and although direct American investments there did not reach the 1929 high until the 1940's they climbed from their low point of the early depression.

Democratic High Tide

After the session of Congress that had passed the unprecedented slate of progressive legislation in 1935, both Republicans and Democrats looked forward to the 1936 elections. Republicans, or at least most of them, hoped for a GOP victory that would mean repudiation of the New Deal, an end of further New Deal measures, and a repeal of some already enacted; Democrats sought the electorate's affirmation, and at least some Democrats thought a victory would be the signal for another round of reform.

The Republicans met first in 1936. The problem of their ticket was serious since they had no nationally popular leader seeking the nomination. The convention nominated Governor Alfred M. Landon of Kansas, who had attracted attention by winning despite the Democratic landslide in 1934. Governor Landon had supported the Bull Moose rebellion in 1912, but his more conservative cohorts were willing to forgive that indiscretion. Landon had little personal flair or political magnetism, and the convention nominated for the second spot Colonel Frank Knox, publisher of a Chicago newspaper, to lend dash to the ticket. The platform was also a problem. Suspecting that the New Deal laws were basically popular, most Republicans were hesitant to call for their repeal. Their platform criticized Democratic administration of the laws, but did not call for their repeal (except, as previously noted, for the Reciprocal Trade Agreements Act).

FDR's renomination was a foregone conclusion. The Philadelphia convention was no more than a huge Roosevelt rally. Roosevelt in his acceptance speech seemed to endorse the idea of further reform when he condemned "economic royalists" who sought to establish "industrial dictatorship." The convention endorsed the New Deal, as everyone expected it to do, and renominated the conservative John N. Garner for the vice-presidency.

Both candidates ran hard, and the campaign generated a great deal of excitement. Roosevelt upon several occasions answered Republican charges that he was against capitalism with assertions that he and his party had actually saved that economic system. "It was this administration which saved the system of private profit and free enterprise after it had been dragged to the brink of ruin by these same leaders who now try to scare you." Landon had difficulty with his campaign. Actually not an extreme conservative at all and calculating that an appeal to right-wing sentiments would only lose votes, Landon was restrained in his criticisms of the Democratic record. But Republican National Chairman John D. M. Hamilton did his best to leave voters with the impression that a Landon victory would mean wiping the New Deal from the books and that a Democratic success would mean the end of political democracy in the United States. Maine in those days voted for state and congressional offices in September—it did not change to conform with the rest of the nation until after World War II—and when the Republicans won in Maine they raised their old slogan, "As Maine goes, so goes the nation." The Republicans were actually optimistic. The *Literary Digest* poll, conducted by postcards with names gathered from telephone directories and automobile registration records, indicated that Landon would win. An overwhelming majority of the nation's newspapers supported the Republican candidate.

Election day was a shock to the Republican party. Roosevelt won the greatest victory of any presidential candidate since James Monroe in 1820. He carried every state except Maine and Vermont—Democratic wags rephrased the GOP slogan to "As Maine goes, so goes Vermont"—even defeating Landon in the governor's home state. With 36.5 per cent of the popular vote Landon had done better than his eight electoral votes made it appear, but the Republicans could find little solace in the returns. They had taken a bad licking in state and congressional races as well.

Some aspects of the election deserve special consideration. Roosevelt's popularity was obvious from even a superficial examination of the election results, but closer examination revealed that he and his party were especially popular among those parts of the population that had been hardest hit by the depression. The *Literary Digest* poll had been so far from accurate largely because its sampling system had ignored those too poor to own automobiles and maintain telephones. Precincts in working-class neighborhoods, especially in the big cities, went for Roosevelt more heavily than did the nation as a whole. Republicans charged that the Democrats had used WPA to coerce voters. Actually, there had been a few cases of Democrats using WPA for political purposes, but Hopkins had been quick to stop such practices wherever he had found them. Most of the WPA employees did vote for Franklin D. Roosevelt and other Democratic candidates, but this was mainly because they calculated that the Democratic party had done more for them and for recovery generally than had the Republican party or than the Republicans would if they should again become the majority party.

Organized labor's role in the campaign was a new development. John L. Lewis and Sidney Hillman of the newly formed CIO established Labor's Non-Partisan League to promote FDR's campaign and to help friends of labor in congressional races. Never before had labor unions been so active in a national election, never so generous with manpower and financial contributions. The size of labor's support indicated that Roosevelt had been successful in adding another element to the Democratic coalition, especially in the industrial states, and in time to come the alliance of the Democratic party with organized labor would become even stronger.

Still another significant aspect of the 1936 election was the change in the political affiliation of the Negro voter. Since the Civil War, the Negro vote, what there was of it, had always gone to Republicans because theirs was the party of Lincoln. But most New Deal administrators had treated Negroes fairly, the Roosevelt family had entertained Negro leaders in the White House to a far greater extent than had earlier first families, and most Negroes who voted—in the North and West—were industrial workers, and industrial workers of all races were predominantly Democratic. Also, the Republicans in 1928, in an effort to win southern white votes, had ignored southern Negro Republican leadership in favor of the "lily whites." The shift had started to reveal itself in 1934. In 1928 a predominantly Negro district on Chicago's South Side had elected a Republican, Oscar De Priest, to Congress, the first Negro to serve there since Reconstruction. The same district in 1934 elected a Negro Democrat, Arthur W. Mitchell, who had been a registered Republican as late as 1930.

The 1936 elections demonstrated the political astuteness of the New Deal's shift to the left for a few months in 1935. The left-of-FDR forces had lost momentum when Roosevelt accepted their most popular programs, or parts of them, and the pseudo-left demagogues who tried to keep the Huey Long movement going with the Union party came out badly on election day. Roosevelt had put together an extraordinary political coalition: southern traditionalists, big-city political machines, industrial workers of all races, trade unionists, and many depression-hit farmers. With such majorities as the Democrats had (all but 19 seats in the Senate and 107 in the House), a reasonable man might have predicted after the Democratic victory that the New Deal would go on to more reform and continued electoral success. But prediction is a hazardous exercise. In fact, New Deal reform was almost completely over, and the extraordinary coalition began to come apart at the seams immediately after its most sweeping political victory.

The Deterioration of the Democratic Coalition

In 1937 and 1938 it appeared that FDR had lost his political magic touch. Everything seemed to go wrong at once. Democrats fought Democrats, and Republicans observed the struggles with glee and capitalized upon them in Congress and at the polls. First there was Roosevelt's proposed reorganization of the Supreme Court and the federal judiciary, which stirred a magnificent row. Then there was an increasing intrusion of problems of foreign policy into the public consciousness, and the Democratic coalition was divided upon these issues. In the campaigns for the congressional elections of 1938, FDR further inflamed already hot intramural Democratic differences. And all these political troubles took place against a background of further economic difficulty, the recession of 1937-1938. Each of these subjects merits further explanation.

The Supreme Court in 1935 and 1936 had declared unconstitutional some critical New Deal measures as well as some progressive legislation enacted by the states. The Court was composed mostly of Republican appointees, and six of the nine justices were over seventy years old. (A popular book in 1936 was Drew Pearson's and Robert Allen's *Nine Old Men,* a vigorous attack on the court.) A group of four justices (Willis Van Devanter, James C. McReynolds, George Sutherland, and Pierce Butler) consistently wrote decisions that would have pleased Herbert Spencer and other nineteenth-century Social Darwinists. At the other end of the Court were three progressives (Louis D. Brandeis, Harlan F. Stone, and Benjamin N. Cardozo). The other two justices, Chief Justice Charles Evans Hughes and Owen J. Roberts, could not easily be classified; sometimes they voted with the conservative four, sometimes with the more progressive three. Roosevelt had no opportunity to make a Court appointment.

On May 27, 1935, the Court had delivered three blows to the New Deal, all of them by unanimous decisions. The most important case, *Schechter* v. *United States,* declared NRA unconstitutional in its entirety. (A January decision had already declared one aspect of the law contrary to the Constitution.) The Court also declared the Frazier-Lemke Farm Mortgage Act null and void and ruled that FDR had illegally removed William E. Humphrey from the Federal Trade Commission. In January 1936, in

Butler v. *United States,* often called the Hoosac Mills case, the Court held, six to three, that AAA was unconstitutional. In the Tipaldo case the court by a five-to-four decision struck down a New York law regulating the hours and wages of women in a decision that was particularly old-fashioned in its legal reasoning and definitions. Roosevelt grumbled privately but restrained himself in his public statements.

Then on February 5, 1937, completely without warning, FDR sent a message to Congress that called for reorganization of the Supreme Court and the judiciary generally. The effect was electric. Roosevelt asked Congress for legislation empowering him to appoint up to fifty additional federal judges, of whom no more than six would be to the Supreme Court, each new appointment to be made whenever an incumbent judge failed to retire within six months after reaching age seventy. His argument was that age prevented judges from keeping abreast of their work, but it took no special intelligence to see that FDR wanted to make enough new Supreme Court appointments to override the four consistently anti-New Deal justices. The newspapers, which were almost unanimously opposed to the proposal, called it FDR's "court packing bill." Republicans in Congress were opposed almost to a man, as were many Democrats, most of them conservatives. Senate Republicans made a tactical decision to let their Democratic colleagues carry the fight against the bill.

In May the Senate Judiciary Committee voted to reject the judiciary bill and denounced the whole idea. At the same time, Justice Van Devanter informed the President that he wanted to retire. This gave FDR his first chance for a Court appointment, but it put him on a spot because before the Court message he had promised the first vacancy to Senate Majority Leader Joseph T. Robinson of Arkansas, who was then leading the fight for the judiciary proposal against his personal wishes. To appoint Robinson would have been inconsistent with FDR's expressed purposes since the Senator was sixty-five years old. Robinson died of a heart attack in July, and his friends in the Senate thought that he had died from overwork on FDR's project. On the way back from the funeral, they determined to force FDR to accept either a compromise or defeat. FDR compromised and accepted the Judicial Procedure Reform Act of August 27, 1937, which provided for no new judgeships but did hasten the process of cases involving constitutionality and inhibited the power of judges to issue injunctions that stayed the execution of federal law.

Roosevelt had to accept much less than he had demanded, but the Court began, even before his defeat, to uphold New Deal legislation. On April 12 it upheld the Wagner Act in three cases, the most important of which was *NLRB* v. *Jones and Laughlin Steel Company*. In *West Coast Hotel* v. *Parrish* the Court reversed its Tipaldo decision and upheld a Washington minimum-wage law. In August 1937 it approved the Social Security Act. The change in the direction of the Court's decisions has led many historians to say that FDR lost the battle for his judiciary proposal but that he won the war for a more sympathetic Supreme Court. This is a valid interpretation, but it should also be pointed out that the battle decimated his army in Congress and that the army never again won a major legislative campaign. Congress enacted very few reform measures after the Supreme Court uproar. The only important one, the Fair Labor Standards Act, twice needed a discharge petition to get out of the House Rules Committee.

Divisions within Congress on matters of foreign policy were by no means along party lines nor along the same lines that divided progressives from conservatives on domestic issues, and the same was true of the country at large. The terms "isolationist" and "interventionist," while by no means descriptive, as we shall see in greater detail in the last chapter, were used to label the two main tendencies. Some isolationists supported FDR on domestic issues; some did not. Some interventionists opposed him on domestic affairs; some did not. In order to gain support on foreign policy questions, FDR sometimes had to bargain and compromise on domestic issues. Foreign policy questions thus blurred the New Deal coalition and led to dissensions within it.

The Democratic party, having within it a greater number of Catholic voters and a greater number who called themselves liberals than the Republican party, was particularly vulnerable to division upon what policy to follow in connection with the Spanish Civil War. The Catholic Church hierarchy generally supported Franco, and the liberals generally supported the Loyalists. Roosevelt, while personally greatly concerned about the strengthening of European fascism by the Spanish war, nevertheless made a decision that in effect aided Franco. The neutrality law in effect when the war began in July 1936 had nothing to say about civil wars, and it thus would have been possible for the United States to have extended aid to the Loyalist Spanish government. Instead, Roosevelt withheld aid, and in January 1937 got Congress specifically to include civil wars under the neutrality legislation. Inasmuch as Germany and Italy were giving Franco massive assistance, the American hands-off position played into Franco's hands.

FDR's positions on foreign policy in late 1937 and early 1938 caused further trouble within his party. In an October 1937 speech at Chicago he rather vaguely supported the idea of a "quarantine" against aggressor nations. Whatever the President had in mind, the idea was far from popular in either party. The sinking of the naval gunboat *Panay* by Japanese aircraft on December 12, 1937, while the *Panay* was convoying Standard Oil tankers in the Yangtze River, caused a reaction against Roosevelt's sanctioning of such duty for American naval vessels rather than a demand for action against Japan. (Japan apologized profusely and made financial restitution.) The most serious battle within the New Deal coalition came on an amendment to the Constitution proposed by Democratic Congressman Louis Ludlow of Indiana. The Ludlow amendment would have required a national referendum before a declaration of war, except in the case of invasion. Roosevelt used great pressure to prevent the amendment's passage, and in January 1938 the House defeated the resolution. But the margin of defeat was only twenty-one votes.

Complicating the entire political picture was the dreary fact of economic recession. If the New Deal was a failure at recovery it had little to commend itself to the voters, and the economic situation was bad indeed in 1938. From 1933 to 1937 the economy had significantly improved. By the latter year, the physical volume of industrial production was up to slightly higher than even 1929, and wholesale prices of non-farm products were about what they had been in 1930. Unemployment had declined but by no means as much as was desirable. The Bureau of Labor Statistics estimated unemployment in 1937 at 7,273,000 out of a total labor force of 52,849,000; this was an improvement over the 12,634,-000 out of 50,403,000 of 1933, but it was still an unemployment rate of 14 per cent. Farm prices had improved until they were almost up to 1930 levels.

In view of this improvement, economic traditionalists called for a return to more conventional fiscal policies. Secretary of the Treasury Henry Morgenthau was a particularly influential advocate of balancing the budget. In fiscal 1936 (mid-1935 to mid-1936) the federal deficit was $4.3 billion. This fell to $2.7 billion for fiscal 1937 and down further to only $740 million for fiscal 1938, which was almost a balanced budget. Roosevelt had always been uneasy about the growing national debt and in his January

1937 budget message had called for a large reduction in federal spending. The cutbacks were effected mostly in smaller WPA payrolls and reduced farm subsidies.

Rather than stimulating business, as traditional economists had predicted, the budget cuts brought on a rather serious recession, beginning in the last quarter of 1937. The physical volume of industrial production fell almost to the level of 1934. Farm prices declined 15 to 20 per cent. Most alarming was the increase in unemployment, 2,637,000 more in 1938 than in 1937, up to 18.7 per cent of the civilian labor force. In 1933 unemployment had averaged 12,634,000 according to BLS estimates, and in 1938 it was 9,910,000, an improvement of only 21.5 per cent. Although federal relief was far more effective than it had been under Hoover, the fact remained that five years of New Deal had not brought about economic recovery. This was a political embarrassment of major proportions for the administration.

For the first few months after the advent of the new depression the President seemed puzzled about what way to turn. Some of his advisers, notably Morgenthau, argued for continued lower spending levels, saying that such policies were necessary for the business community to have faith in the economy's future. Keynesian economists urged a massive resumption of federal spending and a loosening of credit. Some people saw the difficulty as a "strike of capital," a refusal of businessmen for political reasons to undertake new investments. These people urged FDR to embark upon an antitrust program. Roosevelt failed to make significant economic moves until April 1938. He then urged Congress to increase spending for relief and agriculture and set a major antitrust program going in the Department of Justice. The new head of the Antitrust Division of the Department, Thurmond Arnold of the Yale Law School, prosecuted vigorously. In June Congress established the Temporary National Economic Committee, which undertook a vast investigation of the extent of monopoly and the methods used to limit competition.

The year 1939 saw an economic upturn. Physical volume of industrial production rose almost to 1929 levels and unemployment declined by 17.7 per cent. Roosevelt was partly out of the political woods so far as domestic affairs were concerned, although he was more deeply in them in foreign affairs. But until the economy began to improve he was in serious political difficulty, the most serious of his more than twelve years in the White House.

Annoyed by the refusal of the most conservative Democratic

members of Congress to go along with White House suggestions, Roosevelt in June 1938 announced in one of his radio fireside chats what the newspapers promptly called a "purge" in the Democratic congressional primaries. It was highly unusual for a President to go into a senator's state or a congressman's district and campaign in a primary, but this was precisely what FDR did in certain areas in the summer and fall of 1938. The decision was an abrupt reversal of Roosevelt's usual political acumen. The shrewdest politician of the era made one of the greatest political errors of judgment.

In the first place, FDR backed losers in all but two of the primaries where he publicly expressed a preference. Of all the figures he had marked for defeat, only John O'Connor, a representative from New York City, and A. B. "Happy" Chandler of Kentucky, who opposed Senator Alben W. Barkley, actually lost. Roosevelt's choice against Senator Walter F. George of Georgia never had a chance of winning and came in a poor third on primary day. The very conservative Senator Millard Tydings of Maryland (the same one whom Senator Joseph R. McCarthy would later accuse of being a Communist sympathizer) may have won only because of FDR's opposition, and some argued that Senator Ellison D. "Cotton Ed" Smith of South Carolina would have lost if it had not been for Roosevelt's earmarking him for defeat. But, secondly, even in the two cases Roosevelt won he left a bad taste within his own party; those upon whom he had declared open war were not hesitant to reciprocate. Thirdly, other Democratic senators and congressmen, seeing their colleagues survive Rooseveltian opposition and even benefit from it, could more easily be persuaded to oppose the President's wishes in their voting and committee work.

Because of division within Democratic ranks and other factors —largely the 1938 recession—Republicans in the 1938 elections reversed the fortunes that had worked against them ever since the 1930 elections. They gained eighty seats in the House and eight in the Senate and won several governorships. Ever since the 1938 elections Congress has for all practical purposes been under the control of a coalition of conservatives in both major parties. Most Republicans vote with this coalition, and enough Democrats, especially those from the South, so that the conservative coalition has never again permitted a burst of progressive legislation such as Congress enacted in 1935. The conservative coalition's strength derives not only from numbers but also from the seniority system, which gives committee chairmanships to members with long tenure. Most Democratic senators and representatives with long tenure are from Dixie, and many southern members of Congress are fully as conservative as their Republican colleagues.

Thus the elections of 1938 signaled the death of the New Deal. Closer scrutiny reveals, however, that it was almost dead so far as significant legislation was concerned for the previous two years. The most important reform measure after the 1936 elections was the Fair Labor Standards Act of 1938. The law exempted domestic workers, agricultural labor, and sailors from its provisions, but for all other employees engaged in interstate commerce it set a minimum wage of 25 cents an hour and a maximum work week of forty-four hours. The law provided for gradual increase of the minimum wage to 40 cents an hour in 1945 and a forty-hour work week in 1940. Since the original legislation's passage, the law has been amended a few times to raise the minimum wage. This was not the New Deal's first wage-hours legislation. The Walsh-Healy Act of 1936 had set wage-hours standards for employers who had government contracts. Of lesser stature as reform legislation was the National Housing Act of 1937, which provided for the continuation of public housing and slum clearance undertaken by PWA. Congress not only failed in 1937 and 1938 to continue reform, it decisively rejected some reform proposals. Senator Wagner's national health bill of 1938 never got off the ground. The anti-lynching bill that Wagner co-sponsored with Frederick Van Nuys of Indiana, which would have allowed the families of lynching victims to sue the county in which the crime had been committed, fell before a southern threat of filibuster. FDR never offered the measure any support.

The New Deal, then, was dead, gone, but not forgotten, roughly five years after it began. Roosevelt was a New Deal president for less than half of his years in office. Roosevelt himself seemed to announce the passing of the New Deal in his message to Congress of January 4, 1939: "We have now passed the period of internal conflict in the launching of our program of social reform. Our full energies may now be released to invigorate the processes of recovery in order to preserve our reforms."

What generalizations can one make about the New Deal, about Roosevelt, his advisers in the executive branch, and the New Dealers in Congress? Quite clearly, the New Deal was no grand plan of one man or even any group of men. It was the result of the interplay of political and economic forces, often inconsistent, always sporadic and uneven in development as political balances changed and as the basic conditions altered. Roosevelt was the central figure, to be sure, but he always had to reckon with the power of men on Capitol Hill, who in turn, as did FDR, had to reckon with the power of their constituents' opinions.

The New Deal's effects are perhaps more important than its methods or the motives of the men who made it. Economically, if the New Deal did not "save" capitalism, it certainly restored it, revived it, and fortified it. Capitalism in America was stronger in late 1938 or early 1939, when the New Deal died, than it had been in 1933, when Roosevelt took the oath of office. Yet, obviously, the New Deal did not bring the economy back to normal. In June 1940, after the fall of France and the Lowlands, during the battles between the RAF and the Luftwaffe in the skies over England, there were still 5,900,000 unemployed workers in the United States out of a total labor force of 55,700,000, an unemployment rate of 10.6 per cent. It was the war, not the New Deal, that returned prosperity to America, although certainly the New Deal ameliorated economic conditions. The New Deal modified American capitalism—the economy had a closer relationship to federal economic policy than it had previously, and federal law had smoothed the way for the growth of strong labor unions (to be considered in greater detail in the next chapter), which inhibited the policy decisions of capital and management. But, one should remember, the New Deal nationalized no industries nor did it enlarge the government's role in the economy to anything approaching the role of government in democratic and capitalistic nations elsewhere in the world. Indeed, seen from the perspective of Great Britain, Scandinavia, Australia, France, or Mexico, the New Deal's reforms were mild and cautious. In terms of government-provided services and security guarantees for its citizens, the United States, even after the New Deal, was one of the most backward—or most forward if one wishes to apply Herbert Spencer-Robert A. Taft-Barry Goldwater standards—of the industrial nations of the world.

The experiences of 1933-1938 greatly altered the facts of political life in the United States. Majority political strength shifted from the Republican to the Democratic party. In 1929 there were more voters registered as Republicans than as Democrats; ten years later the situation was the reverse. But, aside from numbers, the Roosevelt years altered each of the parties. The nature of the Democratic coalition changed as the giant cities shifted more heavily into the Roosevelt camp and as organized labor and the Negro voter enlisted under its banner. Also, liberal intellectuals flocked to the Democratic party in the 1930's as never before.

The Democratic party changed considerably in the ten years following 1929; the party of Al Smith bore less resemblance to the party of FDR, Robert Wagner, and Felix Frankfurter than it had to the party of Woodrow Wilson and Colonel House. The Republican party changed too. Although many, perhaps most, of its leaders even a generation after the New Deal still preferred Hoover's view of the proper role of the federal government to Roosevelt's, they seldom dared to say so when they had to face a national election. From 1936 forward, GOP presidential candidates usually adopted a "me-too" stance in their campaigns because the party leaders believed, probably correctly, that an avowed conservative "can't win."

Perhaps it was popular ideology that the New Deal and its background of economic depression changed more than anything else. Except for issues of foreign policy, a person who died in 1938 would feel at home in political arguments if he could return in the 1960's. Thirty years after the New Deal people were still discussing balanced federal budgets versus deficit financing, "government interference" versus "the rights of labor." Thirty years, even ten or five years, before FDR's inauguration, most such issues and rhetoric would have had a strange ring indeed. For better or for worse, the New Deal period posed the basic questions and provided the usual answers for years to come.

8

The Moods of the Depression

FROM ABOUT 1931 UNTIL PEARL HARBOR there were more Americans with attitudes of protest and rebellion against the status quo—against things as they were—than at any time since the depression of 1893. For more people than ever before in the twentieth century, the conditions of life and the prospects of better conditions in the near future were such that dissatisfaction was natural. This is not to say that the nation was teeming with revolutionists nor that those who yearned for change wanted a thorough and fundamental revision of American society. Indeed, in view of the hardships that millions suffered, especially in the early depression, one of the wonders of the period is that there was not more widespread revolutionary sentiment than there actually was. But it is to say that dissatisfaction was general, even if often passive.

Rather than in revolutionary ideas or in new or alien philosophies, most of the basic unrest found its expression in a reaffirmation and strengthening of the ideal of Jacksonian democracy. The nation's difficulties, most people believed, had come about because of political, economic, and social privilege. The cure for the difficulties lay in an extension of democracy, in equality of opportunity and an increase in the power of ordinary citizens to make society's basic decisions. The popular heroes of the era, to use the era's clichés, were the "little people," "the common man," "the man in the street." The villains were the privileged who had failed in the previous decade to create a permanently viable and wholesome society: the presidents of stock exchanges, prominent bankers and business leaders, pompous politicans. Roosevelt struck a popular chord with his 1932 glorification of "the forgotten man" and his 1936 condemnation of "economic royalists."

There was nothing new in this popular mood. It was an old and honorable faith. Alexis de Tocqueville had reported its prevalence and written penetratingly about it in the 1830's. Nor had the faith disappeared and then revived in the depression decade. It only became more militant, more widely held, and more firmly believed. If some expressions of the faith seem to a later generation to be a little mystic, slightly fuzzy, and naive, the later generation would do well to remember the record of societies that have belittled the "common man" and glorified the few.

Related to the mood of protest and of militant egalitarian democracy was a rather strong strain of democratic nationalism with, especially in literature and art, a dash of regionalism. This nationalism was by no means chauvinistic; in fact, it was generally opposed to war and military swashbuckling. Americans increasingly took pride in being a "nation of nations," a heterogeneous mixture of people of various ethnic backgrounds. Writers and artists—and their readers and viewers—tended to focus upon what was unique or at least unusual about America or its regions. The nation became increasingly conscious of its own culture, traditions, and customs. Orchestras of the WPA performed concerts of American music; college and university departments of English offered more and more courses in American literature; in New York City the Whitney Museum came into existence to exhibit only American art. There was nothing new about this strain of "I sing America" either; cultural nationalism within an egalitarian and democratic framework was at least as old as Mark Twain and Walt Whitman.

Historical generalizations always have exceptions, and the ones offered here may have historical evidence cited against them. Not by any means were all Americans militantly democratic and egalitarian in the 1930's nor even sympathetic to militant movements. In no period of American history has there been unanimity about political, economic, social, and cultural matters. If there has been a general consensus on some matters, it does not follow that there have not been basic and important differences. Although most voters in the 1930's responded to militantly democratic rhetoric, others were still attracted by the appeals of those who had built the "new era" of the 1920's and even by those who looked yearningly back to the old order before that. Although most citizens during the depression approved of the inhibitions placed by government and labor unions upon the power of corporation officials to make decisions concerning the conduct of their business, there were still some who clung to the slogans of the era of Herbert Spencer. Although such writers of protest novels as John Steinbeck and John Dos Passos received popular and critical acclaim, Kenneth Roberts' *Oliver Wiswell*, which praised the Tories of the American Revolution, was a best seller in 1940.

And although the 1930's were grim and earnest and its keynotes were unrest and protest, one would be wrong to assume that people at all times were serious and heavy-hearted. The decade, sandwiched in as it was between two eras of widespread complacency and sometimes wonderful nonsense, presents a contrast in popular moods, to be sure. But the 1930's saw a certain amount of gay nonsense too. Miniature golf, then commonly called "goofy golf," was a rage in 1931 and 1932, largely because only a minimum of capital was necessary to build one of the courses on a vacant lot. The country continued, as usual, to make silly tunes popular for a few weeks, such as "The Music Goes 'Round and 'Round" in very early 1934. The tradition of campus horseplay stayed alive with the highly publicized goldfish swallowing fad of the late 1930's. Times were hard and people suffered, but people were as wondrously complex and ambivalent then as they are now.

The Labor Movement

One of the most important and permanent results of the mood of democratic egalitarianism of the 1930's was the great growth in the size and power of the labor movement. Weakened during the 1920's, labor unions slipped even farther with the onset of the depression. As employment declined, union membership declined. At the low point in early 1933, there were slightly less than three million members in the nation's unions, both affiliated with the AFL and unaffiliated. What unionism there was existed mainly among skilled workers and outside the basic industries; the United Mine Workers of America was the only fairly strong union in a basic industry. In the steel mills of Pittsburgh and the Chicago area, unionism hardly existed. Auto workers were unorganized. In these industries and most others, corporation officials had almost complete power to make policy concerning the conditions of labor without consultation. Who could be hired or fired, the hours of work, conditions in the plant, wage rates—all were determined by management on a take-it-or-leave-it basis. In national politics labor unions were all but impotent. So weak were they that Roosevelt in 1932 felt no need to make any commitment to organized labor whatsoever.

By Pearl Harbor there had been many changes. Total union membership had grown to about 10,500,000. For the first time in American history, most of the workers in basic industry, skilled or unskilled, were members of unions. In most industries hiring and firing policies, wages, hours, and other working conditions were determined by a labor contract rather than by a corporation official. The labor contract, often a long, complicated, and comprehensive legal document, was the result of bargaining sessions between management and the union. (Collective bargaining, the usual term, means only that the union represents the employees collectively, as opposed to the concept of each employee bargaining with management individually.) By the time the United States entered World War II, organized labor was a political force to be reckoned with. The "labor vote" was not as concrete nor as vulnerable to manipulation as some political and union figures sometimes assumed it was, but no longer could candidates afford to ignore it or national office holders fail to consult union leaders. "Big labor" had come into being as a countervailing power to "big business," as had, to a lesser extent, "big government."

Union strength began to grow while Section 7(a) of the National Industrial Recovery Act was in force. Total union membership increased to about 3,600,000 in 1934 and 3,890,000 in 1935. This was less of an advance than militant and optimistic unionists had expected and hoped for because of, as we have seen in the previous chapter, the growth of company unions and the Roosevelt administration's acceptance of the idea of more than one labor bargaining agent. But another reason for the relatively modest growth was the reluctance of the leaders of most of the craft unions to go out and actively unionize the unorganized.

An explanation of the primary difference between craft and industrial unions is necessary. In a craft union eligibility for membership is determined by a worker's craft or skill, and in industries organized by craft there are many unions for the various functions or crafts. Thus, in the building industry there are separate unions for carpenters, masons, electricians, painters, and so forth. In industrial unions the only condition for membership is employment in the industry and there is but one union for all kinds of workers. Thus, in the automobile industry all production employees, whether they are welders or machinists or relatively unskilled assembly-line workers, belong to the United Auto Workers. From the standpoint of union effectiveness, there are advantages for each kind of union, depending upon the nature of the industry, the status of technology, and the traditions of labor. But, as became evident in the 1930's, craft unionism was not an effective device for organizing workers of basic industries, most of whom had no crafts in the usual sense and only a relatively small degree of industrial skill.

Craft unionists, who dominated the American Federation of Labor, resisted the spread of the principle of industrial unionism to the bitter end. Industrial unionists demonstrated during the NRA that their approach to organization got better results, but they failed to persuade the AFL traditionalists. Craft unions under the NRA increased their membership 13 per cent; there were not many industrial unions then, but those that existed grew 132 per cent. The United Mine Workers (UMW) became over eight times as large, and the International Ladies' Garment Workers Union (ILGWU) increased to four times its pre-NRA membership.

The leader of the industrial unionists within the AFL was UMW President John L. Lewis, a remarkable man by any standards. Lewis was the son of a Welsh-born blacklisted Iowa miner and had gone to work in the pits himself at the age of twelve. He married a teacher and learned from her what he had missed by leaving school. Intelligent, strong, articulate, ruthless, and vastly ambitious, Lewis developed rapidly and advanced in importance in his union. He became its president in 1919 at the age of thirty-nine.

Thousands of workers in basic industries in 1933 and 1934 began to organize themselves into local unions. The AFL granted these new organizations "federal charters," a loose affiliation with the Federation rather than full membership with voting rights on the AFL Executive Council. Craft-union leaders of the AFL intended to augment the membership of the already existent AFL unions by incorporating, according to craft, the members of the federal locals. Industrial unionists, on the other hand, proposed that federal locals be made the nuclei for new industrially organized unions for basic industry. Membership in federal locals increased from 10,396 in 1933 to 111,489 in 1935. At the 1934 AFL convention at San Francisco, Lewis succeeded in getting a half-hearted promise to launch an organizing drive in the steel industry, which he wanted desperately to protect the UMW's position in the closely related coal industry, and to issue provisional charters to industrial unions in autos, aluminum, and cement. The AFL, however, did not come through on its promise, and Lewis was ready for fireworks at the 1935 convention at Atlantic City.

Lewis appeared at the Atlantic City convention armed with a long bill of particulars against the AFL leaders and their failure to carry through their commitments. He introduced a resolution from the convention floor that called upon the delegates to condemn the Executive Council. During the roll call, which Lewis lost by a two-to-one vote, an incident occurred which indicated how serious bad feelings had become. The UMW delegates were seated near the delegates from the carpenters' union, and the carpenters' president, the reactionary William L. Hutcheson, a member of the Liberty League, called Lewis an unprintable name. Lewis and Hutcheson, both huge men, squared off for a brief fist-fight.

The next month, November 1935, Lewis met with representatives of seven other industrial unions within the AFL, most of which were then quite small, and the meeting formed the Committee for Industrial Organization (CIO). They did not then regard themselves as separatists from the AFL, the "house of labor," but they were soon to become separate. President William Green of the AFL declared that the CIO threatened dual unionism, but the CIO in January 1936 appealed to the AFL Executive Council to issue charters for industrial unions in steel, autos, radio, and rubber. Instead of issuing the charters, the AFL ordered the CIO to disband. Ignoring the order, the CIO appropriated $500,000 to organize the steel industry—the funds were provided by the UMW—and set about organizing other basic and mass production industries as well. Labor's civil war was in full battle. In August 1936 the AFL Executive Council suspended the CIO unions from AFL membership, and the convention confirmed its action in the fall. The next year the AFL expelled the CIO unions altogether, whereupon the CIO changed its name to Congress of Industrial Organizations, keeping its old initials. By that time the CIO was very much a going institution. For the next several years competition between the CIO and the AFL was intense. In general, the AFL unions won out in industries in which they already had a toe-hold and CIO unions won in mass-production industries in which there had been little or no prior unionism.

Sporadically there were attempts to restore peace within the labor movement and to merge the AFL and the CIO. Roosevelt personally urged reunification. But emotions and rivalries were too strong to call off labor's civil war. Not until 1955, after the deaths of several of the participants in the events of the 1930's, did the two groups finally get together. In that year they merged their organizations into the present AFL-CIO.

The CIO's plan was first to organize steel before moving on to other basic industries. Early in 1936 Lewis and his lieutenant of several years in the UMW, Philip Murray, reached an agreement with the small and ineffective Amalgamated Iron and Steel Workers which granted the recently organized Steel Workers Organizing Committee (SWOC) jurisdiction in the industry. Murray became head of SWOC. Organizers of SWOC, the best available to the CIO, started to work within the company unions of the industry, most of which had been started under the NRA to head off genuine unionism. Dissatisfaction was widespread in the company unions, and membership in SWOC moved forward steadily. But it was in the auto industry that the CIO had its first great success. The auto workers refused to wait for the organization of steel and took matters into their own hands.

The United Auto Workers (UAW) was a relatively new union and quite weak in the fall of 1936. It had no contracts and only 30,000 members. But auto workers were determined to organize themselves into an effective union, and freed at last from the restraining hands of the AFL craft unions, UAW grew with spectacular speed. Unauthorized, relatively unplanned "quickie" strikes broke out in auto and related industries in December 1936. Workers in the Fisher Body Company plant at Cleveland began a "sit-down" strike, in which they merely sat down in the plant, declared they were on strike, and refused to leave. The idea spread to auto workers in Flint, Michigan. Seeing for the first time a spirit of remarkable militance among the auto workers, the UAW in January 1937 asked General Motors for a conference. General Motors refused, saying that the UAW must consult the superintendents of all its many plants and those of its subsidiaries. The UAW called a concerted sit-down against GM, much to management's surprise.

The great advantage of the sit-down as a tactic was that it made it more difficult for management to bring in strikebreakers. Management was also presented with the problem of possible damage to the plant and machinery if it tried to expel the strikers with police and company guards. In the GM sit-down, management made just one real effort to run the strikers out, but the police withdrew when the strikers began throwing bolts and nuts. The great disadvantage was that sit-downs were of dubious legality because of the laws of trespass, and several state legislatures quickly outlawed them in no uncertain terms. Democratic Governor Frank Murphy of Michigan helped to bring about an agreement between the UAW and GM. The UAW received exclusive bargaining rights in twenty GM plants and the right to represent its own members in forty others. GM agreed to rehire all the strikers and to stop legal proceedings against them. The UAW then struck against Chrysler, and that corporation signed agreements in April 1937.

Part of General Motors' and Chrysler's reasoning in surrendering to the UAW was that the market for cars looked good—the recession did not come until the last quarter of 1937—and management wanted to be in a position to produce without labor interruptions. But Henry Ford did not see it that way, and the difference between GM and Chrysler management on the one hand and Ford on the other revealed a difference in point of view that was rather general in American industry. Chrysler and GM were huge corporations with widely distributed stock ownership. Their executives were professional administrators whose function was to build and sell automobiles, not to establish nor defend ideological positions. Furthermore, these executives were employees themselves, although they owned considerable stock in their companies, and they were relatively anonymous compared with Ford executives. The Ford Motor Company, however, was then almost completely a family enterprise. One could not purchase Ford Motor Company stock on the open market. Henry Ford, a man of strong convictions, refused on ideological grounds to deal with the UAW and the ensuing struggle was long and bloody.

Ford used the so-called Ford Service Organization, headed by an ex-boxer named Harry Bennett, as his primary antiunion weapon. Bennett resorted to strong-arm methods on many occasions, established an effective espionage system within Ford plants to ferret out union sympathizers, and used the blacklist. Ford also controlled the municipal government of Dearborn, Michigan, the site of the main Ford plant. When in May 1937 UAW leaders Walter Reuther and Richard Frankensteen, to make a test case of a Dearborn ordinance against distributing handbills, began to hand out leaflets to Ford employees, company thugs attacked them in full view of the local police and beat them badly. Ford's violence at Memphis and Dallas was even greater. But the Wagner Act's National Labor Relations Board consistently found the Ford Company guilty of unfair labor practices, and after a UAW strike in 1941 even Ford capitulated. In five years the UAW had grown from almost nothing to one of the biggest unions in the nation; the auto industry, one of the most firmly open-shop concerns of the country's mass-production industries, had become thoroughly organized. The UAW then moved into the rapidly expanding airplane industry. By the end of World War II the UAW had approximately one million members.

Just after GM signed with the UAW in early 1937 United States Steel signed with SWOC. Within only a few days, two of the nation's biggest manufacturing corporations had agreed to unionization. United States Steel, in March, signed a contract with SWOC that granted the eight-hour day and forty-hour week, a 10 per cent wage increase, seniority rights, and vacations with pay. SWOC had thoroughly organized U. S. Steel's production units and won the contract even without a strike; conversations between Lewis and Myron Taylor, the company's chairman, resulted in the contract. Some of the other steel companies followed "Big Steel's" example.

But four of the "Little Steel" companies, Republic, Bethlehem, Inland, and Youngstown Sheet and Tube, refused to recognize SWOC and bargain with it. Tom Girdler of Republic Steel was the primary "Little Steel" opponent of unionism. SWOC went on strike in May, a conventional strike rather than a sit-down. Inland agreed to a union contract, but the other three companies fought on in the traditional violent manner and with professional strikebreaking companies. At a Memorial Day demonstration near the Republic plant in South Chicago, local police attacked the pickets, killed ten of them, and wounded many others. A newsreel photographer recorded the police action, and when the film appeared in the nation's theaters public opinion swung to SWOC's side. Yet the three "Little Steel" firms held out against the union until 1941, when again the prospects of good profits made it seem advisable for management to seek labor peace and when "Little Steel" had little further recourse in the courts to appeal NLRB decisions. By Pearl Harbor, SWOC had 600,000 members working under labor contracts. SWOC later reorganized as the United Steelworkers of America.

Autos and steel were the scenes of the CIO's greatest success, but the United Rubber Workers successfully organized most of the nation's tire manufacturing plants and the Mine, Mill, and Smelter Workers Union had contracts in most of the nonferrous metals installations in the West as well as some strength in the brass industry of Connecticut. The needle trades unions, the Amalgamated Clothing Workers and the ILGWU, underwrote the expenses of an organizing campaign in the textile industry. In northern plants the Textile Workers Organizing Committee enjoyed fair success, but it encountered great difficulty in the South.

One generalization about the growth of unionism in the late 1930's that even a brief review of the history makes clear: organized labor achieved what it did because of its own efforts; its successes did not come on a silver platter as a gift from the Roosevelt administration. The administration was friendly, to be sure, and NLRB decisions were a positive aid to union growth. But, it will be remembered, the Wagner Act that created the NLRB was not an administrative measure.

The Negro in the New Deal Era

The depression decade's mood of democratic equality also served to give the Negro a boost in his long struggle for equality and against discrimination. The Negro's gains during the period between 1929 and Pearl Harbor were nowhere near as great as the labor movement's, but he nevertheless advanced and, perhaps more important, laid the foundation for further advance after World War II.

The depression's economic effects on Negroes were harder than they were on any other group because the Negro went into the depression the least well prepared, both in terms of job skills and in savings, to weather the hard times. Undoubtedly the hardest hit of all was the southern Negro sharecropper. Already in bad shape because of boll weevil ravages and low cotton prices during the 1920's, Negro sharecroppers—indeed, sharecroppers in general—were reduced to a starvation level by the further drop in farm prices. Often the money that sharecroppers received for their cotton crop was insufficient to pay the bill they had run up at the local store for "furnish." Cotton-farming conditions improved somewhat with the AAA, but often landlords used their government checks to buy tractors and stopped the sharecropping system. Then there was nothing for the Negro sharecropper to do but move into an urban slum, from which he frequently commuted to the cotton fields as a day laborer during the picking season. Private charitable institutions and county relief programs in the poor southern areas either did not exist at all or were dreadfully inadequate for the tasks they faced.

The urban Negro's lot, whether in the North or South, was not much better. Negroes were, as they said, "the last to be hired and the first to be fired" when the business cycle fluctuated. Many colored workers in domestic and personal service had to take wage cuts when their white employers, who likewise suffered from the hard times, were unable to maintain the old level. Cities, however, did have relief systems, although few had good ones and none could do better than keep a relief family at the subsistence level. In October 1933, between one fourth and two fifths of all Negroes in several cities were on relief, a much higher proportion than in the white population. Some cities, most of them southern, openly discriminated against Negro families in extending relief, and others as a matter of routine policy made smaller monthly relief payments to Negroes than to whites.

One effect of the depression was vastly to slow down the rate of Negro migration from the South to the North and West. Between 1930 and 1940 the net migration of Negroes out of the southern states was only about 317,000, roughly half what it had been in the previous decade and much less than it would be in the 1940's and 1950's. (Although total migration was less, Negro migration to the West Coast increased. California's Negro population grew by slightly more than one half during the 1930's.) With employment opportunities few and far between in the industrial cities of the North, southern Negroes who were getting by were hesitant to run the risk of moving north; those who were destitute in the South did not have the funds to travel.

The evidence is scanty, but it was the subjective impression of most people that the 1930's saw an increase in the number of whites outside the South who were opposed to discrimination against the Negro. There was a slow change in white attitudes towards Negroes. In the very early 1930's one of the most popular radio programs, a late-afternoon comedy show, was "Amos 'n Andy." Amos and Andy were stock Negro comic characters, more stereotypes than characterizations, that made the Negro appear to be a silly, ineffectual, happy dolt. By the end of the depression this stock comic caricature had by no means disappeared from plays, movies, and radio, but it was far less common and popular than it had been a few years earlier. The popularity of Richard Wright's novel *Native Son* in 1940 was an indication of a changing attitude toward Negroes among whites. A Book-of-the-Month-Club selection, *Native Son* told the story of a Negro youth of Chicago brutalized by slum life. If the evidence of changing attitudes is scanty, there is an abundance of evidence to indicate that whites were sympathetic to Negroes involved in certain outrageous incidents. When Jesse Owens, the great Negro sprinter and broad-jumper from Ohio State University, was first handicapped badly by Nazi track officials at the 1936 Olympic Games at Berlin and then snubbed by Hitler, who refused to give Owens his gold medals personally as he did to "Aryan" athletes, the outcry in the press was considerable. The Daughters of the American Revolution came in for a great deal of criticism in 1939 when they refused to rent their Washington auditorium, Constitution Hall, for a concert to be given by the Negro contralto Marian Anderson. Secretary of the Interior Harold Ickes, a former chairman of the Chicago chapter of the National Association for the Advancement of Colored People (NAACP), made the Lincoln Memorial available for the concert, and on Easter Sunday Miss Anderson sang for an audience of 75,000 people.

White CIO leaders pursued a more liberal policy toward Negroes than had most trade unionists up until then. Historically, there was widespread distrust between unions and Negroes. The Negroes complained with justification that unions in the skilled trades were just another device to keep a white monopoly, and unionists pointed out that during strikes in the North Negroes had often cooperated with management and served as strikebreakers. When Negroes were in trade unions, they almost always were required to stay in segregated locals.

The CIO's leaders recognized that their bargaining position vis-à-vis management would be stronger if they represented all the workers in a plant, not just the white ones. CIO unions also refused to segregate their locals or to accept contracts with different wage rates for Negroes and whites. (The Textile Workers Organizing Committee made an exception to the policy against segregated locals in its drive to organize the South.) Negro workers at first were skeptical about the CIO. The many Negroes in the steel mills were hesitant to sign up with SWOC because they did not believe that SWOC would live up to its promises. But Negro organizations, such as the Urban League, urged them to trust the CIO promises, and most Negro steelworkers joined. In Detroit there was some opposition to full acceptance of Negroes in the UAW by the whites. Many of the auto workers were from southern backgrounds. The UAW leadership, however, insisted upon full Negro participation, and this view carried the day.

Negro-white relations in Detroit remained tense nevertheless, and during the war the auto city was the scene of the nation's worst race riot since 1919.

But however much the Negro benefited from changing attitudes and policies of their white fellow citizens, they themselves had to bear the main weight of the struggle for equality. To an increasing extent during the depression decade, Negroes, particularly in the North, demonstrated that they were militantly determined to achieve full, first-class citizenship.

The NAACP, predominantly Negro in membership and in its national leadership, entered a series of suits designed to gain Negroes the right to vote in southern primary elections and to attend public, tax-supported graduate and professional schools. In most southern states, the Democratic primary election rather than the general election in the fall was the one that actually counted. A Texas law specifically made Negroes as a race ineligible to vote in its Democratic primaries. The NAACP entered a test suit, and the Supreme Court of the United States declared the Texas law unconstitutional. Texas attempted to circumvent the Court's decision with a new law that granted the executive committee of the state's political parties the right to determine who was eligible to vote in the primaries. The Democratic state committee then excluded Negroes. Again the NAACP contested the law, and again the Supreme Court struck down the work of the Texas legislature. The Court took the position that the law made the party committee an agent of the state. Then the NAACP suffered a setback. The Texas state Democratic convention, without any action from the legislature, voted not to permit Negroes to vote in its primary. The Supreme Court in 1935 refused to accept the NAACP's contention that this action was contrary to the Fifteenth Amendment. But courts change their composition and justices change their minds. In 1944 the Court reversed itself and held that exclusion of Negroes as Negroes from primary elections was a clear violation of the Fifteenth Amendment.

The NAACP suits of the 1930's concerning Negro attendance in tax-supported graduate and professional schools led ultimately to the Supreme Court's famous school desegregation decision of May 17, 1954. When Negroes insisted upon going to a graduate school or professional school, many former slave states which had no tax-supported graduate or professional schools for Negroes had the practice of paying the students' tuitions to an institution outside the state. The only state tax-supported law school in Missouri was at the University of Missouri. In 1936, Lloyd Gaines, a

Negro, applied for admission to the University law school. He was refused. He took his case into the state courts and lost, but he appealed in the federal courts. In 1938, the Supreme Court of the United States upheld Gaines's contention that Missouri had to provide legal education within the state for all its citizens, white or black. Missouri thereupon created a segregated law school for Negroes, as did some other states. Some others merely hastily created inadequate law departments in the already existing Negro state colleges. Other states increased their appropriations for tuition in other states, hoping that no Negro would go to court but would accept the states' offer. Eventually, in 1950, the Supreme Court held that even state-supported legal schools that were segregated were not actually the academic equal of the regular state university law schools and that, not being equal, they did not meet the criterion of "separate but equal" laid down by the Court in its 1896 decision, *Plessy* vs. *Ferguson*. Not until the May 1954 decision did the Court overturn the Plessy precedent and rule that separation was inherently unequal.

Negroes also took matters into their own hands early in the depression concerning stores in overwhelmingly Negro neighborhoods, whose customers were almost altogether Negro, that refused to hire Negro clerks and other workers. St. Louis Negroes organized a boycott against a chain store that had a lily-white hiring policy. Other northern cities with large Negro populations soon had the same situation. Most merchants succumbed to the economic pressure, grudgingly to be sure, but well aware of where their economic interest lay. The greatest resistance, curiously, was in Harlem. Harlem Negroes got many of the jobs in their neighborhood that they felt should be theirs, but the situation remained tense. A riot broke out in March 1935, the Negroes complaining of continued hiring discrimination and brutality of white policemen. The administration of Mayor La Guardia assigned more Negro police to Harlem precincts.

Surely the case of Negro militance that won more economic improvement than any other in the depression decade was A. Philip Randolph's threatened march on Washington in 1941. During 1940 defense contracts at last began to end the persistent problem of unemployment. Jobs in defense industries generally paid better than other employment, and many workers left nondefense positions for the new openings. Negroes got many of the jobs that were left vacant, but they encountered discrimination in getting defense jobs. In the last days of 1940 President Roosevelt used the term "great arsenal of democracy" to describe the

American effort to supply beleaguered Britain with arms. The arsenal did not seem very democratic to Randolph, the president of the Brotherhood of Sleeping Car Porters. In January 1941, he proposed a march on Washington of fifty to one hundred thousand Negroes to demand federal action against discrimination in defense industries, the same tactic that Jacob S. Coxey had used with his "army" in 1894 and that the veterans had used in 1932. Negro response was favorable; preparations for the march began.

The White House was in an embarrassing position. To refuse to accede to the Negro demand would be good propaganda for Hitler; to accede might alienate the South. Roosevelt and several administration officials conferred with Randolph in a futile effort to get him to call off the march. Mayor La Guardia and Mrs. Roosevelt urged him to cancel the plan, arguing that it would cause reprisals against Negroes. Randolph was unmoved. Finally, only a week before the march was scheduled to begin on July 1, Roosevelt submitted to Randolph's demand and issued an executive order decreeing that "there shall be no discrimination in the employment of workers in defense industries or Government because of race, creed, color, or national origin." The order also created the Fair Employment Practices Committee to investigate complaints of discrimination. The FEPC was relatively powerless legally, but the unfavorable publicity the FEPC could give a company practicing discrimination was effective in most sections of the country.

Literature and Art

One of the primary evidences of a shift in the American mood, particularly among intellectuals, was the inability of the giants of American letters of the prosperity decade to come to terms with depression America. H. L. Mencken, Sinclair Lewis, Ernest Hemingway, Scott Fitzgerald, Eugene O'Neill—all seemed, in varying degrees, to be either wrong-headed or irrelevant in the days of the locust. Lionized in the 1920's, they were out of tune with the 1930's.

In the days when Calvin Coolidge lived in the White House it had been a refreshing thrill to read Mencken's and Lewis' barbs about the shallow, the complacent, the pompous, and the phony. Mencken and Lewis had written that the emperors of the decade had no clothes, and readers were excited by their revelations; but in the 1930's the newspaper headlines revealed the former emperors' nakedness every day, and Mencken and Lewis were old hat. Lewis at least made an effort to adjust to the new spirit. In 1935 he came forth with a novel against fascism, *It Can't Happen Here*, in which he portrayed a nightmare of a fascist America. The WPA Theater Project dramatized it and produced the play in several cities, and the reviewers were polite. But the book did not have the punch of *Main Street* or *Elmer Gantry*. Mencken, it seemed to most readers, had deserted to the Philistines he once had flayed so belligerently. His 1932 book on the Roosevelt election, *Making a President*, a paste-up of his news stories and editorials, fell deservedly flat. H. Allen Smith, later to be a popular writer of humor but then book editor for the United Press, wrote of it: "His publishers charge $1.50 for his new book. If you've got $1.50, get it changed into nickels and take 30 rides on a street car. You'll have more fun."

O'Neill's dramatic innovations and psychological torments seemed not very important to a society deeply concerned about its daily bread. Scott Fitzgerald went to Hollywood. Hemingway's themes of the 1920's no longer had their old appeal, although he was still honored as a literary craftsman and much imitated. His preoccupation with bull fighters, muscles, and sex no longer attracted the American reading public. Of his novels during the decade, only *For Whom the Bell Tolls* (1940), whose hero was an American college instructor fighting for the Spanish Loyalists, had a very popular response.

The major novelists most in tune with the mood of militant democratic egalitarianism were John Dos Passos, James T. Farrell, and John Steinbeck. Dos Passos, who had already attracted attention with *Manhattan Transfer*, wrote a major trilogy, *U.S.A.*, in the depression years that was in many respects a left-wing history of the United States from early in the twentieth century into the early depression. The first volume, *The 42nd Parallel*, appeared in 1930, *Nineteen Nineteen* in 1932, and *The Big Money* in 1936. Dos Passos employed unusual devices to put his fictional action into historical context. He included impressionistic profiles of actual figures from the past and with what he called "The Camera Eye" recreated historical newspaper stories. Some of his fictional images had an enormous emotional impact; his picture of "Vag," broken and without hope, trying to thumb a ride on the desert while a sleek, silvery airliner filled with wealthy and comfortable people droned overhead, was one that depression-affected readers were not likely to forget.

Farrell, like Dos Passos at that time a political radical, also produced a major proletarian triology. The Studs Lonigan books portrayed in a rather heavy-handed but powerful way the troubles and deterioration of a Chicago working class Irish-American family. Like his friend, sponsor, and idol, Theodore Dreiser, Farrell disliked the commercial quality of American life and made his morally decaying characters symbols of the greater decay, the greater tragedy, that he thought America had become. The contrast between Mr. Lonigan, a solid union man who worshiped Debs and worked hard as a teamster, and his aimless son Studs, a boozy, sensual, frustrated degenerate, was the difference between what had been the promise of America and what had become the reality.

Surely the most popular of the protest novelists was John Steinbeck. Steinbeck burst upon the public consciousness in 1939 with *The Grapes of Wrath,* one of the great American novels of the century. Hollywood turned the novel into an honest film and made it even more popular. Then readers went back to Steinbeck's earlier books, which were not as powerful, some of them bordering on the sentimental, but which shared with *The Grapes of Wrath* the trait of portraying the dispossessed and the defeated with compassion and understanding. Probably a major reason for Steinbeck's being more popular than Dos Passos and Farrell was that he was not ideological. He dealt sometimes with political and economic subjects, such as the Okies in *The Grapes of Wrath* and a strike of agricultural workers in *In Dubious Battle* (1936), and he sometimes put bitter political-economic comments into the mouths of his characters, yet his obvious concern for his characters as people rather than as social symbols lifted him above the purely ideological novelist.

The harmony of Dos Passos, Farrell, and Steinbeck with the dominant mood of the 1930's was revealed further by their subsequent careers. All of them continued to write actively during and after the war. Dos Passos reversed his ideological course, but the other two continued in largely the same vein they had worked in during the depression. But none of them after the war loomed as large in the national literary consciousness as they had in the Roosevelt years. Steinbeck won the Nobel Prize for Literature in 1962, it is true, but it seemed to most people that the judges had recognized him more for his prewar work than for what he had done later.

William Faulkner was one of the giants of the American novel in the 1930's—and later as well—who was difficult to classify. His first novel to attract attention was *As I Lay Dying* (1930). He followed it quickly with other complex and difficult books about his mythical (and yet realistic) Yoknapatawpha County, Mississippi—"Area, 2400 Square Miles; Population, Whites, 6,298, Negroes, 9,313; William Faulkner, Sole Owner and Proprietor." There was an element of social protest in the novels, more despairing than militant; at least he was critical of the commercialization and urbanization of the South. There was also a strong element of regionalism. But yet Faulkner was far more. One of the outstanding literary figures of the 1930's, he transcended his generation and his environment. His Nobel Prize in 1949 was more understandable to those who had never known the Great Depression or who had managed to forget it.

The "I sing America" theme or style had a great vogue in the literature of the 1930's. It was closely related to the general emphasis on the lives and problems of ordinary people, and much of it was expressed in a regional context. In some ways the most gifted of the depression decade's novelists, Thomas Wolfe, was in this tradition. Wolfe was a sensitive, intense physical and emotional giant from modest circumstances in Asheville, North Carolina. He graduated from the University of North Carolina, attended Harvard as a graduate student, and taught English at New York University before he devoted his prodigious energies entirely to writing. Romantic power ran through his novels: *Look Homeward, Angel* (1929), *Of Time and the River* (1935), *The Web and The Rock* (1939) and *You Can't Go Home Again* (1940). His words, hundreds of thousands of them, gushed forth in a strong flood that revealed a strange mixture of southern pride and alienation from the South. Uprooted and feeling not quite at home anywhere, a feeling commonly found among American intellectuals from provincial origins, Wolfe appeared torn between gratification that he had grown out of provincialism and regret that he could not "go home again." For all this writing power and articulateness, the giant North Carolinian never became a disciplined literary craftsman. He did not construct his novels; he just wrote them in huge bursts of energy. To his editor, Maxwell Perkins, fell the task of cutting and fitting together, discarding and rearranging, the great boxes of manuscript that Wolfe submitted. Wolfe might have developed literary discipline and become one of the world's major authors of the century. Unfortunately, he died in 1938 when only thirty-eight years old.

Easily the most exuberant writer in the Whitman-Wolfe tradition of the decade was a second-generation Armenian of rural California, William Saroyan. Primarily a writer of short stories, Saroyan was extraordinarily inventive and imaginative. His collection of stories, *The Daring Young Man on the Flying Trapeze*, made a great stir when it appeared in 1934. His *The Time of Your Life*, a wonderfully wild and noisy play, appeared on Broadway and won a Pulitzer prize in 1940. Although Saroyan was entertaining and often very funny, he appeared to be trying to do more than merely entertain. But anyone would have been hard-pressed to say just what it was that Saroyan was trying to express beyond a conviction of the importance of the dignity of individuals, especially of unimportant and lowly people such as the young man who played a pinball machine through all of *The Time of Your Life* or the intellectually backward small-town boy in one of his short stories who learned to play just one tune on a cornet.

Several of the more widely read poets of the 1930's focused on what was at least generally thought to be distinctively American by employing a regional approach. Robert Frost, who began first to be widely read during the depression decade and to appear in the school anthologies, dealt with universal themes in a rural New England setting. Edgar Lee Masters, who published *Poems of People* in 1936, did the same with Illinois settings. Carl Sandburg was more clearly in the social protest tradition with his *The People, Yes* in 1936, but he nevertheless continued to sing America. When he tried his hand, most successfully, at biography, it was natural that he choose the midwesterner Abraham Lincoln as his subject. His first two volumes, *Lincoln: The Prairie Years* appeared in 1929; the next four volumes, *The War Years*, appeared ten years later.

American art showed many of the same tendencies during the 1930's as literature. Realistic social-protest painting was plentiful, and there was a tremendous interest in the work of artists who concentrated on the distinctively American scene. The modernists —those who concentrated on artistic innovation, especially those who distorted superficial reality as not to be clearly representational—and the outright abstractionists faded badly from the public consciousness. It was a socially conscious age, and people wanted a socially conscious art. Modernists who wanted to concentrate altogether on working out the special technical problems of their medium had to await a decline in the popular mood of social urgency before they would again be restored to popular favor. (Their time came; in the late 1940's and the 1950's they so held the limelight that the realists were all but forgotten.)

Some of the social-protest artists were frankly political and propagandist in their work or in much of it. To them, artistic talent and imagination were weapons to be used for a social purpose.

This was an old and honorable tradition in the history of art; Goya, Hogarth, and Daumier all exemplified it. If the conception is worthy and the execution is excellent, a political or social painting can be great art. On the other hand, it always risks being no more than an angry, quickly dated, political caricature or cartoon, even if a strong and powerful one. William Gropper, who contributed many excellent drawings to leftist magazines, sometimes appeared to be more of a propagandist than an artist, not because of his purpose in painting but because he sometimes did not quite succeed. His "Legislative Paunch," one of the more widely reproduced paintings of this period, portrayed a group of grotesque legislators with death-like heads and obscenely bulging bellies. It packed a hard emotional punch, to be sure, and perhaps Gropper intended no more than that. But most people would place "Legislative Paunch" on a lower level of artistic achievement than Peter Blume's "Eternal City," which also was a savage indictment of a political figure. "Eternal City" was a condemnation of fascist Rome, done in an almost surrealistic style; the focal point of the picture, an extremely ugly likeness of Benito Mussolini done in a bright green, irresistibly attracted the viewer's eye.

A good deal of social protest appeared in the works of many "I sing America" painters where their subjects were the ordinary man and woman in the street who bore the brunt of the economic crisis. Their paintings often evoked the viewer's sympathy *for* the ordinary man, rather than, as with the more frankly political artists, passion *against* the forces or persons that oppressed him. They often painted more with compassion than with anger. This was certainly true of the so-called 14th Street School of New York (Morris Kantor and Raphael and Moses Soyer, for example), of Reginald Marsh, and of Edward Hopper. Kantor and the Soyers painted the common people and the scenes of downtown New York in the old Ash Can tradition—tired workers, poorly dressed shop girls, and the depressed and depressing neighborhoods where they lived. Most of their painting suggested weariness and poverty. Marsh, who selected similar subjects, was far gayer in his mood. He was enormously impressed with the vitality of city people. He filled his canvases with masses of people crowding the beach, rushing to the subway, shopping in a bustling street. To Marsh the crowds did not suggest fatigue but dynamism and animation, and he obviously loved the quality. He avoided the economically comfortable and successful, the chic women who shopped on Fifth Avenue. As he put it, "Well bred people are not fun to paint." One of his most famous works, "The Bowery," portrayed the inhabitants of that distinctly run-down neighborhood. Hopper's works evoked still a different mood: loneliness and anonymity. He was a master at light and shadow, which gave his paintings a feeling of harsh reality. His "Nighthawks," now at the Art Institute of Chicago, which shows a small group of people in the coldly glaring light of an all-night diner, is one of the masterpieces of American twentieth-century realism.

The so-called "regionalists," Thomas Hart Benton, John Steuart Curry, and Grant Wood, were perhaps the most widely reproduced and popular painters of the decade. All of them midwestern, they were in open rebellion against the tides of artistic taste of New York and Paris. They constituted a sort of artistic Populist revolt. They chose rural subjects, but urban people, yearning for the simpler, easier, less tense society they thought preindustrial America had been, were deeply interested in their work. The Missouri-born and bred Benton, a grandson of the eminent Senator Thomas Hart Benton of the Jacksonian era, was at his best as a muralist, and he often took his themes from nineteenth-century American history. Curry, a Kansan, glorified life on the Great Plains. Wood, from Cedar Rapids, Iowa, had an impish sense of humor. His "Daughters of the American Revolution" was a laugh-provoking satire, as was his "Parson Weems' Fable," which portrayed the young George Washington chopping down the cherry tree. Probably his best painting was "American Gothic," a harsh portrait of his sister and a friend with an Iowa farmhouse in the background, done in the style of early European primitives.

American primitive painters enjoyed a great vogue during the decade. If art had a special interest because it was about ordinary, unsung people, it was even more interesting when the painter himself was untrained, ordinary, and unsung. Some obscure people who had painted for years for their own pleasure, without thought of ever selling their work, now found that they had a market. A few of these obscure hobbyists became lionized in urban art circles. John Kane, an old man of Pittsburgh who had been a coal miner and a house painter, had for years painted crude pictures of big picnics which only his relatives and a few friends had seen. Then the poor old man was "discovered" and told that he was a priceless primitive. Far and away the most popular primitive was Grandma Moses of Eagle Bridge, New York, whose farm scenes and snowscapes brought very good prices in the New York market.

If the primitives' works were more a record of artistic aspiration than of esthetic achievement, they at least had the advantage of being ideologically safe in an era that saw many conflicts between artists and outraged social and artistic conservatives. Most of these conflicts were over murals in public buildings. People who never would have visited a gallery or museum saw murals in the local post office or in the schools and sometimes they took rather violent exception both to the artist's esthetic principles and to his social philosophy. The Mexican muralists, who were political leftists, were the subject of great controversy. Some Dartmouth College alumni protested vociferously when José Orozco did a mural for the New Hampshire institution, and when the Detroit Institute of Arts commissioned Diego Rivera to do murals for its walls, a group of local right-wingers protested that the institute had engaged "an outside, half-breed Mexican Bolshevist." Rivera also had trouble at the new Rockefeller Center in New York. When he included a likeness of Lenin in his work, the managers of the project fired him and covered the Russian with canvas. They later destroyed the mural altogether. Peter Blume had trouble even with museum managers. In 1939 the authorities of the Corcoran Gallery at Washington refused on political grounds to hang his "Eternal City." The same year, after a debate that reflected depths of prejudice and ignorance such as Gropper had skewered with "Legislative Paunch," Congress cut back WPA appropriations for its art and other cultural projects almost to nothing. Little of the debate had to do with such legitimate questions as the economic advisability of continued federal subsidy of the arts or of the proper relationship of government to the arts.

But perhaps even the occasional public uproar over a work of art was an indication of a healthier and wider interest in art than there had been in the 1920's. Art was at least coming increasingly into the lives of people. Not even President Coolidge would have been unaware by the end of the 1930's that the United States had a vigorous group of contemporary artists.

Education

One of the most surprising—and culturally encouraging—aspects of the Great Depression was that the long-term trend toward universal education through high school continued and even became stronger despite economic adversity. In the first few years of the depression, as we saw briefly in Chapter 5, many communities tried to solve their public financial problems by seriously reducing expenditures for education. After 1933, however, when the federal government assumed a greater share of the financial burden of relief and thereby eased the problem for the states and municipalities, most school districts were able again to keep the schools open for thirty-four or thirty-six weeks of the year.

Late in the 1930's the nation's total public school budget was the equal of the predepression figure, and the figure for 1940 was roughly 10 per cent higher than it had been for 1930. Much of the increase reflected higher costs of materials. Teachers' salaries improved only very slightly over the decade as a whole. The national average public school teacher's salary in 1930 had been $1,420; in 1940 it was only $1,441.

Due to the declining birth rates of the 1920's and 1930's, there was a decrease in the national public school enrollment during the depression decade, but a higher percentage of the school-age population attended school. In 1930, 81.3 per cent of the nation's children from age five to seventeen were enrolled in public school; the figure stood at 85.3 per cent in 1940. Counting private and parochial school students, almost all youngsters up through high-school age attended school. Most of the increase was at the high-school level; school attendance of younger children had been almost universal, except for a few areas, since World War I. Indeed, except for the nation's biggest cities with large slum populations and the poorest agricultural areas, four years of high school and usually graduation became the norm.

Changes in the law and depressed economic conditions were the primary reasons for nearly universal high-school attendance. Some states strengthened their school attendance laws and many of them stiffened their enforcement. The NRA codes forbade employment of children under sixteen, as did the Fair Labor Standards Act of 1938, which raised the minimum age to eighteen in certain dangerous industries. Some communities gave higher allowances to relief families with children in school, which was an additional pressure against dropping out. But perhaps the most important reason was that the poor labor market presented high-school students with no attractive alternative to staying in school. Even poor full-time jobs were difficult to find, and most youngsters and their parents realized that it was better to be in school than on the streets.

School administrators and teachers failed to solve the problem of devising a curriculum that fitted the aspirations, abilities, and needs of such a heterogeneous high-school student body. In most schools the instruction was least adequate for the brightest and the dullest students, for the former because it was not sufficiently challenging intellectually, for the latter because it was too difficult. Vocational education improved relatively little during the decade, primarily because it was expensive and school budgets were tight. The public at large remained oblivious to this problem of universal secondary education until after World War II, when it began, largely because of Cold War pressures, to become alarmed and even hysterical about the failure of most high schools to stretch bright adolescents to their full capabilities.

Colleges and universities, far from being the isolated and insulated ivory towers they often are alleged to be, demonstrated conclusively during the 1930's that they were quite sensitive to the society of which they were a part. Enrollments dropped significantly in the depression's first years as family incomes shrank. The low point was the 1933-1934 academic year, when enrollments nationally were down 8 per cent from what they had been three years earlier. But then enrollments began to increase, despite a progressively smaller college-age population, until by the last full academic year before Pearl Harbor (when already selective service had begun to make inroads) there were 1.5 million college students in the country. This was an increase of approximately 25 per cent in ten years. Roughly 15 per cent of the college-age population was in school. Again, the main reason for the increase was limited job opportunity. Good jobs for college-age people were scarce indeed, and one's chances improved with a bachelor's degree or at least college attendance.

Tax-supported institutions grew more rapidly than the national average because they were less costly for the student. Many cut expenses by living at home and commuting to the campus, and there was a significant rise in the number of students "working their way through." At several state universities and colleges over one half the students, both men and women, were helping to support themselves through part-time jobs, and at some institutions as many as one fourth were wholly dependent upon their own earnings. In February 1934 the Roosevelt administration began to direct FERA funds to the most needy students, and NYA after 1935 subsidized still more. Many universities helped students to organize cooperative boarding houses, which enabled them to cut their living expenses to the bone. The co-ops at the State University of Iowa cost only $15 a month for room and board, and the students received a rebate for one month's bill at the end of the year. Thousands paid as little as $2 a week for a room and had "meal jobs" that provided their food.

With many students living close to the margin of subsistence, it was not surprising that campuses, particularly the state and municipal ones, had an earnestness that had not been prominent in happier times. The "rah-rah" atmosphere of the 1920's did not entirely disappear, but students clearly were more serious and more concerned with the world around them than they had been before the depression. American university students have never been as political as their counterparts in most other nations, but there was a distinct increase in political interest and activity during the depression years. More students than ever before elected to take courses in history and the social sciences in an effort to understand what had happened to their society and to seek ways to improve it. Marxist study and discussion clubs became rather commonplace. Student peace demonstrations became almost annual events by the late 1930's, and national associations of students attempted to influence national policy by lobbying in Washington and by efforts to shape public opinion.

The greatest change in what was taught in colleges and universities was the gradually increasing requirement that all students take more courses, particularly in their first two years, relating to the cultural heritage of the Western world. After Harvard President Charles W. Eliot introduced the elective system at his university in the late nineteenth century the idea had spread to such an extent that at some institutions a student might take almost no courses outside his major interest. Columbia College introduced a required program in the history and culture of the West, which in modified form became common all over the nation. The "great books curriculum" that President Robert M. Hutchins introduced at the University of Chicago failed to attract a large number of imitators, but it clearly did stimulate other institutions to put a greater emphasis upon teaching their students more of their cultural heritage. Reforming the college curriculum in this manner was no easy task during the depression because students were naturally anxiously interested in their vocational futures. But most professors and university administrators became convinced of the need for reform, and the introduction of required general education programs came rapidly in the economically easier times after the war.

The Business of Popular Taste

The fact of the depression did not change the essential nature of the problem of mass culture. That people had less money to spend did not affect cultural commercialism. Publishers, show-business producers (the term itself is revealing), and radio sponsors still sought as large an audience as possible, which continued to mean aiming the product at the lowest common denominator of taste and interest.

Book publishing differed significantly from other enterprises engaged in selling a cultural product to the public. Overhead costs were relatively small, as compared for example with motion pictures, most of the people in the business were intellectuals, publishing firms seldom had to yield to bankers' wishes about the nature of their product as did film companies, and the nature of the book-buying public was different from the toothpaste or Hollywood market. Book publishers were willing to publish manuscripts they thought worthy if their probable sale were enough to prevent the firm from losing money. Indeed, publishers sometimes brought out books they felt certain would lose money when they thought the book was culturally worth the monetary loss, if it would add to the prestige of the publisher to have the book or author on his list, and if the publisher had enough profitable titles to compensate for money-losers. But even so, publishers still had to bring out some profitable pieces of what they knew to be trash in order to keep out of the red. Sterile, formula detective novels that the reader forgot within a few days after finishing continued to be a reliable source of income, as did maudlin, cloying, and pretentious romances, the "soap operas" of the book world. Long novels of adventure or romance in an American historical setting became a rage in the depression decade. Some of them were good stories and ably written. Such a book was Margaret Mitchell's *Gone with the Wind,* which appeared in 1936 and was an enormous commercial success. That this novel was high on the best-seller lists during the campaign and election of 1936, the sit-down strikes in the auto industry, and the Munich crisis of 1938 indicates a great deal about the ambivalence of the American people and the escapist aspect of book reading.

Two developments during the 1930's broadened the base of the book-buying public. The Book-of-the-Month-Club became very popular during the depression, probably because of its bargain prices, and soon there were several smaller book clubs for people with specialized interests. Then in 1939, with the first appearance of the *Pocket Book* series, there came the beginning of a revolution in book distribution methods. Inexpensive paperback books were not new; very cheaply printed volumes, bound by stitching or the less expensive staples, had been for sale for years, particularly in Europe. The new paperbacks were bound with a newly developed flexible glue. More important, these books were sold for as little as twenty-five cents at drug stores and newstands as well as at book stores, which were rapidly disappearing from the American scene except in the business districts of the biggest cities and in college towns. Most of the new paperbacks were not calculated to raise the level of American culture, but publishers soon found that some quite good books sold rather well.

But even with paperback books selling at the rate of ten million a year, as in 1941, they came into the lives of far fewer people than did the products of Hollywood and the general press, and there was little from these sources to bring smiles to the person concerned about the state of American culture. The motion-picture industry thrived financially during the depression. Going to the movies was the most common and least expensive kind of entertainment. Admission prices were only from fifteen to forty cents, and exhibitors often offered two features, a news reel, and a short subject. Hollywood only occasionally made a great film—one almost felt it was an accident when it did—because film companies did not often attempt to make great films. Producers knew the formulas that made profits and concentrated upon cranking out as many sure money-makers as possible. Through a "block booking" scheme, which was not broken up until a Department of Justice action in 1940, film distributors required exhibitors to accept films they did not want in order to get the ones they wanted. Exhibitors had no choice but to change their programs frequently and to show double features.

Newspaper publishing changed greatly during the depression years. Publishers did not suffer from decreased circulations after the first years of the depression, but radio advertising so cut into their total revenues that they had to increase their circulations dramatically in order to be able to compete with the new advertising medium. Many newspapers were unable to compete. Between 1930 and 1941, nearly one half of the independently published newspapers of the country disappeared as economic entities; they either stopped publishing altogether or became part of a newspaper chain. By World War II, only 120 cities in the United States had competing newspapers. Rural and small-town weeklies almost quit trying to compete. Most of them ceased trying to cover more than strictly local news, yielding general news coverage to city journals that spread out from metropolitan centers.

Many of the newspapers that survived did so because of reasons other than the quality of their news reporting. They added more and more "features," many of which had nothing whatsoever to do with the news or the questions of the day. Newspapers that sold largely through newstand sales, as in the biggest cities, strived for sensationalism in their headlines and front-page stories so as to attract the purchaser's preference. They more and more tended to sell themselves rather than to inform their readers. (In this respect it should be noted that American newspapers were not unique; British and French newspapers became even less informative, dignified, and reliable.)

One of the curious and widely noted phenomena of newspaper publication in the 1930's was that newspapers quite obviously failed to influence a majority of voters in presidential elections to mark their ballots as their editors and publishers preferred. In 1932, 60 per cent of the nation's dailies opposed Roosevelt, 63 per cent in 1936, and 75 per cent in 1940. There was considerable talk of the "failing power of the press." But, on closer examination, it does not appear that the power actually failed. Although a majority of newspapers failed to get their readers to vote their way, they nevertheless, through daily political injections, conditioned their readers for certain policies and people and against others. In state and congressional elections, especially in non-presidential years when Democratic candidates did not have FDR's coattails to cling to, the voting results were much closer to the newspapers' editorial policies.

Magazine publication had the same problems as newspapers: increasingly critical competition and an intense struggle for existence. Scores of magazines that had long been family stand-bys were unable to keep publishing or were forced to change so much that they became quite different magazines. The two big commercial successes of the decade were *Life,* begun in 1936, and the *Reader's Digest. Life* was an extension of Henry Luce's smorgasbord principle, developed in the news magazine field, to the field of general magazines with an added bonus of scores of interesting photographs. Each issue had a tidbit for many tastes. Rather than search out the single lowest common denominator of public interest, Luce provided a little bit for many kinds of interests. *Reader's Digest* was an even greater success. From a circulation of about one-quarter million at the beginning of the depression, it grew to almost seven million by World War II. Its secret was to aim at low-brow mentalities with middle-brow aspirations, to appear to be a "mentally improving" kind of reading matter. Those whose cultural horizons would not be expanded by such an approach were not numerous enough for the *Digest* to bother with. It also attracted some attention by its "crusades," usually against such safely opposed evils as disease and highway deaths.

The great new mass media of the 1930's, radio, demonstrated well the pitfalls and possibilities of mass culture. Although commercial radio had begun well before the depression, it was not until small, inexpensive receivers began to be made in volume during the 1930's that it became truly a mass media. In 1929, about twelve million families had a radio; by Pearl Harbor, there were over twice that number. People listened to radio fully as much as they watched television in the 1950's. Most radio programs had little to commend them to anyone other than their commercial sponsors. That was not their purpose. Their purpose was to attract an audience for the ad-man's pitch. On the other hand, radio proved that it could be a powerful cultural leaven when it tried to be. Low-powered transmitters were not prohibitively expensive to build and operate, and a few noncommercial stations came into being, some of them operated by colleges and universities. Although the technical proficiency of these broadcasters was frequently below that of the commercial stations and although they made no effort to attract a mass audience, many of their programs had a surprisingly strong and wide response. The national networks during the 1930's set aside Saturday and Sunday afternoons, not good commercial times, for a special effort at musical education. The Saturday operas and the Sunday symphonic concerts gradually gained wide audiences. Public opinion polls and sales of concert tickets and phonograph recordings indicated a steady and impressive growth in the numbers of people interested in serious music. To the national networks' experiment in musical programming must go much of the credit for increased interest.

Perhaps the most encouraging popular cultural development of the decade, however, was the continued growth of huge metropolitan centers. Cities and their suburbs increasingly constituted such a large cultural market that they contained enough people of moderately well cultivated tastes and interests to make aiming at them commercially feasible. Ten per cent of the population in a city of 50,000 was not enough of a market for mass media to aim for; but 10 per cent of the population of the Greater New York City population was a commercially significant group. The radio station of *The New York Times,* WQXR, a station that accepted advertising, was both commercially and culturally successful. Perhaps, in the failiure of society to come to grips with the problem of cultural commercialism directly, the only path toward progress lay with the gradual development of more such minority cultural markets.

9

The Road to Pearl Harbor

MYTHS ABOUT HOW THE UNITED STATES entered World War II became widespread even before all the returning soldiers had picked
up the threads of civilian life. The myths are largely partisan in
origin, and President Roosevelt is the central figure in them. In
one version of how the war came, FDR is a villain; in the other,
he is a hero. In the one interpretation, Roosevelt "tricked us" or
"lied us" into a disastrous, senseless conflict against the majority
will of the people; in the other, Roosevelt, with rare political cour-
age, led Americans to recognize that the Axis powers endangered
their security and safety and thereby saved them from Axis domination. As in most partisan interpretations of history, neither hits
the mark, neither fits all the pertinent and ascertainable facts,
neither satisfies a reasonable and dispassionate inquirer who
seeks to understand rather than to vilify or glorify. But also, as
with most enduring myths, neither view is entirely without foundation. History, to the distress of those who like easy simplicity,
is painted in tones of gray and seldom if ever in pure darks and
lights.

Wherein does the "villainous Roosevelt" interpretation, or "revisionist" view as it is commonly called, have anything to support
it and wherein is it a distortion? For the view this much is clear:
FDR from the beginning of the European war in September 1939

214

wanted an Allied victory; at the same time, at least early in the neutrality period, he did not want his country to become a full-scale belligerent; in time, with Allied defeats, he came to believe that defeat of the Axis was worth the risk of American involvement; and even later, by the fall of 1941, he apparently believed that American participation would be necessary to bring about Axis defeat. It also is clear that Roosevelt was not candid with the nation. He and his administration sometimes withheld information from the public that might have handicapped his policies, as with the *Greer* affair (see page 232), for example, and in general he conducted his foreign policies so as seriously to reduce the range of choice available to the people through their democratic processes. But this revisionist interpretation has serious defects. First, to accept the revisionist view wholly requires disagreement with FDR's judgment that Axis defeat was desirable and that American belligerency was necessary to bring about that defeat. This, of course, is a matter of judgment and values for each side. We cannot experiment with history, go back and try it again with different policies. Second, it is very doubtful that Roosevelt was as far "ahead" of public opinion, that is to say, more willing to take positions that might involve the nation in war, as revisionists assume. Public opinion polls indicated that the people at large followed the same pattern of thinking as did the President, not moving on to the next and riskier position as quickly as he but responding in the same way to actions of the Axis nations. As Hitler invaded and defeated Denmark, Norway, Holland, Belgium, and France in the spring of 1940, pounded England with aerial bombardment, and invaded the Soviet Union in June 1941, and as Japan formed a military pact with Germany and Italy in September 1940 and continued her militaristic expansions in Asia, both FDR and the public generally became increasingly apprehensive and willing to risk war. And it should be remembered that FDR suffered no significant reversals in Congress on issues relative to war and peace—although some of the votes were very close. Sometimes, however, Roosevelt did not ask for all he actually wanted, and he resorted to political sandbagging to get the votes. Third, the keystone of the revisionist interpretation, that Roosevelt baited Japan into attacking Hawaii in order to get into war with Germany, does not stand up under close scrutiny.

Some of the merits and defects of the "heroic Roosevelt" interpretation have emerged in consideration of this view's extreme opposite. For those who worship at the Roosevelt war shrine it should be said that fascism, particularly in Germany, was evil by any reasonable standard of social ethics and a thorough denial of American ideals. If Hitler's enemies, Great Britain, France, and Russia, fell short of democratic standards they did not fall short as far as Germany—not even the Soviet Union —and they did not doctrinally deny the ideal of democracy as did the Nazis. (The Soviets, of course, defined democracy quite differently from the usual concept of it in the United States.) Of course, it is a matter of judgment whether or not the United States should have played the role of defender of world democracy. Clearly on the debit side of the "heroic Roosevelt" ledger is the assumption, often unstated in historical accounts but frequently stated in the months before Pearl Harbor, that the Axis constituted a military threat to the safety of the continental United States. Given the difficulties that the Axis powers faced in Europe and Asia and the state of their military technology in 1941, the United States was not in danger of serious attack. If later the Axis nations had subdued all of Europe and Asia and further developed their weaponry, what might have happened is a matter for conjecture.

Before starting the narrative of how the United States moved from neutrality in September 1939 to a declaration of war in December 1941, it is necessary to survey some of the background, the economic, diplomatic, and legal setting, as well as American public opinion.

In view of the amount of attention historians have accorded the economic background of World War I, it is surprising that there has been so little interest in the international economics of World War II. We have seen earlier in this volume how foreign markets and resources were a serious concern of American foreign policy. The diplomatic basis of American markets in Asia was the Open Door policy, adopted at the turn of the twentieth century in an effort to maintain American commercial rights in China in the face of growing colonial imperialism there by Western powers. In effect, the United States insisted upon protection of its right to receive the economic benefits of colonial imperialism while opposing colonial imperialism itself. The Open Door was the American trade entrance to Asia.

Japan was becoming an industrial nation with spectacular speed. Japan accepted the Open Door principle formally in the Washington treaties of 1922, but she successfully closed the door to Manchuria during the Hoover administration. In July 1937 Japan broke the truce with China and embarked upon a major military campaign that in the next eighteen months drove the

Chinese government into the interior. Japan controlled the major ports. Wherever the Japanese armies advanced they slammed the Open Door tightly, and in November 1938 the Japanese government officially announced a new economic order for East Asia that reserved the area for the exclusive exploitation of Japan. The United States consistently protested these violations of its Open Door policy and of Japanese treaty obligations, but American public opinion at the time would not permit a stronger reaction. The conflict between American economic interest in China and Japanese imperialism was central to Japanese-American relations. The long negotiations between the two nations in 1940 and 1941 always stumbled on the matter of the Open Door. There were many other important points at issue between the United States and Japan, such as militarism, aggression, and treaty commitments, but to a significant extent Japanese-American conflict had an economic basis.

American economic concern with the events of Europe was not so clear-cut as it was in Asia. American animosity to Germany and Italy had its main roots in shocked disapproval of their domestic policies, their aggressions against their neighbors, and sympathy for the more democratic nations that suffered from fascist expansion. Yet there was concern for America's economic future in western Europe and considerable anxiety about German economic penetration into Latin America. It was significant that one of the more popular anti-Nazi books was *You Can't Do Business with Hitler* (1941) by Douglas Miller, and that the title became a common saying.

Only relatively few people were concerned about economic considerations, although they were politically and economically powerful; the public at large was anxious lest the nation become involved in a war. There was a strong reaction against the decision to go to war in 1917. A majority of people felt that World War I had been a tragic mistake. When war began again in Europe, a public opinion poll indicated that only a minority thought the 1917 decision had been justified. Opinion was to change, particularly after the German successes of the spring of 1940, but widespread and intense opposition to war and preference for neutrality were major facts of political life. Americans were torn two ways. They thoroughly despised fascism, particularly Nazism and Japanese militarism, but they felt they had been duped in 1917. Not until 1940 did sympathy for the Allies and revulsion against Hitler begin to outweigh the desire for peace and neutrality.

A great deal of the neutrality sentiment grew from the anti-business attitudes prevalent during the depression. Antiwar feelings centered upon the role of bankers and munitions makers in World War I. In early 1934 the Senate appointed a special committee headed by Gerald P. Nye, Republican of North Dakota, to investigate the adequacy of laws on government regulation of the international activities of munitions companies. For nearly three years the Nye committee made headlines with revelations of enormous wartime munitions profits. People came to believe that if it had not been for the "merchants of death" there would not have been acres of American military cemeteries in northeastern France. Public opinion demanded legislation to maintain neutrality in the event of another war, and the legislation enacted was designed to prevent a repetition of the events of 1914 to 1917. The events of 1939 to 1941 turned out to be somewhat different from those of the earlier era, but by then the public was beginning to have second thoughts on the whole subject of war and peace.

The First Neutrality Act, which became law on August 31, 1935, required the White House, upon finding an international war, to impose an American embargo on arms to both belligerents; prohibited American ships from carrying munitions to or for a belligerent; and created a government agency whose permission was necessary to export arms to any country, whether at war or not. The law was to be in effect until the end of February 1936. During this period fascist Italy invaded Ethiopia and with its vastly superior arms subjugated the small African nation. Two days after the invasion FDR "found" the war, thereby making the embargo effective. There was some criticism of this policy because it tended to maintain the Italian margin of superior strength. The law said nothing about an embargo on other than munitions, and Mussolini needed oil for his military ventures. Secretary of State Hull declared a "moral embargo" on oil shipments to Italy and requested American oil companies to restrict their shipments there to normal peacetime quantities.

On the day the first measure expired Congress passed the Second Neutrality Act, which was effective until May 1, 1937. The new law extended the provisions of the previous one and in addition forbade any person living in the United States to lend money to a belligerent foreign government. In the two years preceding American entry into World War I American banks had lent over $2 billion to the British and French governments for purchases in the United States, thereby partially tying the domestic economy to Allied military success. Congress did not want to repeat the process. In a gesture toward hemispheric solidarity, the Second Neutrality Act exempted from embargo any American nation that became involved in war with a non-American country. While this law was in effect the civil war began in Spain. Congress hastily amended the law to extend it to civil as well as international wars, and the Third Neutrality Act (April 30, 1937) also included the coverage of civil conflicts. The 1937 law also forbade American citizens from traveling on ships of belligerent nations, a provision designed to prevent American involvement in another *Lusitania* disaster.

The Third Neutrality Act was in effect when Japan renewed her assault on China. Japan had the greater military power, and Roosevelt realized that applying the neutrality law, thereby denying help to China and Japan alike, would work to Japan's advantage. Consequently, Roosevelt refused officially to "find" a war in China. The American position in connection with the Chinese-Japanese war was ambiguous for its first two years. The war did not officially exist so far as the government of the United States was concerned, but on the one hand the government made loans to China and used the "moral embargo" device to persuade American exporters not to send munitions to nations which bombed civilians in open cities—in other words, Japan. American arms also reached China through sales to Great Britain. On the other hand, the government made some bows in the direction of neutrality and American firms continued to sell oil, copper, and scrap iron to Japan. The neutrality bows consisted of a ban on vessels owned by the Maritime Commission (that is, government-owned ships) from transporting arms to either China or Japan, a ban later relaxed so far as China was concerned, and a warning that privately owned ships flying the American flag carrying arms to either belligerent did so at their own risk. This warning did not apply to American-owned private ships that flew "flags of convenience," ships that officially were registered as Panamanian or Liberian. Roosevelt deplored the sale of oil and metal to Japan, but as he pointed out to newsmen, even invoking the Third Neutrality Act would not have prevented Japanese ships from carrying these commodities from American ports since that law, as had the earlier neutrality Acts, applied only to munitions.

The ambiguity of the situation reflected the ambiguity of popular opinion: opposition to fascism and militarily aggressive nations but reluctance to become involved in situations that might lead to war for the United States. In early October 1937 in a speech at Chicago, Roosevelt made a vague reference to a "quarantine" of aggressor nations. Whatever FDR meant precisely, and a close reading of the speech offers few clues, the public feared that he meant adherence to some kind of collective security organization and expressed itself against such an idea. A public opinion poll revealed that less than a third of the population favored leaving the tasks of neutrality to Roosevelt rather than to stricter neutrality laws. When in December 1937 Japanese bombers sank a United States gunboat, the *Panay,* in the Yangtze River, there was almost no demand for war against Japan. Rather, people demanded to know why the vessel had been convoying Standard Oil Company tankers.

Whatever Roosevelt would have done if he had had an entirely free hand in foreign affairs, the fact was that in late 1937 and 1938 the President's political strength was at its lowest ebb. The Supreme Court fight, the recession, and the "purge" in the 1938 Democratic primaries had weakened FDR's political position to such an extent that he was hesitant about bolder foreign policies. When Hitler threatened war to gain the German-speaking area of Czechoslovakia in the fall of 1938 and when France and England gave in to Hitler's demands on the Czechs at the Munich conference in late September in exchange for the dictator's promise to refrain from further demands, the general reaction in the United States was one of relief. War in Europe had been averted. It cannot be determined whether Roosevelt's course would have been different given a stronger political position at home. At any rate, he urged the potentially warring governments to negotiate, and when the Munich pact was announced the State Department announced that the agreement brought "a universal sense of relief."

The fall of 1938 was the high tide of neutralist sentiment in the United States. In 1939, even before the outbreak of war in Europe on September 1, as Hitler took the rest of Czechoslovakia and pressed Poland, as Mussolini took Albania, and as the Japanese continued their advances in the undeclared war against China, public opinion, while still utterly opposed to war for America, began to shift toward countenancing stronger American policies. Opinion was particularly exercised about Japanese purchases of oil and scrap. In the absence of a war declaration in Asia and of official United States refusal to recognize that a war existed, to have prohibited these sales would have been a violation of the Japanese-American commercial treaty of 1911. The treaty required that a six-month notice be served before the treaty could be abrogated, and congressional resolutions calling upon Roosevelt to start the abrogation process had been introduced. On July 26, 1939, before such a resolution passed and over a month before the beginning of the war in Europe, the State Department announced that it had sent Japan the six-month notice.

The Neutrality Period

After months of fruitless negotiations looking toward a defensive alliance of Great Britain, France, and Russia against Germany, the war developed rather quickly. The main stumbling block to a British-French-Russian alliance was fear of Russia in the countries between Germany and the Soviet Union. The British and French refused to enter an arrangement that ignored the wishes of these countries (the Baltic states, Poland, and Rumania), and no alliance developed. Instead, Russian Foreign Secretary Molotov began secret talks with the Germans that resulted in the Russian-German nonaggression agreement of August 23, 1939. Free from the threat of resistance from Russia, Germany invaded Poland on September 1. (Russia stormed into Poland from the eastern border.) On September 3, acting upon commitments to Poland, Great Britain and France declared war against Germany. The war that the world had feared for years had begun.

Yet it had not really begun. German and Russian troops took Poland so quickly that the Western powers were unable to start action in western Europe, and the war settled down to a winter of glaring at one another across the presumably impenetrable lines of fortifications. The only serious warfare during the winter of 1939-1940 was between Finland and Russia. Russia invaded Finland in late November and settled for her minimum demands in March. Although American opinion was strongly for Finland, neither the White House nor Capitol Hill would go beyond a "moral embargo" on shipments to Russia, which was effective, for fear of strengthening the unexpected, unnatural, and, as it turned out, unlasting Russian-German alliance. Finland later invaded Russia, when Germany did so in June 1941; was invaded by Russia again in late 1944; and ended the war by fighting the German divisions remaining on her soil.

When war had begun in Europe in August 1914 Wilson announced, "We must be neutral in thought as well as in act." In September 1939 Roosevelt declared in a radio address, "This nation will remain a neutral nation, but I cannot ask that every American remain neutral in thought as well." FDR "found" the European war, thereby invoking the Third Neutrality Act and blocking exports of munitions to either side, and immediately began to urge amendment of the neutrality legislation. He argued that if the arms embargo were repealed "the United States will more probably remain at peace than if the law remains as it is today." The Fourth Neutrality Act passed Congress by wide margins in early November. It empowered the President to prohibit American ships from sailing in combat areas, and Roosevelt promptly banned sailing to the ports of the belligerents, the Baltic and North Seas, and the waters around Great Britain. The act relaxed the embargo. It permitted belligerents to buy products, arms, or any other commodity, at American ports on a "cash and carry" basis. Since Great Britain controlled the Atlantic, subject to danger from German submarines, the "cash and carry" provision meant in effect that Britain and her allies could buy American arms and that German and Italy could not. The United States had adopted the policy of aiding the Allies but of requiring them to pay cash and make their own deliveries.

The nature of the war and of American opinion about it changed rapidly in the spring of 1940. On April 9, 1940, Hitler's troops made a surprise attack upon neutral Denmark and Norway. Denmark could do no more than offer token resistance. Norway held out longer but was no serious problem for the Nazi invaders. On May 10 the Nazis struck like lightning through Belgium and Holland and the next day were in France. They broke through the Allied lines with their Panzer divisions. The British managed to escape to sea with heavy losses at Dunkirk. Paris fell on June 14, and Hitler received the French surrender on June 22. Meanwhile, Mussolini's troops invaded France from the southeast. After six weeks of war Britain stood alone. Throughout the summer the Luftwaffe and the Royal Air Force battled over Britain. Unable to knock the RAF out completely, the Germans shifted tactics in the fall and began heavy bombing of London and other English cities.

The United States stepped up its production for Britain and even began indirectly to provide her with arms from the American armed forces. The navy delivered some of its planes to the manufacturer on a "trade in" for new planes to be obtained later.

The manufacturer delivered them to the Canadian boundary, where the Royal Canadian Air Force took possession of them. Canada had declared war in the fall of 1939. Royal Canadian Air Force crews trained at Florida air fields. Such circuitous devices by no means met with unanimous approval, but public opinion obviously was shifting away from hard neutralism. After the fall of France and the Battle of Britain, a public opinion poll indicated that for the first time a majority thought aid to Britain was more important than maintaining American neutrality.

Although public opinion was shifting, the national debate became more intense. For those who favored heavy aid to Great Britain, the situation was more urgent because of the punishment England was taking. For those who favored neutrality at all costs, the situation was more urgent because they feared the United States was again drifting toward war. The first camp, commonly but inaccurately called "interventionist," was personified by the Committee to Defend America by Aiding the Allies, of which the Kansas newspaper publisher William Allen White was chairman. The other camp, usually called "isolationist," a poor description of most people in it, was personified by the America First Committee. These two propaganda groups worked furiously to bring public opinion around to their points of view. The views of the White Committee gradually gained strength, but it is probable that the change in public opinion was due more to the drift of events in Europe and Asia than it was to the committee's work. Certainly the America First position remained strong. The two groups tended to solidify the nation's thinking.

The one thing that most interventionists and isolationists agreed upon was that stronger continental defenses were desirable. Federal appropriations for defense had grown slightly since 1938, but armed strength was still surprisingly low by later standards. At the end of June 1940 the army had a total of 267,767 officers and men, including the air force, the navy's total was 160,997. Just after the German thrust into France, FDR asked Congress for a larger defense budget. By July Congress had appropriated $12 billion. Nine months later defense appropriations reached a total of $35 billion, more than the total American cost of World War I. Administering such a vast defense mobilization was a formidable task. Roosevelt both made the administration of the armed services more efficient and accomplished a political coup when in June 1940, just before the Republican national convention, he appointed two Republicans to the cabinet. Henry L. Stimson, who had been Secretary of War under Taft and Secretary of State under Hoover, again became head of the War Department; Frank Knox, who had been the GOP vice-presidential candidate in 1936, became Secretary of the Navy. Industrial mobilization was a far more complicated and delicate problem. There was a great deal of confusion and ineptitude, false starting and administrative reshuffling, in the whole area of beefing up production for defense under government direction. Not until after Pearl Harbor did Roosevelt arrive at a satisfactory arrangement. Still, for all the confusion, American production by the time of Pearl Harbor was greater than that of any nation, including Germany. Furthermore, the construction of even more industrial facilities was well under way.

Politics in 1940 reflected the basic anxieties of the people about growing fascist power and involvement in a bloody war. The Republican national convention opened just two days after France's surrender. So-called isolationists, or men leaning in that direction, had been the front-runners for the GOP presidential nomination until the last days before the convention began. Senator Robert A. Taft, son of the former president, had attracted a great deal of attention in the two years he had served in the Senate. Senator Arthur H. Vandenberg of Michigan, like Taft a firm neutralist, had a strong following, as did District Attorney Thomas E. Dewey of New York City. In the last few weeks of the preconvention jockeying a group of eastern interventionists came forward with the name of Wendell L. Willkie, until then almost unknown. Willkie was an attractive figure. A general supporter of New Deal measures—indeed, he did not register as a Republican until 1940 and had been a delegate to the 1924 Democratic convention—he had nevertheless led the battle of privately owned power companies against TVA. In general a supporter of the administration's foreign policies, he was not identified in the public mind as either an interventionist or an isolationist. Although his professional political support came primarily from the East originally, he was unmistakably midwestern in appearance, accent, and manner. (The acid-tongued Harold Ickes called him a "bare-foot boy from Wall Street.") Willkie was behind Dewey and Taft on the first ballot, but he gained thereafter and won the nomination on the sixth. Senator Charles McNary, co-sponsor of the McNary-Haugen bills, became his running mate.

Sensing the popularity of the New Deal's domestic policies, the Republican leaders who wrote the platform mildly endorsed its reforms and even promised extension of the Social Security Act but criticized the Democrats' administration. Since it appeared likely that Roosevelt would run again and since they wanted to make gains on the third-term issue, the Republicans urged a constitutional amendment to restrict the president to two terms. The platform straddled the main foreign policy question: it stated strong opposition to America's going to war but supported aid to nations under attack from aggressors.

The Republicans were correct in anticipating FDR's renomination, but the President had been extremely coy about the question of a third term. He did not say he would run; he did not say he would not run. He did not object when his supporters entered his name in primaries, each of which he won easily. By keeping quiet he put other hopefuls—Postmaster General James Farley, Vice President John N. Garner, and former Governor of Indiana Paul V. McNutt—at a bad disadvantage. By allowing the possibility of not running again he brought dissidents within his camp out into the light; by leaving the way open to a third nomination, which he clearly could have if he wanted it, he kept them from gaining much strength because delegations did not want to come out for a sure loser. Alben Barkley, the Democratic leader in the Senate, told the convention that Roosevelt wanted him to make it clear to the delegates that they were "free to vote for any candidate." This included Roosevelt himself, of course, and the announcement prompted a big demonstration. Delegates placed some other names before the convention, but FDR received the nomination on the first ballot with 946 votes to 147 for all the others. The real battle of the convention—Democratic conventions usually provide a dramatic fight—came over the nomination of FDR's running mate. Roosevelt insisted upon Secretary of Agriculture Henry A. Wallace, but the Iowan was never close to the party's machine leaders and he was able to beat out McNutt and Speaker of the House William B. Bankhead, the southern delegates' favorite, only after a hard struggle. To no one's surprise, the platform emphasized the domestic reforms of the previous eight years and straddled on foreign policy as had the Republicans.

Although Willkie was off and running hard in mid-August, Roosevelt postponed his real campaigning until October. Indeed, before he began campaigning actively Roosevelt took two actions relevant to the war issue that were extremely risky in an election year: Selective Service and the Destroyer-Bases Deal. In his acceptance speech to the Democratic convention Roosevelt urged peacetime conscription to strengthen the armed forces. Never had the United States had a draft during peacetime, and even during wartime it had not been a popular way to staff the armed services. In June a conservative Democrat had joined with a Republican to introduce a conscription measure, and Roosevelt pushed for its passage. Congress sent the bill through with big margins, and Roosevelt signed it on September 16, only about seven weeks before election day. On October 16 all men between the ages of twenty-one and thirty-six registered for the draft. A week before election day came the drawing of the draft numbers, and the first draftees left for camp before the end of November. The draftees, limited to 900,000 a year, were to receive twelve months of military training and were not to be sent outside the Western hemisphere. The base pay of a draftee was only $21 a month. Another law authorized the chief executive to call National Guard units into federal service. During the depression many young men had joined guard units to get the drill pay without thought that their enlistment would incur more than that. The National Guard units went off to army camps along with the first draftees.

The passage of the draft measure and conscription preparations took weeks and thereby prepared people for the departure of the draftees. The Destroyer-Bases Deal came as a surprise. The British had their backs against the wall. They did not have enough destroyers properly to convoy freighters through the submarine zones of the North Atlantic and they expected an invasion attempt by the Germans. The United States had a fleet of about 175 World War I destroyers that had been reconditioned after being brought out of storage. In exchange for fifty of these destroyers, the British leased to the United States for ninety-nine years a series of air and naval bases in the Caribbean and transferred title altogether to bases in Bermuda and Newfoundland. The transfer agreement was signed in early September. The deal did not violate the letter of the neutrality laws, but it required ingenuity on the part of Attorney General Robert Jackson to find a legal route. Jackson's reasoning was that since the ships had not been built specifically to be given to a foreign belligerent power they did not come under the ban of the 1939 neutrality law. A naval appropriations bill had specifically prohibited transfer of naval equipment to another power without the permission of the Chief of Naval Operations and Army Chief of Staff, who had to certify that such equipment was not necessary to American defense. Admiral Harold R. Stark and General George C. Marshall so certified. The deal was not inconsistent with American law, but it certainly was without precedent. And, since Roosevelt had not consulted Congress about the transfer, the action had lent a new dimension to the power of the White House to conduct foreign affairs. Further, the transfer was a clear violation of the spirit of neutrality. American neutrality in the war between Great Britain and Germany was no more than a technicality after the Destroyer-Bases Deal. Prime Minister Winston Churchill later wrote in his memoirs that Hitler could have justified a declaration of war against the United States by interpreting conventional neutral behavior strictly. (Hitler, of course, was not foolish enough to declare war; since there was no chance that America would fight on his side, it was in his interest to keep the United States as neutral as possible.)

There was quite a bit of protest against the destroyer transfer but not as much as might legitimately have been expected. Willkie, who had already come out for aid to Britain, objected only to Roosevelt's failure to consult Congress before going through with the deal. Since there was consensus on the need to strengthen continental defenses, the bases part of the arrangement headed off potential criticism.

Nevertheless, there was widespread misgiving about the drift of foreign affairs and Republican leaders urged Willkie to exploit this misgiving. He did so, and for the first time his campaign caught fire. The Willkie strategy was to portray FDR as seeking war and to imply that his re-election would make war inevitable. "If his promise to keep our boys out of foreign wars is no better than his promise to balance the budget, they're already almost on the transports." Public opinion polls, which had shown only a bare majority approving the destroyer transfer, indicated that Willkie was gaining fast in October. Roosevelt at last took to the stump.

Again the old campaigner deftly countered the attack. First, he made explicit answer to Willkie's new tack: "I have said this before, but I shall say it again and again and again: Your boys are not going to be sent into any foreign wars." Second, he challenged the genuineness of the Republican espousal of the New Deal's reforms. He pointed out, quite accurately, that Republican newspapers, senators, and congressmen had either opposed the New Deal measures outright or had dragged their feet.

The voters followed FDR for the third time. His popular vote was 27,243,466; Willkie received 22,304,755. The electoral vote was 449 to 82. Still, it was a considerably smaller margin than 1936. Besides Maine and Vermont, Roosevelt lost Indiana (Willkie's home state), Michigan, Iowa, North and South Dakota, Nebraska, Kansas, and Colorado. The races for Congress were a stand-off; the Democrats gained six seats in the House but lost three in the Senate.

The Undeclared War

In the twelve months following the 1940 elections the United States came ever closer to full war against Germany. Before Pearl Harbor brought full war to America, the nation had already moved to a status that has been described as "shooting nonbelligerence." America and Germany had exchanged blows on the high seas, the United States had almost completely abandoned its legalistic neutrality, and the President had, in effect, joined in a statement of war aims with the Prime Minister of Great Britain.

While on a vacation cruise in early December 1940, Roosevelt received a long letter from Prime Minister Winston Churchill. Churchill wrote that Britain needed great quantities of arms and planes to prevent defeat and begin the military build-up that would be necessary eventually to defeat Germany. Interestingly, Churchill wrote that his letter was not intended as an appeal for aid but as a "statement of the minimum action necessary to the achievement of our common purpose," the purpose being the defeat of "Nazi and Fascist tyranny." Roosevelt immediately began efforts to increase the flow of arms from American ports to Great Britain. Rather than conventional international loans, which had been a source of friction between the Allies of World War I and the United States in the years after 1918, Roosevelt preferred a system of lending goods, rather than money, to be repaid after the war in goods and services. This concept became the basis of the Lend-Lease Act.

The Lend-Lease bill began its course through Congress on January 10, 1941. During the two months the measure was before Congress the national debate over foreign policy became shrill and bitter. Both sides exaggerated wildly. Senator Burton K.

Wheeler charged that passage of the Lend-Lease bill would mean "plowing under every fourth American boy," an allusion to the plowing under of cotton at the beginning of AAA in 1933, and Roosevelt in a press conference in December likened the whole matter of supplying arms to Britain to a man lending his garden hose to a neighbor whose house was on fire. The President said that the man would not say, "Neighbor, my garden hose cost me $15; you have to pay me $15 for it." Although opposition to Lend-Lease was highly vocal, the bill passed Congress by large margins, 260 to 154 in the House and 60 to 31 in the Senate. Willkie, the titular leader of his party, publicly supported the measure, but a majority of the Republican membership in each house voted against it. Roosevelt signed the bill on March 11. It empowered him to "sell, transfer, exchange, lease, lend or otherwise dispose of" any commodites "to the government of any country whose defense the President deems vital to the defense of the United States." Congress soon appropriated $7 billion for Lend-Lease. By the end of the war, total Lend-Lease aid amounted to over $50 billion.

Roosevelt, besides sponsoring Lend-Lease, also subtly in his public statements came around to the view of American-British relations that Churchill had adopted in his December letter. Rather than merely aiding a friendly power, the President said, the United States should be an ally against totalitarian tyranny. In his radio speech of December 29, although he said he believed "there is far less chance of the United States getting into the war" if the nation helped Britain, he stated that the Axis was an enemy. Americans should help "the nations defending themselves against attack by the Axis" rather than "acquiesce in their defeat, submit tamely to an Axis victory, and wait our turn to be the object of attack in another war later on." Britain, in other words, was fighting America's battles against a common enemy. "We must be the great arsenal of democracy." In his State of the Union message to Congress on January 6, 1941, he continued to assume an alliance with Britain, an alliance of democracies, against the Axis. The United States should supply the strength "to regain and maintain a free world." He also stated his belief that a world based upon the "four freedoms" —freedom from want, freedom from fear, freedom of speech, and freedom to worship as one chooses, all denied in Axis nations—was "attainable in our own time and generation." The distinction between ordinary aid and partnership against a common enemy was subtle, but it was an important shift in America's status because it involved a commitment to defeat the Axis. From the passage of Lend-Lease to Pearl Harbor the United States worked increasingly closely with Great Britain and came ever closer to outright war against Germany.

Two weeks after the signing of Lend-Lease Hitler extended the war zone westward to include the waters between Greenland and Iceland, and German submarines intensified their campaign against shipping to Great Britain. The submarines were unable to cut off the flow of supplies but they did hinder British aid considerably. In the spring of 1941 they sank over 500,000 tons of shipping each month. Roosevelt countered with a series of actions. At the end of March, using powers granted under the Lend-Lease Act, he permitted the British to repair one of their battleships at an American port. He ordered the Coast Guard to take possession of all Axis shipping in American ports as well as thirty-five ships under the flag of defeated Denmark. In June he ordered the seizure of French ships as well. In early April the United States assumed the defense of Greenland, which formerly had been Danish. On April 10 Roosevelt proclaimed that the neutral zone around the Americas set by the Panama Conference of 1939, a conference of the twenty-one American republics that met just after the declaration of war in Europe, be moved eastward to the 25th meridian. The 25th meridan lies just to the west of Iceland and about half-way between the bulges of the South American and African continents. The German-proclaimed war zone and the American-proclaimed neutral zone thus overlapped in the area between Iceland and Greenland. In June the United States froze all German and Italian assets in the country and closed all their consulates.

On July 7, for the first time, American troops moved overseas. Iceland had been Danish territory. Upon Denmark's defeat Iceland had declared herself independent. With a total population of only a little over 100,000 and almost no defense establishment, Iceland did not object to the Canadian and British troops that landed there to defend the island, strategic because of its position near North Atlantic shipping lanes. American troops replaced the Canadians and British in July, and the navy began constant convoy patrol between North American ports and Iceland. British destroyers escorted the convoys on to Great Britain. There was not yet an American "shoot-on-sight" order. American naval vessels could only track submarines, lead evasive action, and notify British planes and ships of submarine locations. With Germany having declared the sea just west of

Iceland in the war zone, the United States having declared it a neutral zone, and the American navy engaged in convoy escort there, a conflict between German submarines and American naval vessels was almost a certainty. Somewhat surprisingly, there was no incident for almost two months.

By the time the incident came, in early September, the United States and Great Britain had come into closer cooperation through a meeting at sea between President Roosevelt and Prime Minister Churchill. From August 9 to 12, 1941, Roosevelt and Churchill and their staffs conferred off the coast of Argentia, Newfoundland. Many of the discussions were technical, having to do with long-range supply problems and general strategy. Churchill tried unsuccessfully to get Roosevelt to agree to come to Britain's aid if Japan attacked British areas in the Pacific. Roosevelt agreed only to warn Japan against such an attack and did not accept the British draft of the warning. The only aspect of the Argentia conference to be publicized at the time was the Atlantic Charter, in effect a Roosevelt-Churchill statement of war aims, which was released to the public on August 14 when the first news of the conference was announced. In the Charter, Roosevelt and Churchill enumerated eight "common principles in the national policies of their respective countries on which they based their hopes for a better future for the world." First, they declared their countries sought no aggrandizement, territorial or otherwise. Second, they desired to see no territorial changes that did not accord with the wishes of the people concerned. Third, they respected the right of all people to choose their form of government and wished to see self-government restored to those who had been forcibly deprived of it. (India soon pounced upon this point as justification for its demand for sovereignty.) Fourth, they wished all nations to have equal access to trade and necessary raw materials. Fifth, they desired international economic cooperation to improve all living standards and economic security. Sixth, after the destruction of Nazism, they hoped for a peace which would assure all people to live their lives free from fear and want. Seventh, such a peace should provide for freedom of the seas. And eighth, they believed that, pending the establishment of a permanent system of general security after the war, national disarmament was essential. Interventionists hailed the document and isolationists condemned it. Public opinion polls did not indicate any significant change of opinion one way or the other.

Public opinion at the time was far more exercised about the

extension of Selective Service. In June Roosevelt began a campaign in Congress to extend the term of service of draftees from twelve months to the duration of the emergency and to remove the ban on draftees serving overseas. Leaders of Congress told him that his requests were a political impossibility, that such proposals would surely meet congressional defeat. Roosevelt compromised, dropping the overseas feature and reducing the time extension to an additional eighteen months. Debate in Congress was very sharp. The Senate passed the amendment to the Selective Service Act on August 7. On August 12, while the President was still in conference with Churchill, the House passed it by one vote, 203 to 202. Democrats supported the bill almost three to one; Republicans voted against it about six to one.

The nature of the war in Europe changed abruptly and profoundly when on June 22, 1941, the Nazis invaded Russia in force with a surprise attack. The German armored divisions moved with such speed that it appeared to many that the Soviet Union would soon be forced to capitulate as had France. Within five months after the attack German troops were at the gates of Leningrad in the north, near Moscow in the center, and almost to Rostov in the south. But Russia was a huge area and its winters were bitter. With the coming of cold weather the Russian lines began to hold, and before the end of another year the Germans were in retreat.

The United States and Great Britain implicitly brought the Soviet Union into their informal anti-Axis alliance. Earlier in June, when the White House froze German and Italian assets in America, it had included Russian assets as well. With the attack the assets were again made available. In July, when in London to arrange for the Argentia conference, Lend-Lease administrator Harry Hopkins received Churchill's suggestion to go on to Moscow to confer with Josef Stalin, the Soviet dictator. Hopkins did so and found Stalin eager for American help. Congress defeated a proposed amendment to the Lend-Lease Act to forbid help to the Soviet Union, and in November Roosevelt officially declared Russia eligible for Lend-Lease. Russia eventually received over $11 billion in Lend-Lease equipment, most of it after the American declaration of war.

The almost inevitable incident in the North Atlantic came on September 4. A German submarine fired two torpedoes at the American destroyer *Greer*. Each of them missed. The *Greer* dropped depth charges but could not detect their effect. A week later Roosevelt announced by radio that an American naval ship had been fired upon and announced that henceforth the navy would protect all merchant vessels, American and otherwise, "in our defensive waters." He closed with a warning: "From now on, if German or Italian vessels of war enter the waters the protection of which is necessary for American defense, they do so at their own peril." The shoot-on-sight order went out to the Atlantic fleet.

The President was not frank with the public in the *Greer* affair. There were aspects of the destroyer's encounter with the U-boat that he did not mention. The *Greer,* bound for Iceland with troops and mail, had been notified by a British patrol plane that a submarine lay submerged about ten miles ahead. The *Greer* located the submarine and tracked it for several hours, meanwhile radioing the U-boat's position to the British. It was then that the submarine released the torpedoes.

After the shoot-on-sight order there were more incidents. A torpedo hit the destroyer *Kearny,* killing eleven men but not sinking the ship; the *Reuben James,* also a destroyer, sank after torpedo hits. With undeclared naval warfare in the North Atlantic and Lend-Lease, the neutrality act on the books was partly an anachronism. On October 9 Roosevelt requested Congress to repeal that part of the act prohibiting the arming of American merchant ships. He said he hoped Congress would also repeal the section of the law that prevented American ships from going to belligerent ports, but he did not expressly ask for this repeal. The House rescinded the ban on arming merchant ships by a big margin, and the size of the vote encouraged FDR to ask for the lifting of the ban on visiting belligerent ports. After acrimonious debate the Senate passed the bill as Roosevelt had requested but by a margin of only thirteen votes. When the changed bill went back to the House it had another close call, this time, by a margin of eighteen votes.

On November 13, when Roosevelt signed the recent changes in the Neutrality Act of 1939, all that was missing to complete the picture of war was a war declaration. American and German naval vessels had exchanged blows. American armed merchant ships were free to sail to British ports. The United States was sending billions of dollars' worth of war supplies to Germany's enemies, and the American President had joined the British Prime Minister in a statement of war aims. Still, most Americans did not regard the nation as at war and continued to hope that they could avoid it. All aid short of war was the majority position until the attack on Pearl Harbor. It is likely that if President Roosevelt had made a formal request to Congress for a war declaration in November or early December 1941, such as Wilson had done in April 1917, Congress would not have complied. A November public opinion poll revealed that slightly less than 35 per cent of the people would vote for war if there were a referendum on the issue.

The Open Door and the Rising Sun

In considering the strained and tangled relations of the United States and Japan in the period before the war one must keep in mind certain constant situations and policies in the background of the complicated diplomatic tugging and hauling. Most basic was the conflict of Japanese and American plans for Asia, particularly China. The United States remained always fully committed to the Open Door, through which would march American commercial and manufacturing interests in search of markets and resources. Japan was fully committed to the reverse: closing the Open Door, making Asia a private imperial reserve for Japanese industry and commerce, and creating what she called the Greater East Asia Co-Prosperity Sphere. This scheme amounted to a vast economic and military empire in Asia, directed by and for Japan, the only industrialized nation of the Orient. Despite a high density of population on the Japanese islands, "living space" for the Japanese was not a major consideration. The Japanese had controlled Korea since 1905 and Manchuria since 1932, and Japan had peopled those areas only with soldiers, civil administrators, and businessmen.

One must remember also the facts of economic geography. Japan, an industrial power, did not have sufficient raw materials for her industry in the home islands. She yearned for the resources of Southeast Asia, particularly oil and rubber, which were controlled by the Dutch (in the East Indies, present-day Indonesia), the French (in Indo-China), and the British (in Malaya and Burma). For scrap iron, essential in the manufacture of steel as well as bombs and shells, she was dependent upon American supplies. The United States also had a strategic interest in the resources of Southeast Asia. Before the greater exploitation of oil fields in the Middle East, Southeast Asian oil was more important to America than it is today. America imported huge quantities of raw rubber from Southeast Asia, becoming less dependent upon imports only after she developed synthetic rubber during the war, when the Japanese cut off the Asian supply. The United States also imported Asian tin. Thus, Japan sought to gain Southeast Asia's resources and the United States sought to protect its access to them.

Still another factor was Japanese politics. So far as American-Japanese relations were concerned Japanese political forces could be divided into moderates and expansionist extremists. The moderates, for example Prince Fumimaro Konoye, were committed to the integration of China into the Japanese industrial complex, but they feared war with the United States and sought to avoid it. Although by the late 1930's the Japanese navy was stronger than the combined Pacific fleets of its potential enemies (the United States, Great Britain, and the Netherlands), the admirals were cautious about war. Japanese generals, on the other hand, were confident their armies could defeat any military force likely to confront them and constituted the most extreme force in politics. Nor were they averse to using force, terror, and assassination as weapons in domestic politics. The most prominent military figure in politics was General Hideki Tojo.

Japan's expansionists took the opportunities presented by difficulties in Europe. When Hitler broke his Munich pledge and took the remainder of Czechoslovakia in early 1939, Japan seized the large Chinese island of Hainan in the South China Sea, which put her in a strong position vis-à-vis the northern part of French Indo-China. Germany's successes in the spring of 1940 further encouraged Japanese militarists. They forced the moderate government that had come to power in January 1940 to begin negotiations looking toward a military alliance with Germany, and in July they were able to overthrow that government altogether. The new cabinet, although headed by Prince Konoye, had General Tojo in it as Minister of War and an ally of the militarists, Yosuke Matsuoka, as Minister of Foreign Affairs. The new government quickly pressed for advantage. It wrung from the collaborationist Vichy French government permission to occupy northern Indo-China and did so in September. It demanded of Churchill that he close the Burma Road, vital to the Chinese capital, Chungking, in the Chinese interior. The British Prime Minister, being in no position to resist, acquiesced for three months, and opened the road again in October.

But although happy about these opportunities as a result of German successes in Europe, Japanese expansionists were wary of possible German interest in reviving its power in Asia, dormant since Versailles. The Japanese had no wish to destroy the British, French, and Dutch colonial empires and the American

Open Door commercial empire, only to be confronted with a new German empire in Asia. Accordingly, the Japanese began negotiations with Germany and her junior partner Italy, which resulted in the Tripartite Pact of September 27, 1940. In this agreement "Japan recognizes and respects the leadership of Germany and Italy in the establishment of a new order in Europe" and the Nazis and Fascists reciprocated by recognizing Japan's leadership in "Greater Eastern Asia." The three countries agreed "to assist one another with all political, economic and military means" if one of them were attacked by a power not then engaged in either the European or Chinese-Japanese war. The only possible two countries to which this article could apply were the United States and the Soviet Union, and since another article of the treaty specifically exempted Russia, the Tripartite Pact was a defensive alliance against the United States.

Japan herself did have to contend with the Soviet Union in the Far East: Russian Siberian provinces were contiguous with Manchuria and the port of Vladivostok was not far from the Japanese home islands. On April 13, 1941, more than two months before the German attack on Russia, Japan and Russia signed a five-year neutrality pact that committed each of them to neutrality should either become engaged in war with another power or powers. This agreement freed Japan for its military operations elsewhere, but it also enabled Russia to pit her total strength against Germany when Hitler's attack came.

The United States responded to these actions of Japan with diplomatic warnings and economic pressures. The State Department sent strongly worded messages to Japan that warned against expansion into Southeast Asia. Threats to its sources of rubber, tin, and oil "would not be tolerated." But economic leverage against Japan caused the Japanese more concern. In the latter half of 1940, after Congress gave him the authority, Roosevelt began to impose embargoes upon exports of petroleum and its derivatives and scrap metal to Japan. He did so cautiously at first for fear that shortages would prompt Japan to move quickly into Southeast Asia at a time when his main concern was stopping Hitler in Europe. The administration also, through the Export-Import Bank, lent funds to China. That the embargoes had an effect upon Japan was evident from the curious story of the proposals that Japanese moderates sent informally to Washington by two American priests.

Bishop James E. Walsh and Father James M. Drought were in Japan in the winter of 1940-1941 on affairs connected with their religious order. They had unofficial conversations with Japanese moderates in the government, and eventually they were asked to carry some proposals to President Roosevelt. The moderates proposed to yield a great deal in China if the United States would relax its embargo. Secretary Hull doubted that Japan would actually deliver on such a proposal and suggested that nothing more be done until the new Japanese ambassador, Admiral Kichisaburo Nomura, arrived in Washington. (Admiral Nomura, incidentally, had once attended Annapolis.) The negotiations with Nomura proceeded with promise but no conclusion until Foreign Minister Matsuoka returned to Japan from Russia, where he had been negotiating the neutrality agreement. Matsuoka was disturbed at what had happened in his absence and insisted that Nomura demand hard terms. The discussions thereupon came to an end.

In late July 1941 Japanese-American relations took a turn for the worse. Indeed, the two countries were on the verge of war from that time forward, just as were the United States and Germany. Hitler's early success in the war with Russia was probably a factor in Japan's decision to step up her expansionist pace. On July 25 Japan announced she was extending her control over all of French Indo-China, having occupied the north of the country since the previous September. Roosevelt retaliated quickly. "Magic," the American navy's code-breaking operation, had recently solved one of the important Japanese codes, and the information thereby gained confirmed Washington's suspicions that the purpose of the Indo-Chinese move was to put Japanese troops in better position to attack Malaya and the Dutch East Indies. The day after the Japanese announcement Roosevelt took three important steps. First, he froze all Japanese assets in the United States, which made it almost impossible for Japan to buy or sell in America. The Dutch government in exile and Great Britain quickly did the same, and Japan's main sources of rubber, oil, and scrap iron were thus completely cut off. Second, Roosevelt brought the armed forces of the Philippine Commonwealth into the American army and appointed General Douglas MacArthur commanding general of United States forces in the Far East. Third, he closed the Panama Canal to Japanese shipping.

It was at this point that Roosevelt and Churchill had their meeting off Newfoundland. Although Japanese-American relations had reached a new low point, FDR still was unwilling to adopt as hard a position vis-à-vis Japan as Churchill desired.

When Roosevelt returned from the Argentia conference he found that Ambassador Nomura had come forward with a conciliatory proposal. Roosevelt conferred with Nomura the day he returned.

Nomura relayed to Roosevelt a proposal from Konoye that the American President and the Japanese Prime Minister meet to attempt to resolve the difficulties between the two countries. Konoye had apparently decided, given the economic stranglehold the United States had on Japan and the political strength of Japanese militarists, that either there would have to be a Japanese-American agreement quickly or there would be war. Roosevelt was interested. Joseph C. Grew, the American ambassador in Tokyo, strongly supported such a conference. But Secretary Hull insisted that Japan must indicate just what it was willing to concede on China before the United States agreed to a conference. Japan would do no more than agree to withdraw its troops from Indo-China "as soon as the China Incident is settled or a just peace is established in East Asia." This was not enough for Hull; there was no Pacific conference. On October 14 Konoye made one last move. He appealed to General Tojo to pull at least some of his troops out of China. Tojo refused. Two days later the Konoye government fell and the new one was headed by General Tojo himself.

Not even the new Tojo government was able to go to war immediately. Pressure from Japanese moderates prompted Emperor Hirohito to call a conference of political, military, and naval leaders for November 5. The conference decided to make one more effort for peace with the United States and spelled out what Japan would concede. The government sent a second ambassador to Washington, Saburo Kurusu, to help Nomura. But if no accord were reached with America by late November Japan would go to war. The Japanese ambassadors in Washington knew the situation.

The Roosevelt administration knew the situation also because "Magic" had intercepted and decoded important messages to the Japanese embassy in Washington. The State Department and Roosevelt knew that Japan had two proposals ready, the second to be presented if America rejected the first. Neither proposal made any concessions on the central American-Japanese point of difference, China. On November 22 "Magic" decoded still another message. This one informed the Japanese embassy in Washington that the deadline for negotiations had been extended from November 25 to November 29. If there were no results by then, "things are automatically going to happen." This was obviously some kind of warlike move, but the Unitted States did not know precisely what.

The Japanese ambassadors set their second proposal before the State Department on November 20, five days before the old deadline and nine days before the new one. Between then and November 26, when Hull replied to the second proposal, the administration worked feverishly. Army and navy commanders in the Pacific received warnings that attacks, possibly surprise attacks, on Guam and the Philippines were possible. The administration decided not to accept the second Japanese proposal, which in effect meant a decision to accept probable war sooner or later, and to present Japan with a counterproposal of a three-month truce. During these three months, thought Secretary of War Stimson, enough B-17 bombers could be sent to the Philippines to prevent a Japanese movement to the south. But the State Department could not draft a short-term *modus vivendi* proposal that would both deter Japan from what the administration knew was her intention and would be satisfactory to other powers consulted, Great Britain, China, and the Netherlands. When Hull met with Nomura and Kurusu on November 26 he presented them with nothing more than a summary of American demands, including Japanese withdrawal from China and Indo-China. He knew that the demands would be unacceptable. Indeed, on the same day he told Stimson that the whole situation was now in the hands of the military. Thus, by November 26, both Japan and the United States had taken hard, "take-it-or-leave-it" positions which they had no reason to believe the other would accept. However, Japan had the advantage. She had an offensive strategy. The United States expected Japan to strike, but Washington did not know where the blow would land. The best reasoning was that Japan would strike toward the south, possibly the Philippines, certainly the East Indies and Malaya.

In the internal administration discussions from November 20 to 26 one of the main problems was what to do if and when the Japanese launched an attack on Southeast Asia. The administration wanted to declare war in the event of such an attack but did not think that public opinion would accept such a decision. FDR's speech writers worked on a proposed message to Congress arguing that a Japanese advance to the south was justifiable cause for a war declaration. An entry in Stimson's diary for November 25 has given the "villainous Roosevelt" interpreters more ammunition than any other bit of evidence. Stimson wrote that the "war cabinet"—Roosevelt, Hull, Stimson, Knox, Marshall, and Stark—considered "the question of how we should maneuver them into the position of firing the first shot without allowing too much danger to ourselves." Revisionist historians have argued that this meant that Roosevelt anticipated, even welcomed, the attack on Pearl Harbor in order to become involved in the European war. In the context of the whole discussion within the administration, however, a better interpretation of the Stimson diary entry, which described a meeting and discussion which quite certainly did take place, is that "we" meant the British and Dutch as well as the Americans and that the attack would be in the western Pacific or Southeast Asia. The surmise that the Japanese would attack toward the south was correct; they did in fact make their main thrust in that direction. The attack on Pearl Harbor was a raid, although a very strong one, and the Japanese did not have plans to make it more than a raid. The administration did not have evidence to lead it to anticipate a raid on Hawaii until the last hours before the attack. The military and naval establishments were grossly inefficient in sending further warnings to the commanding officers in Hawaii, but the "Pearl Harbor bait" argument does not stand up under careful analysis.

The weight of the evidence points to the conclusion that Roosevelt and his subordinates had accepted probable, almost certain, war with Japan by November 26. Yet there is one fact that indicates at least a bit of ambivalence on Roosevelt's part. Washington received intelligence on December 6 that Japanese troops were on their way to Malaya. (They made their landings before the raid on Hawaii.) Roosevelt's response was to send a desperate personal appeal for peace to Emperor Hirohito. The cable did not arrive in time for Hirohito to make any reply before the shooting began.

The Japanese blow to Hawaii was one of the best planned and executed military and naval maneuvers in history. On November 25 a task force of aircraft carriers, submarines, and supporting vessels left the waters around the Kurile Islands with orders to attack Pearl Harbor and Hawaiian air bases early on Sunday morning, December 7. Given the weekend habits of peacetime American military and naval personnel, the selection of a Sunday morning was cunning. The task force had been alerted to turn back if it received orders to do so. The orders never came. At 7:55 A.M., Honolulu time, the Japanese planes struck. The American defenders were thoroughly surprised. The first wave of the attack wrought such thorough destruction that the second wave, fifty minutes later, was almost unopposed. Only a handful of American planes were able to get into the air and few antiaircraft batteries were ready for action. By 9:30 A.M. the American forces on Hawaii were reduced to impotence. Over three thousand servicemen were dead or missing. Half the planes in Hawaii were destroyed or disabled. Five battleships were sunk or seriously damaged. So great was the destruction that Washington withheld the extent of the damage from the public for fear of panic. The same day the Japanese struck elsewhere. At noon their planes surprised and wrecked American air bases in the Philippines. Saipan-based Japanese bombers blasted Guam at 8:30 A.M., and Japanese troops had landed in Malaya before dawn.

It had been the Japanese plan to have her ambassadors in Washington deliver the official reply to the American message of November 26 early in the afternoon of December 7, Washington time, just before the attack on Hawaii. In one of the few slip-ups in the whole operation, personnel of the Japanese embassy had difficulty decoding the message and did not have it ready to present until after the attack. When Nomura and Kurusu met with Hull to deliver the message that the Japanese government considered it impossible to reach an agreement with the United States through further negotiations, all three men knew of the attack and realized that their meeting was meaningless. Japan officially declared war about two hours later.

Thus, twenty-three years and twenty-six days after the armistice of 1918 the United States was again at war. On Monday, December 8, Congress almost unanimously passed a resolution declaring that a state of war existed between the United States and Japan. (The lone dissenting vote was that of Representative Jeannette Rankin, Republican of Montana, the first woman to sit in Congress and an opponent of war in 1917. She explained that even with Pearl Harbor it was proper for one vote to be cast against war and that a woman should do it.) The same day Great Britain declared war upon Japan, and Japan requested Germany to declare war upon the United States. Germany, as well as Italy, complied on December 11. A few hours later Congress passed a war resolution against Germany and Italy, this time without a dissenting vote.

It would be an exaggeration to say that the American people welcomed the war. They did not. But it was something of a relief for them to know that the war-peace issue was settled and the problem they faced, defeating the Axis, was a clear one although certainly not a simple nor easy one. The uncertainty at last was over. So also was the division within the Republic over foreign policy. The Pearl Harbor attack unified American opinion as nothing else could have. The Sunday morning raid seriously damaged American fire power but enormously stimulated and strengthened the nation psychologically. Still there was little of the forced-draft, evangelical, "Over There" spirit of World War I. The people regarded the war as a grim but necessary task, and they set about the task with high determination.

Selected Bibliography

This bibliography makes no attempt at being comprehensive. Its purpose is to enable the reader to make rational selections of other titles that offer more detail than the present volume can. When a title in this bibliography is available in a paperback edition, an asterisk (*) follows the date of publication. In view of the flood of paperback volumes appearing, the reader may well find other titles here in inexpensive reprints.

The bibliography is divided into two parts. The first includes works that amplify the material in the first four chapters of this book, the period from 1919 to 1929. The second part is devoted to subjects treated in the last five chapters, which concern the period between the Wall Street crash and Pearl Harbor. Some titles are relevant to both periods. In some cases they are mentioned in each section, with the fuller bibliographical information appearing only at their first mention.

I

The best treatment of Wilson's negotiations at Paris and the defeat of the Treaty of Versailles are the companion volumes by Thomas A. Bailey, *Woodrow Wilson and the Lost Peace* (1944)* and *Woodrow Wilson and the Great Betrayal* (1945).* Ray Stannard Baker, *Woodrow Wilson and World Settlement* (3 vols., 1922) contains many documents. Denna F. Fleming, *The United States and the League of Nations, 1918-1920* (1932) is a valuable work, and W. Stull Holt, *Treaties Defeated by the Senate* (1933) is useful.

Unfortunately there is not yet a book that concentrates on Wilson's domestic policies for the last two years of his presidency. Arthur S. Link's thorough and scholarly multi-volume biography of Wilson has not yet reached the postwar period. One can find some relevant information in Arthur C. Walworth, *Woodrow Wil-*

son (2 vols., 1958); H. C. F., Bell, *Woodrow Wilson and the People* (1945); John A. Garraty, *Woodrow Wilson* (1956); and John M. Blum, *Woodrow Wilson and the Politics of Morality* (1956). See also James R. Mock and Evangeline Thurber, *Report on Demobilization* (1944).

There are several general histories of the 1920's. An excellent place to begin is John D. Hicks, *Republican Ascendancy, 1921-1933* (1960)*. Frederick Lewis Allen, *Only Yesterday: An Informal History of the Nineteen Twenties* (1931)* continues to be very popular, particularly for social history, but William E. Leuchtenburg, *The Perils of Prosperity, 1914-1932* (1958)* is a more perceptive work. Harold Underwood Faulkner, *From Versailles to the New Deal* (1950) is brief but more objective than Karl Schriftgiesser, *This Was Normalcy: An Account of Party Politics during Twelve Republican Years* (1948). Preston W. Slosson, *The Great Crusade and After, 1914-1928* (1930) is strongest in social history. The last two volumes of Mark Sullivan, *Our Times: The United States, 1900-1925* (1926-1935) constitute an easily read account by a conservative journalist.

There is no thorough biography of Warren G. Harding, but Samuel Hopkins Adams, *Incredible Era: The Life and Times of Warren Gamaliel Harding* (1939) is a readable book of the Ohioan's public life with emphasis upon the scandals of his administration. William Allen White's *A Puritan in Babylon* (1938) is a masterful biography of Calvin Coolidge. On dissident Republicans of the prosperity decade see George W. Norris, *Fighting Liberal* (1945), Belle and Fola La Follette, *Robert M. La Follette* (2 vols., 1953), Claudius O. Johnson, *Borah of Idaho* (1936), Marian C. McKenna, *Borah* (1961), and Russel B. Nye, *Midwestern Progressive Politics* (1951). For the 1924 La Follette movement see Kenneth McKay, *The Progressive Movement of 1924* (1947). The best single-volume treatment of the Democrats during the period, although it focuses on Franklin D. Roosevelt, is Arthur M. Schlesinger, Jr., *The Crisis of the Old Order, 1919-1933* (1957).

A very good general economic history of the era is George Soule, *Prosperity Decade* (1947). The relevant chapters of Thomas C. Cochran and William Miller, *The Age of Enterprise* (1942)* are good for the history of business. There are many excellent studies of business developments during the decade. One of the most important is Adolph Berle and Gardiner Means, *The Modern Corporation and Private Property* (1932). See also Arthur R. Burns, *The Decline of Competition* (1936) and Harry

W. Laidler, *Concentration of Control in American Industry* (1931). James Prothro, *The Dollar Decade* (1954) considers the social thought of businessmen, and Otis Pease, *The Responsibilities of American Advertising: Private Control and Public Influence, 1920-1940* (1958) is a thoughtful treatment of an important aspect of business. For the farmer during the decade see John D. Hicks and Theodore Saloutos, *Agricultural Discontent in the Middle West, 1900-1939* (1951) and Harold Barger and H. H. Landsberg, *American Agriculture, 1899-1939* (1951). On labor, the most interesting book for the period is Irving L. Bernstein, *The Lean Years: A History of the American Worker, 1920-1933* (1960), but one must consult the pedantic volumes of Philip Taft, *The A.F. of L. in the Time of Gompers* (1957) and *The A.F. of L. from the Death of Gompers to the Merger* (1959). There are two good surveys of American labor history: Foster Rhea Dulles, *Labor in America* (1949) and Joseph G. Rayback, *A History of American Labor* (1959).

On foreign relations in the 1920's see Frank H. Simonds, *American Foreign Policy in the Post-War Years* (1935), Robert H. Ferrell, *Peace in Their Time* (1952) on the Kellogg-Briand Pact, and a provocative essay by William Appleman Williams, *The Tragedy of American Diplomacy* (1959)*. General diplomatic histories of the United States such as those by Samuel Flagg Bemis and Thomas A. Bailey are useful for the basic facts. All too often diplomatic histories neglect the economic aspects of foreign policy. One that does not is Herbert Feis, *The Diplomacy of the Dollar: First Era, 1919-1932* (1950).

For immigration and the immigrant see Carl Wittke, *We Who Built America* (1939)*, a general history of immigration, and the relevant chapters of the excellent book on the role of the immigrant in American life by John Higham, *Strangers in the Land* (1955)*. Oscar Handlin, *The Uprooted* (1951)* does a fine job of portraying the difficulties of immigrants in American cities. Roy L. Garis, *Immigration Restriction* (1927) and William S. Bernard, *American Immigration Policy* (1950) suffice for immigration laws. Joseph J. Huthmacher, *Massachusetts People and Politics, 1919-1933* (1959) considers the role of immigrant groups in politics.

The best single volume on the Negro in American history is John Hope Franklin, *From Slavery to Freedom: A History of American Negroes* (2d ed., 1961). One of the most thorough investigations of the Negro ever done was that reported on in Gunnar Myrdal, *An American Dilemma* (2 vols., 1944). This long work, which is sociological, economic, and psychological as well as historical, is condensed in Arnold Rose, *The Negro in America* (1948)*. E David Cronon's *Black Moses: The Story of Marcus Garvey and the Universal Negro Improvement Association* (1955)* is the best account of this most dramatic Negro development of the 1920's.

Despite widespread interest in the phenomenon of prohibition there is no fully satisfactory book about it. But see Andrew Sinclair, *Prohibition: The Era of Excess* (1962), Charles Merz, *The Dry Decade* (1931), and Herbert Asbury, *The Great Illusion, An Informal History of Prohibition* (1950), a racy, popular account.

The most thoughtful treatment of the Ku Klux Klan of the 1920's is in Higham, *Strangers in the Land,* already cited, but see also John M. Mecklin, *The Ku Klux Klan* (1924) and Emerson Loucks, *The Ku Klux Klan in Pennsylvania* (1936). On fundamentalism, see Ray Ginger, *Six Days or Forever?* (1958) on the Scopes trial, and Norman F. Furniss, *The Fundamentalist Controversy, 1918-1931* (1954).

There is no thorough biography of Alfred E. Smith. Henry F. Pringle's *Alfred E. Smith* (1927) was written before the most important era of Smith's life; Oscar Handlin, *Al Smith and his America* (1958) is full of insights but too brief. For the election of 1928 the best work is Edmund Moore, *A Catholic Runs for President* (1956), but see also Roy Peel and Thomas Donnelly, *The 1928 Campaign: An Analysis* (1931).

The best writing on education in the 1920's will be found in volumes that treat the subject more broadly. The best survey of the history of education in America is R. Freeman Butts and Lawrence A. Cremin, *A History of Education in American Culture* (1953). Cremin's *The Transformation of the School: Progressivism in American Education, 1876-1957* (1961) is particularly good for the 1920's. Merle Curti, *The Social Ideas of American Educators* (1935) contains excellent chapters on educational philosophies prevalent in the prosperity decade. For the colleges and universities see Richard Hofstadter and C. DeWitt Hardy, *The Development and Scope of Higher Education in the United States* (1952).

On journalism, movies, radio, and other aspects of mass culture in the 1920's see Frank Luther Mott, *American Journalism, A History, 1690-1950* (3d ed., 1962); L. C. Rosten, *Hollywood* (1941); Margaret Thorp, *America at the Movies* (1940); Gilbert Seldes, *The Seven Lively Arts* (1924); and Lloyd Morris,

Not So Long Ago (1947). Merle Curti in the important *The Growth of American Thought* (1943) has a chapter on popular thought during the decade.

Curti's book and Harold Stearns, ed., *Civilization in the United States* (1922) are excellent starting places for reading of more intellectual developments of the 1920's. See also James Truslow Adams, *Our Business Civilization* (1929). Robert and Helen Lynd's *Middletown* (1929)*, a searching analysis of a midwestern small city, describes among other things the community's level of culture.

Histories of literature, volumes of criticism, and biographies of writers exist in plenty. Among the best general ones are Frederick Hoffman, *The Twenties* (1955)* and *The Modern Novel in America, 1900-1951* (1951)*, J. W. Beach, *American Fiction, 1920-1940* (1941), and John Hutchens, *The American Twenties* (1952). Alfred Kazin, *On Native Grounds* (1942)* is excellent. For biography see Arthur Mizener, *The Far Side of Paradise* (1959)*, a life of F. Scott Fitzgerald; Mark Schorer, *Sinclair Lewis* (1961), and William Manchester, *Disturber of the Peace* (1951)*, a life of H. L. Mencken.

Easily the best work on American art during this period is Milton W. Brown, *American Painting from the Armory Show to the Depression* (1955). Useful also are Oliver W. Larkin, *Art and Life in America* (1949) and John Baur, *Revolution and Tradition in Modern American Art* (1951), each of which treats a broader time period.

II

For the crash of 1929 the most clearly written and economically accurate work is John Kenneth Galbraith, *The Great Crash* (1955)*. Broadus Mitchell, *Depression Decade: From New Era Through New Deal, 1929-1941* (1947) is excellent for the crash and subsequent economic history. David A. Shannon, ed., *The Great Depression* (1960)* emphasizes the depression's effects upon human beings. See also Gilbert Seldes, *Years of the Locust: America, 1929-1932* (1933).

The most thorough book on the Hoover administration is Harris G. Warren, *Herbert Hoover and the Great Depression* (1959), but there is more exciting reading in Schlesinger, *The Crisis of the Old Order* and Bernstein, *Lean Years,* both previously cited. Charles A. and Mary R. Beard's *America in Mid-*

passage (1939) has a good account of the Hoover administration. Hoover's *Memoirs* (3 vols., 1951-1952); W. S. Myers and W. H. Newton, *The Hoover Administration* (1936); and Ray Lyman Wilbur and Arthur Hyde, *The Hoover Policies* (1937) are standard works that defend the administration. There are provocative interpretations of Hoover in Richard Hofstadter, *The American Political Tradition and the Men Who Made It* (1948)* and William Appleman Williams, *The Contours of American History* (1961).

Of books about Franklin D. Roosevelt and the New Deal there is almost no end. An excellent survey of the subject is William E. Leuchtenburg, *Franklin D. Roosevelt and the New Deal, 1932-1940* (1963)*. The best accounts of FDR before he became President are Bernard Bellush, *Apprenticeship for the Presidency: Franklin D. Roosevelt as Governor of New York* (1951), and the three volumes published to date of Frank Freidel's masterly life of Roosevelt: *The Apprenticeship (1952), The Ordeal* (1954), and *The Triumph* (1956). Arthur M. Schlesinger, Jr., *The Coming of the New Deal* (1958) and *The Politics of Upheaval* (1960), volumes II and III of his *The Age of Roosevelt,* carry the story down to the election of 1936. The Schlesinger volumes and James M. Burns, *Roosevelt: The Lion and the Fox* (1956)*, which is excellent until the time when foreign affairs began to become FDR's primary problem, constitute a first-rate history of the New Deal. Other useful volumes are Rexford G. Tugwell, *The Democratic Roosevelt* (1957), Harold F. Gosnell, *Champion Campaigner, Franklin D. Roosevelt* (1952), and Robert E. Sherwood, *Roosevelt and Hopkins* (1948)*, especially good for the war period. Edgar E. Robinson, *The Roosevelt Leadership, 1933-1945* (1955) is critical from a conservative position, John T. Flynn, *The Roosevelt Myth* (1948) is critical from a reactionary position, and Mauritz A. Hallgren, *The Gay Reformer: Profits before Plenty under Franklin D. Roosevelt* (1935) and Alfred M. Bingham, *Challenge to the New Deal* (1934) are critical from a left-of-FDR position. For FDR letters and documents see Samuel I. Rosenman, ed., *The Public Papers and Addresses of Franklin D. Roosevelt* (13 vols., 1938-1950) and Elliott Roosevelt, ed., *F.D.R.: His Personal Letters* (4 vols., 1947-1950). There are many memoirs and autobiographies relating to the New Deal: Hugh S. Johnson, *The Blue Eagle from Egg to Earth* (1935); Harold L. Ickes, *Autobiography of a Curmudgeon* (1943) and *Secret Diary* (3 vols., 1953-1954); Marriner S. Eccles, *Beckoning Frontiers* (1951); James A. Farley, *Behind the Ballots* (1938) and *Jim*

Farley's Story (1948); Raymond Moley, *After Seven Years* (1939); Edward J. Flynn, *You're the Boss* (1947); and Eleanor Roosevelt, *This Is My Story* (1937) and *This I Remember* (1949).

On various aspects of the New Deal see Leverett S. Lyon *et al.*, *The National Recovery Administration* (1935); G. Griffith Johnson, Jr., *Treasury and Monetary Policy, 1933-1938* (1939); E. G. Nourse *et al.*, *Three Years of the Agricultural Adjustment Administration* (1937), and also for agriculture the Saloutos and Hicks and Barger and Landsberg titles cited earlier. For other aspects see Paul H. Douglas, *Social Security in the United States* (1939), Donald S. Howard, *The WPA and Federal Relief Policy* (1943), and James C. Bonbright, *Public Utilities and National Power Policies* (1940).

Herbert Hoover's *The Challenge to Liberty* (1934) and *Addresses upon the American Road* (1938); George Wolfskill, *The Revolt of the Conservatives: A History of the American Liberty League, 1934-1940* (1962); Donald R. McCoy, *Angry Voices: Left-of-Center Politics in the New Deal Era* (1958), and Harnet T. Kane, *Louisiana Hayride* (1941), on Huey Long, illustrate some of the political battles of the mid-1930's. For the Supreme Court controversy see Merlo J. Pusey, *The Supreme Court Crisis* (1937) as well as the relevant parts of his *Charles Evans Hughes* (2 vols., 1951), Joseph Alsop and Turner Catledge, *The 168 Days* (1938), and biographies of Supreme Court Justices such as Alpheus T. Mason, *Harland Fiske Stone: Pillar of the Law* (1956), Samuel J. Konefsky, *Chief Justice Stone and the Supreme Court* (1945), and Joel Paschal, *Mr. Justice Sutherland* (1951). An outstanding book is C. Herman Pritchett, *The Roosevelt Court: A Study in Judicial Politics and Values, 1937-1947* (1948).

For business developments during the 1930's, besides the Broadus Mitchell book already cited, see Merle Fainsod and L. Gordon, *Government and the American Economy* (1941). For concentrated business power see Clair Wilcox, *Competition and Monopoly in American Industry* (1940) and a very useful summary of the TNEC investigations, David Lynch, *Concentration of Economic Power* (1946). For labor during the decade see Walter Galenson, *The CIO Challange to the A. F. of L.* (1960); Irving Bernstein, *The New Deal Collective Bargaining Policy* (1950); Edwin Young and Milton Derber, eds., *Labor and the New Deal* (1957); and James O. Morris, *Conflict within the A. F. of L.* (1959).

For the Negro in the 1930's see the Franklin and Myrdal works already cited and Horace R. Cayton and G. S. Mitchell,

Black Workers and the New Unions (1939) and Herbert S. Northrup, *Organized Labor and the Negro* (1944). Walter White, *A Man Called White* (1948) is a memoir by the leader of the NAACP.

For the subjects considered in Chapter 8 of this volume, besides the works of Curti and Mott, already cited, see Dixon Wecter, *The Age of the Great Depression, 1929-1941* (1948), a very useful social history. The Beards' *America in Midpassage* has in its last half a perceptive account of cultural developments during the 1930's. On literature see the previously cited Kazin and Hoffman works, plus John W. Aldridge, *After the Lost Generation* (1951)*, Leo Gurko, *The Angry Decade* (1947), and Maxwell Geismar, *Writers in Crisis: The American Novel, 1925-1940* (1961)*. Milton Crane, ed., *The Roosevelt Era* (1947) is a representative anthology. On art during the era see the previously listed works and Thomas Hart Benton, *An Artist in America* (1937).

For foreign affairs in the 1930's before the war-peace issue after 1939, see Richard N. Current, *Secretary Stimson* (1954) and Elting E. Morison, *Turmoil and Tradition: A Study of the Life and Times of Henry L. Stimson* (1960)*, two books written from quite different points of view; and Robert Ferrell, *American Diplomacy in the Great Depression* (1957), Alexander De Conde, *Herbert Hoover's Latin American Policy* (1951), Raymond L. Buell, *The Hull Trade Program* (1938), and Edward O. Guerrant, *Roosevelt's Good Neighbor Policy* (1951).

The most thorough work on American involvement in World War II is the two-volume study by William L. Langer and S. Everett Gleason, *The Challenge to Isolation, 1937-1940* (1952) and *The Undeclared War, 1940-1941* (1953). The most solid works from the revisionist point of view are by Charles A. Beard, *American Foreign Policy in the Making, 1932-1940* (1946) and *President Roosevelt and the Coming of the War, 1941* (1948). Basic to understanding Beard's point of view is his *The Open Door at Home* (1935). Other general works are Department of State, *Peace and War: United States Foreign Policy, 1931-1941* (1943), and Forrest Davis and Ernest K. Lindley, *How War Came, An American White Paper: From the Fall of France to Pearl Harbor* (1942). See also Wayne S. Cole, *America First, The Battle against Intervention, 1940-1941* (1951) and the book by Walter Johnson on the White Committee, *The Battle Against Isolation* (1944).

For relations with Japan in the pre-Pearl Harbor era see P. W.

Schroeder, *The Axis Alliance and Japanese-American Relations, 1941* (1958), Herbert Feis, *The Road to Pearl Harbor* (1950), and Harold S. Quigley, *Far Eastern War, 1937-1941* (1942). For Pearl Harbor itself see Walter Millis, *This Is Pearl!* (1947) and a popular account by Walter Lord, *Day of Infamy* (1957)*.

Picture Credits

WOODROW WILSON	*United Press International Photo*
ROBERT LA FOLLETTE	*The Bettmann Archive*
KU KLUX KLAN	*Wide World Photo*
HOOVERVILLE	*Franklin D. Roosevelt Library*
MIGRANT WORKERS	*U. S. Department of Agriculture*
COMMUNIST PARADE	*United Press International Photo*
HUEY P. LONG	*Wide World Photo*
SIT-DOWN STRIKE	*U. S. Department of Agriculture*
FRANKLIN D. ROOSEVELT	*Franklin D. Roosevelt Library*
"EYES TESTED"	*Collection of Lawrence A. Fleischman*
F. SCOTT FITZGERALD	*Brown Brothers*
H. L. MENCKEN AND G. J. NATHAN	*Brown Brothers*
SINCLAIR LEWIS	*Brown Brothers*
"THE EMPEROR JONES"	*Harvard University Theater Collection*

Index